£1 2|23

D1577059

NEW REVISED EDITION

JACK THE RIPPER

THE FINAL SOLUTION

'Here comes my noble gull-catcher'
Twelfth Night

NEW REVISED EDITION

JACK THE RIPPER

THE FINAL SOLUTION

STEVEN KNIGHT

CHANCELLOR PRESS

For Margot
Ma Belle Marguerite

First published in Great Britain in 1976 by
George G. Harrap & Co Ltd.

Revised in 1984 by Treasure Press
an imprint of Octopus Publishing Group Ltd.

This revised edition published in 2000 by
Chancellor Press, an imprint of Bounty Books,
a division of Octopus Publishing Group Ltd,
2-4 Heron Quays, London E14 4JP

Reprinted 2002

ISBN 0-75370-369-6

Printed and bound by Mackays of Chatham, England.

FOREWORD

by Nigel Cawthorne

When Stephen Knight published *Jack the Ripper: The Final Solution* in 1976, he not only came up with a new, thoroughly convincing and meticulously researched theory on the Jack the Ripper murders, he also revealed the flaws in all the theories to date. At that the time, much of the background to Knight's theory – that the Ripper murders were a conspiracy rather than the work of a single madman and that they were connected to a morganatic marriage entered into by the heir to the throne Prince Eddy – seemed novel and farfetched. Now this background is widely accepted. However new books are being written about Jack the Ripper all the time. Each develops a theory more off the wall than the last. It is a wonder that no one has yet suggested that Jack the Ripper was an alien who abducted East End prostitutes to perform bizarre anatomical experiments on them. Perhaps it is coming.

In 1987, Martin Fido fingered *David Cohen* – the John Doe of an unknown Jewish madman incarcerated in Colney Hatch lunatic asylum in December 1888. He died there in October the following year. The last murder known for sure to have been the Ripper's occurred on 9 November 1888. Fido believes that *Cohen* was identified by Joseph Lawende, a witness who had seen a man talking to the Ripper's fourth victim Catherine Eddowes shortly before she was murdered. But Lawende refused to testify against a fellow Jew, knowing that he faced the hangman's rope, so the police detained *Cohen* under the Lunacy Act instead to keep him off the streets. Fido also believes that the police were convinced of his guilt but rivalries between the Metropolitan and City Police have obscured his real identity. It is a nice theory but hardly satisfying as nothing more is known about *Cohen* – other than he was a foreign-born Jew, a tailor living in a homeless shelter in Whitechapel aged 23 in 1888, who was extremely violent and had to be kept in a strait jacket. However, his wild assaults on other patients, his shouting and dancing, his noisy acts of vandalism, his inability to take care of himself and his need for restraint all seem at odds with the Ripper who slipped unnoticed in and out of the shadows, cutting up his victims with the practised skill of a surgeon.

In 1991, Northamptonshire police officer Paul Harrison concluded that Joseph Barnett, the common-law husband of the Ripper's last known victim Mary Kelly, was Jack. Harrison contends that Barnett was a sensitive man who thought he could save Mary from the streets. Instead she dragged him down into the gutter with her. An earlier, unrelated murder of a prostitute had persuaded her to suspend her activities as a streetwalker. When she started again, he was driven half-mad with jealousy. He tracked down other prostitutes she knew and killed them in the most gruesome way possible, hoping to scare her back off the streets. When this failed, he murdered and mutilated her. Having rid himself of the source of his psychological problems, Harrison maintains, Barnett had no reason to kill again. But Harrison draws a comparison between Barnett and the serial killers Peter Sutcliffe, the Yorkshire Ripper, and Dennis Nilsen. Neither Sutcliffe nor Nilsen stopped killing until they were caught, but Barnett went on to live a long and untroubled life as a costermonger. As far as I am aware, there is little outlet for the Ripper's raging bloodlust in the retail fruit trade.

In 1992, David Abrahamsen, a fellow of the American College of Psychoanalysts, brought his psychological insight to bear and named Prince Eddy and his Cambridge tutor J.K. Stephen as the murderers. It is an interesting theory from the psychological point of view, but Stephen Knight had already explained how Prince Eddy and J.K. Stephen fitted into the Ripper plot.

Ripperology was revivalised in 1993 with the publication of *The Diary of Jack the Ripper*. This concluded that the author of the diary, said to be a 49-year-old Liverpudlian cotton-merchant James Maybrick, a substance abuser with a history of domestic violence, was Jack the Ripper. For several years Ripperologists debated whether the diaries were fake. However in his 1997 book *Jack the Ripper: The Final Chapter*, Paul Feldman, who believes the diaries are genuine, tied Maybrick into Stephen Knight's conspiracy theory.

In 1994, Melvin Harris resurrected the story that the journalist and devil-worshipper Roslyn D'Onston – or Dr Roslyn D'O Stephenson – was the Ripper. D'Onston himself wrote the police in 1888 accusing Dr Morgan Davies, a surgeon at the London Hospital in Whitechapel. A failed doctor and a drug addict, D'Onston was said to have killed the women to give his journalistic career a fillip. It was said that his stories in the newspapers carried details about the murders that were never released by the police. Soon after the murders, his fellow devil-worshipper Aleister Crowley claimed that D'Onston had performed his ritual murders in an attempt to become invisible. Crowley himself claimed in court to have killed many times for the purposes of black magic. He was never prosecuted. The case against Onston was effectively dealt with and dismissed by Stephen Knight, but still it persists.

In 1995, Stewart Evans and Paul Gainey dismissed the Ripper diary and came up with a new suspect – Francis J. Trumblety, a Canadian woman-hater and fraudster who was arrested in America in connection with the assassination of President Lincoln. After his release, he moved to England. In 1888, the year of the Ripper murders, he was in London, lodging in Whitechapel, Evans and Gainey maintain. On 2 December 1888, he was arrested for unnamed sexual offences. Released on bail, he headed for Le Havre where he took a ship back to New York. The New York police were alerted and kept an eye on him. Detectives were also despatched from England. But Trumblety gave then all the slip and went on to continue his murderous campaign in Jamaica and Nicaragua. He returned to New York in 1891, where he killed again. All this was covered up, Evans and Gainey say, because the Metropolitan Police were embarrassed that they had had the Ripper and released him. Trumblety, they maintain, ìkilled for no apparent motive other than enjoymentî. In which case, after a couple of years of murderous pleasure, he must have stinted himself for the last 12 years of his life. He died in Rochester, New York, in 1903, without, apparently, sating his bloodlust again.

In 1996, former private eye Bruce Paley again accused Joseph Barnett, Mary Kelly's common-law husband, of the crime. Paley claims Barnett fits the FBI's psychological profile of a modern serial killer. Most are white males in their twenties or early thirties. Barnett was thirty at the time of the murders. They come from dysfunctional families, though it would be hard to find a family that was not dysfunctional in the Whitechapel area in the late 19th century. According to top FBI psychological profiler Robert K. Ressler, serial killers come from families where the mother is cold and unloving, while the father is usually absent. Barnett was six when his father died and his mother had disappeared by the time he was thirteen. Paley says that she possibly abandoned her family. This fits with Ressler's theory that the most important single factor in creating a serial killer is a sense of loneliness and isolation consolidated between the age of eight and twelve.

Serial killers usually suffer from a physical defect. Barnett had a speech impediment. Serial killers tend to be intelligent men, stuck in jobs below their capabilities. Barnett was a fish porter though he was well spoken and had had some schooling. A serial killer's first crime tends to be precipitated by a period of stress. Barnett had lost his job shortly before the killings started, forcing Mary to return to prostitution. This gave Barnett a motive for killing her, and it could have given him a reason for venting his wrath on other prostitutes. As a fish porter, he would have been a familiar figure on the streets of the East End in the early morning and, through Mary, he would probably have been known to all the victims. Being a fish porter also meant he was skilled with a knife, boning and gutting fish.

However, according to the FBI, serial killers tend to have been emotionally or sexually abused as a child and come from a family where drugs or alcohol were abused. It is not known if this was the case with Barnett. They also continue to kill until they are caught. But for following 38 years, Barnett led a blameless life. Although he certainly continued having relationships with women – electoral rolls show that he lived with a common-law wife for at least seven years – he never felt that murderous rage well up inside him again. And, it seems, in all that time he never ever felt the urge to tell anyone of his crimes or record the fact that he was the world's most notorious killer for posterity.

In 1997, James Tulley used the same psychological profiling methods to identify the Rippers. But he absolved Barnett and picked one James Kelly instead. In 1883, Kelly had stabbed and killed his wife. He admitted the crime and was sentenced to death, but was reprieved and sent to Broadmoor. In January 1888, he escaped and hid out in the East End of London, before fleeing to France at the end of the year. He returned to England in 1892 to sail to the U.S. In 1896, he gave himself up at the British Consulate in New Orleans. Instead of having him arrested, the vice-consul arranged for him to work his own passage back to Liverpool. Arriving in England, he absconded again, this time heading for Canada. In 1901, he surrendered himself at the

British Consulate in Vancouver, but again he gave the authorities the slip. For the next 26 years he travelled back and forth across the Atlantic, spending more and more time in England. Eventually in 1927, he turned up at the gates of Broadmoor, where he surrendered himself once more. He died in the asylum in two years later. Tulley says the authorities kept quiet about Kelly because they had let the Ripper escape in the first place. The fact that they made no effort to apprehend in North America or when he was back in Britain, Tulley says, was part of the cover-up. Once again, there is no indication that Kelly killed again in the 39 years he was at liberty after the Ripper murders, even though he was a dangerous fugitive from justice. It seems you can kill five prostitutes in a couple of months, then give it up just like that, cold turkey.

In 1998, South Wales magistrate Bob Hinton again use those self-same psychological profiling methods. But he came up with was George Hutchinson, a witness who gave a detailed description of a man he said he saw with the Ripper's last victim Mary Kelly the night she died. Again Hutchinson was a white male, at 28 in the right age group, and as a barman and labourer in the right sort of menial job. With those criteria, the East of London in the 1880s must have been brimming over the serial killers. Hutchinson certainly knew Kelly and admitted giving her money – presumably for services rendered. His own testimony put him at the scene of the crime. Hinton also says that senior policemen discounted Hutchinson as a witness – a point that Stephen Knight covered in his book 22 years earlier. Hinton systematically trashed Hutchinson's evidence and believes that he stopped killing because Mary Kelly 'the object of his obsession [was] obliterated'. Hinton was not sure when Hutchinson died, but says he must have been either the George Hutchinson who died in Newark in 1929, the George Hutchinson who died in Bradford in 1934 or the George Hutchinson who died in Darlington in 1936. So again Hutchinson lived at least another 41 years without feeling the urge to kill again, or tell anyone that he was Jack the Ripper.

In 1999, Stephen Wright, reviewing all the literature from an American angle, concluded like others that the Ripper's diary was a hoax. He dismissed all the other theories, then claimed to be the first to finger George Hutchinson as the Ripper. Maybe Hinton's book had not cross the Atlantic when Wright was at work, but Wright makes no more convincing case than Hinton does. The most recent theory is that Walter, the pseudonymous author of the Victorian pornographic classic *My Secret Life was the Ripper*. The clues, apparently, are all in the book.

Ripperology is a strange discipline and seems to attract strange people. But Stephen Knight was no full-time Ripperologist. He stumbled across his remarkable new theory of the Jack the Ripper murders while working as a researcher for the BBC. Here he presents it for the first time. Unlike other theories, Knight's tale ties up all the loose ends: why the police were seemingly so inept, why the public and the establishment reaction was so quickly fired up and so soon abated, why the murders just suddenly stopped and why the police came so briskly to the conclusion that the Ripper murders were over though they had no one in custody and had named no credible suspect. *Jack the Ripper: The Final Solution* is a remarkable piece of work. Although other books have flown off on other tangents, many have confirmed what Stephen Knight says. Other books may have added fresh detail, but Stephen Knight's book has never been bettered.

Preface

Researching and writing this book has been one of the most difficult tasks I have ever undertaken. It has also been one of the most rewarding. It has led me to people I would have been unlikely otherwise to meet, people who began as contacts and whom I am now privileged to count as friends. That well-worn tribute, 'without whom this book could not have been written', applies to so many people in the present case that I am at a loss to know where to begin in thanking them.

At the top of the list of those to whom I owe a huge debt of gratitude are Paul Bonner and Ian Sharp. Without their initial research, and that of Karen de Groot and Wendy Sturgess, I should have been at an immense disadvantage in embarking on the quest for Jack the Ripper. For making their invaluable material available to me, and for their time and advice, given so generously despite the rigorous demands of their own lives and livelihoods, I am deeply grateful.

I wish to thank Joe Gaute, not only for his expert advice and encouragement but also for his open-mindedness in being prepared to listen to a beginner who thought he had something worth while to say. To Ken Thomson I should like to say thanks on a hundred different counts, notably his unfailing approachability, sensitive guidance and his many thoughtful suggestions about text and illustrations. To Ken must go the credit for the present title, an apter and far more memorable one than my own *The Real Jack the Ripper*.

For reading and making vital comments upon my synopsis and manuscript I must thank Robin Odell, whose own *Jack the Ripper In Fact and Fiction* is one of the few really good Ripper books.

Richard Whittington-Egan, that most audacious and tenacious of modern literary detectives, has contributed a foreword to the book. For Richard's charm and friendship, for his

Holmesian percipience and his most illuminating criticism—
offered always in the spirit of helpfulness—I can only say,
most sincerely, thank you.

There comes a time for almost every author where he
wonders if the book on which he has toiled will ever be published, so great and so numerous seem the obstacles. I am
grateful for the kind words of encouragement given me by
Donald Rumbelow when I reached my own, mercifully
short-lived, period of uncertainty. Don's constant interest,
consideration and many ideas have contributed in great
measure to the present form of this book.

My good friend Bernard Taylor is to be thanked for pointing
out some subtle and not-so-subtle errors in grammar that
everyone else had missed.

Others who have read sections of my unfinished manuscript,
or submitted themselves to my own readings from it, and whose
views have been invaluable are Harry Jackson, my brothers
Leonard, Richard and Adrian, Dr Anthony Storr, John
Wilding, my stepdaughters Natasha and Nicole and my
mother. Of especial importance was the inspiration provided
by my friend Joan Moisey. Without her this book could, but is
unlikely to, have been written.

The following people have contributed by giving their time
for often lengthy interviews: Karen de Groot, Wendy Sturgess,
Michael Parkin, Alan Neate, Robert Mackworth-Young,
Harry Jonas, Elwyn Jones, William Ifland, Anthony Storr,
Terese Stevens, Emily Porter and of course Joseph Sickert. I
have spent many hours with Marjorie Lilly, and her reminis-
cences have provided rich background material. Here it is
important to point out, however, that any conclusions reached
in this book are my own.

Many people have helped by taking the trouble to write me
letters, some extremely long and informative, others quite
brief, all of them courteous. These include Michael Harrison,
Timothy d'Arch Smith, H. Montgomery Hyde, Frederick
Bratton, Alan Neate, the Marquess of Salisbury, Donald
McCormick, Wendy Baron, Sir John Gielgud, Dame Peggy
Ashcroft, Donald Rumbelow, Dr J. Mason, G. Lüdemann,
Nigel Morland, Michael Thomas, Algernon Greaves, T.
Tindal-Robertson, John Symonds, Dr Alan Barham Carter,
Martin Cresswell, Lady Muriel Dowding, Thomas Orde, Sir
Philip Magnus-Allcroft, Mavis Pindard, the Law Society, the
Honourable Society of the Inner Temple, the Director of

Public Prosecutions, H. G. Pearson of the Home Office, Nellie J. Kerling and Constance-Anne Parker.

I am grateful to Mrs Edwina Browning and the many Freds of Scotland Yard's record department for their charming hospitality and for the help given by Mr T. H. East of the Home Office. Thanks are due to Mr Eric Harvey, Departmental Records Officer at New Scotland Yard, for permission to examine the Yard file on the Whitechapel Murders, to the Rt. Hon. Roy Jenkins, M.P., for permission to examine the Home Office papers on the case, and to Her Majesty the Queen for permission to see some of the unpublished private correspondence of Queen Victoria.

Thanks are due to the Royal College of Physicians for permission to reproduce part of a letter from Sir William Gull; to Michael Joseph, Ltd. for permission to quote from *Jack the Ripper* by Daniel Farson, to Joseph Sickert for permission to include several family photographs in the book, and to Faber and Faber for permission to reproduce the photograph of young Walter Sickert, from *The Life and Opinions of Walter Richard Sickert* by Robert Emmons. Photographs and transcripts of Crown copyright records in the Public Record Office appear by permission of the Controller of H.M. Stationery Office.

I wish to offer my sincere thanks to my friend Harry Jackson for his help whenever needed. Two of his splendid photographs are included in the book. I have met no one with more enthusiasm for the subject than Harry, and I have spent many happy hours talking Ripper with him and his charming wife Belinda.

I am grateful to my friends in general for tolerating my anti-social behaviour during the preparation of the book. Many of them I virtually ignored for eighteen months. I must particularly thank Terry and Janice Sweeney who, as always, were there when needed, notably when the paper ran out. Several people have lent me books which have proved most useful. They include Dave Bootle, Brenda Lyons, Richard and Leonard Knight, Harry Jackson and Joe Gaute.

Two high-ranking Freemasons have helped with information and comments. To both I am grateful, and comply with their wish to remain anonymous.

Others who have helped in the production of this work are Ron Rothery, Rod Southwood, Margaret Adey, Jack Hammond, Pauline Silver, Christopher Falkus, David Newnham and the resourceful staff of the British Museum Reading Room and of Tower Hamlets Libraries, especially the Local History Library and the Music and Art Library at Whitechapel.

Mr R. F. Armitage and Joyce Hatwell contributed more than they know.

Roy Minton made many suggestions that were both practical and imaginative. I am grateful for his expertise.

The two lives of the author who also has a full-time job are not always compatible. I have to thank Chris Coates for his help and understanding in allowing me time to carry out research. No one could ask for a finer News Editor.

Finally I must express my deepest gratitude to my wife Margot and our daughters Natasha and Nicole. They have listened with patience and encouragement to long and often complicated monologues about the Whitechapel Murders. I am grateful for the love with which they accepted Jack the Ripper as our house guest for nigh on two years. Most of all I am thankful to Margot for her faith in me, unwavering even at times when I had little faith in myself. Without her this book would never have been contemplated.

STEPHEN KNIGHT

31st August 1975

PREFACE TO THE REVISED EDITION

Several people have contributed ideas and comments on the first edition of the book, which I have found valuable to incorporate in this edition. Foremost among those to be thanked is my friend and literary mentor David Richardson. Others to whom I am grateful include Leslie Farmer, Alan Hooker, L.L. Johnson, Maggy Hallam and Joyce Boyce.

S.K.

8th October 1976

NOTE

Certain inconsistencies in spelling proper nouns have appeared in previous books on the Whitechapel Murders. Documents – notably police reports – reproduced in this book contained many errors and these on the whole have been retained. Where practical I have denoted such errors with a '[sic]'. For the record, the correct spellings of the four most troublesome names are: Mary Ann *Nichols*; *Bucks* Row; *Berner* Street; and *Miller's* Court.

Contents

Illustrations

CHAPTER ONE

New Light on an Old Mystery

Jack the Ripper is a misnomer. The name conjures up visions of a lone assassin, stalking his victims under the foggy gaslight of Whitechapel. It is just this mistaken notion, inspired almost solely by that terrifying nickname, which rendered the murders of five East End prostitutes in 1888 insoluble. For Jack the Ripper was not one man but three, two killers and an accomplice. The facts surrounding their exploits have never before been teased from the confused skein of truths, half-truths and lies which has been woven around this case. Falsehoods deliberate and accidental have hopelessly enmeshed the truth. The idea of the solitary killer has been propagated by author after author, each striving to prove that his own particular suspect was without a doubt the most notorious criminal in history. It explains the wide gulf of inconsistency into which every theorist's 'logical' reasoning has ultimately fallen. It is the root of widespread disagreement, even over such a basic point as how many Ripper killings there were. Some say as few as four, some say more than twenty. Most experts, however, agree with Sir Melville Macnaghten, who joined Scotland Yard as an Assistant Chief Constable with the Criminal Investigation Department in 1889, the year after the murders. In a batch of confidential notes he wrote:

The Whitechapel Murderer had 5 victims and 5 victims only.

Macnaghten's official notes list the five victims thus:

(i) 31st Aug '88. Mary Ann Nichols—at Buck's Row—who was found with her throat cut—& with (slight) stomach mutilation.
(ii) 8th Sept. '88. Annie Chapman—Hanbury St:—throat cut—stomach & private parts badly mutilated & some of the entrails placed round the neck.
(iii) 30th Sept. '88. Elizabeth Stride—Berner's Street: throat cut, but nothing in shape of mutilation attempted, & on same date Catherine Eddowes—Mitre Square, throat cut, & very bad mutilation, both of face & stomach.
(iv) 9th November. Mary Jane Kelly—Miller's Court, throat cut, and the whole of the body mutilated in the most ghastly manner.

Macnaghten was right in identifying these five alone as the victims of Jack the Ripper, but not for the reasons previous writers have ascribed to him. Elizabeth Stride, for instance, has been accepted as a Ripper victim on the most tenuous evidence, namely that she was killed on the same night as an established victim and that her throat was cut. On that shallow reasoning there is nothing to connect Stride with this series of murders; she was neither mutilated in the customary manner of the Ripper, nor, numerous writers have stated, was her throat cut from left to right like all the other victims, but in the reverse direction. That Stride's murder *was* one of the series is shown by new evidence, gleaned from secret Government and police papers and from a post-mortem report which was suppressed, even at the inquest. It shows that Long Liz Stride's throat was cut in precisely the same left-to-right sweep that dispatched the other victims.

There is also more concrete new evidence which entangles Stride in the web and turns the popular vision of the crimes topsy-turvy: four of the five victims knew each other. These were no random killings perpetrated by a sexual lunatic, but the systematic elimination of specific targets. Marie Kelly, in common with the other four women, was no hapless harlot who just happened to run into Jack the Ripper. She was the *intended* final victim. And in her hitherto obscure history lies the solution.

One of the myriad seemingly inexplicable details arising from Stride's murder was the butchery of Catherine Eddowes so soon after. Of all the theories propounded with such abandon, none has explained how Eddowes was found as far as half a mile from Stride, less than three-quarters of an hour later, and yet was murdered and elaborately mutilated by the same hand. At last the answer is available.

It is common knowledge that in some recess at Scotland Yard there is a secret file relating to the Whitechapel Murders. Rumour-mongers have insisted that the solution to the riddle, even the name of the killer, is concealed there. I have been given access to the Scotland Yard file, which was due to remain closed until 1992, and also to the secret Home Office papers on the case, which will not be open to public inspection until 1993. Neither file identifies Jack the Ripper, but both provide crucial evidence in support of the thesis examined in this report. The fascinating information contained in the secret documents is published for the first time here.

The truth about Jack the Ripper is ugly. Many would rather not hear it, others will revile it.

But it is the truth.

The basic story which led to this book is no fantasy dreamed up by a nobody desperate for publicity, for the source of the information was New Scotland Yard itself. It was not released in an official statement but via a furtive leakage of intelligence from those who have maintained for years they have no knowledge to impart. The new facts gleaned from the Yard led eventually to an unknown artist who lived in contented anonymity with his family and pets in a large but unspectacular north London house. He repeated an unpleasant and incredible story told him by his father, a famous painter and renowned raconteur. The artist had no proof of the story's veracity, just an unshakable conviction that his father had not lied.

The first steps in the quest were taken early in January 1973. A revival of interest in Jack the Ripper which had started more than two years before and showed no signs of abatement prompted BBC Television to explore the possibility of a series of feature programmes on the murders. From the beginning shadowy Jack had haunted the febrile imagination of the public like no other killer in history. He had featured in more than a hundred books, numerous films and plays and countless magazine and newspaper articles. In November 1970, just as it seemed there was nothing left to say, interest in the subject reached a new intensity with the publication of a sensational and groundless article denouncing Queen Victoria's grandson, Prince Albert Victor, Duke of Clarence, as the Ripper. The article was reprinted and discussed by three thousand news-

papers all over the world, and almost every week between late
1970 and the time the BBC became involved the Whitechapel
Murders were featured somewhere in British newspapers and
periodicals, and two major theories, one completely new, were
published in book form.

After prolonged deliberation the BBC decided not so much
to climb on the bandwagon as to find out the reasons behind
the sustained upsurge of 'Rippermania', and then to attempt to
produce the definitive account of the case. Perhaps, the
producers pondered in their more heady moments, they
might even solve the mystery. It would be a fitting com-
memoration for the eighty-fifth anniversary of the murders.

For the first time since television began the BBC decided on a
joint effort between their features and drama departments.
The series was to be utterly factual; but the material would be
presented and discussed by fictional characters, the popular
detectives Barlow and Watt, to endow a serious documentary
with the audience-attracting power of a thriller.

On the features side Paul Bonner—a man who had been
responsible for several major programmes, including a controversial investigation of the *Lusitania* disaster—was chosen to
produce the series. He was responsible for researching the
entire factual content of the series, and was to head a team of
researchers, all of whom shared his own enthusiasm for the
subject. Customary sources of information such as newspapers,
libraries, public records offices, the British Museum, articles
and contemporary writings all had to be minutely examined.
But this was to be the final word on Jack the Ripper, not an
amalgam of previous words cleverly dressed up.

The centre of operations eighty-five years before had been
Scotland Yard, headquarters of the Metropolitan Police. It
seemed the logical place to open the new investigation. The
Yard, since removed from their Victorian location at Whitehall
to an imposing new building off Victoria Street, Westminster,
had for years remained silent about the case, except for the odd
comment to professional inquirers who were invariably told,
'The case is closed. We know nothing which has not already
been published.' Yet this know-nothing stand was incompre-
hensible, Bonner reasoned. They must know something, if it
were only the background details of an abortive investigation.
Along with Elwyn Jones, the creator of Barlow and the man
selected to write the *Ripper* scripts, Bonner went to New Scotland
Yard to see if the police were prepared to help in any way.

They had lunch with a senior Yard man, whom Jones already knew. Though his name cannot be disclosed, he is regarded as an impeccable source. They quickly outlined their plans. A tense hour followed during which they underwent a long grilling about the intentions behind the proposed documentary. The contact was anxious to be assured that their treatment of the subject was to be conscientious in the extreme, and that they genuinely hoped to provide the definitive account of the Ripper murders. Once satisfied that this was the case— and it was no easy task convincing him—he produced a scrap of paper from his pocket. It bore several handwritten notes. He would not specify the source of the information he was about to give, but attributed it to 'one of our people'. He also re- quested that what he told them should be in confidence.

He asked if they had had any contact with 'a man named Sickert who has some connection with the artist'. He said the man knew of a marriage between the Duke of Clarence, son of Edward VII and Heir Presumptive to the throne until his death in 1892, and an Alice Mary Cook. The clandestine ceremony had taken place in 'St Saviour's' and the two witnesses present were later to become victims of the Ripper. Alice Mary died in 1920. No other information was given. Ian Sharp, a research assistant who worked on the series, described what followed:

Thinking this could be a test to see how thorough we were in our research we were determined to find out, on what little information there was, whether a marriage certificate existed which would substantiate the story. The major problem turned out to be finding the place the wedding was supposed to have happened. Even hospitals and infirmaries had chapels attached to them at that time. But as Elwyn and Paul were not certain if their informant had mentioned "in- firmary" or "church", it seemed a good idea at first to try just plain St Saviour's Church. There was a St Saviour's Parish at that time south of the river, so I went along to Southwark Cathedral, formerly St Saviour's, and saw the verger Mr Philip Chancellor. He kindly showed me the records for the years 1880 to 1889, but there was no sign of a certificate containing any of the names mentioned.

The British Medical Association were more productive, and after several days they returned my phone call with the news of a St Saviour's Infirmary in Osnaburgh Street, just off Euston Road. Unfortunately, it no longer existed and the

area has now been converted into offices and flats. The
Marylebone Records Office had no trace of any papers
belonging to the chapel of the infirmary, which was within
their boundaries, and assured us they would be there if anywhere.

In the meantime two other researchers and I personally
ransacked Somerset House in an attempt to track the
wedding, and the existence of an Alice Mary Cook. We drew
blanks all round. After a fortnight we had come up only with
the existence of a St Saviour's Infirmary, which was anyway
a long way from the area we expected it to be in—the
environs of Whitechapel, or at least within a cock-stride of
the area where three East End prostitutes would have been
liable to stray.

So it was decided that we should try our Yard man for
more information, and preferably the whereabouts of
Sickert, if he still (or even) existed. I remember very clearly
Paul Bonner ringing the informant and in urbane and
diplomatic tones inform him we had found nothing, without
actually saying so. He then asked if Sickert was still around.
And then to Paul's astonishment he provided him with
Sickert's phone number within a couple of seconds. Since
this was a fortnight after their meeting and there had been
no contact during that time, it appeared very odd that he
should now lay hands on the phone number instantly. He
may well have had it on the slip of paper, but why hadn't he
given it to them at the time? The excitement was too much
and the entire team retired to licensed premises for mouth-
to-glass resuscitation.

That evening I rang Sickert and told him what I had
heard without disclosing any sources, other than the fact that
the BBC were interested, as they were doing a series of
documentaries on the subject. He seemed very surprised and
asked me to repeat what I had said to another man who was
very well-spoken, sounded much older and was a little deaf.
The old chap then handed the telephone back to Sickert and
we made an appointment for the following morning.

The address I was given was an artist's studio in Myddel-
ton Square, Islington, which belonged to a Mr Harry Jonas,
the old chap. The studio belongs to another world, a fabulous
old place which is utterly shambolic. There were canvasses,
paints, brushes, pots, empty bottles, disused milk cartons,
tins of paint and beans, and in the centre one of those splendid old stoves with a pipe reaching out through the roof.
There were no windows, and the only source of daylight
were two huge skylights. Harry Jonas and Sickert were there.

For three hours I was subjected to intensive cross-examination as to how I had got the information, what exactly had been said and by whom. They gave absolutely nothing away but it was during the course of this that I realised why the previous fortnight had been spent in abortive research. The names, places and events described by our informant at the Yard were slightly wrong. Jonas and Sickert spent a considerable time discussing whether Scotland Yard had deliberately given us wrong information, so that we would find it necessary to drop them and contact Sickert himself. They assured me they had not spoken to Scotland Yard.

They created a remarkable atmosphere of conspiracy, and I confess they did look worried and were extremely cautious. Sickert stressed that this was a personal story, and that his part in it was only "a small chapter in a very large book". They were agreed that if the story were told, the BBC would not be able to broadcast it.

Eventually we parted on the understanding that I would get more detailed accounts of the source of our information, and as soon as I had done so I was to contact them, and we would meet again. I left wishing I was working on *Holiday 73* or some nice cushy little number in an anonymous corner of Quiz Unit.

A couple of days later I returned and this time the atmosphere was more relaxed. We went out to a café round the corner and Sickert bought the meal, despite my banging on the counter with my handkerchief.

Slowly the story began to emerge, that the Ripper episode had its origins in Cleveland Street, which at that time was the artistic centre of London where Sickert's father, Walter Richard Sickert, had his studio. At No. 22 Cleveland Street there was a confectioner's and tobacconist's shop in which Annie Elizabeth Crook worked. Her assistant, or the girl who worked in the shop with her, was Marie Kelly, the same girl who was the last Ripper victim. It was here that Prince Eddy, Duke of Clarence, had met Annie Elizabeth on one of his secret visits to the area.

There *had* been a wedding in St Saviour's Chapel but there was only one relevant witness, Marie Kelly. In 1888 there was a police raid on certain premises in Cleveland Street and two people were taken away, the Duke of Clarence and Annie Elizabeth, the latter being confined at various institutions until she died in 1920, insane. Marie Kelly had seen what had happened and also had care of a child, Alice Margaret. She fled to the East End, where she hid in a convent and the next time she was heard of was November 9th.

All this information did not come in clear, precise, chronological order but I had to glean it from rambling and sometimes vague discussion as names and places descended on me by the dozen. They went backwards, forwards and sideways, and I was fairly confused. But out of all this the story began to take shape. The actual Ripper episode was hardly mentioned and no names were disclosed as to his or their identities, but I was given the impression that more than one person was involved.

So it went on. Sharp, Bonner and company patiently continued their research, and repeatedly visited Sickert and Jonas in an attempt to pry further information from their wary lips. Jonas would say nothing without the say-so of Sickert, and despite his earlier confidence in the BBC men, Sickert now seemed disposed to remain silent after all. But the team seemed so professional in their approach to the subject that after further prolonged debate, patience reaped its reward.

Sickert, a shy and troubled man, at last realized he could completely trust his new friends, and felt he could mention, in confidence, a few names. But even then the story did not come either concisely or completely. The same rambling conversations were carried on, with no attempt at all to convince, merely to talk. He seemed to find some sort of relief in telling his story at last. And finally, the unbelievable narrative which his father had handed down to him began to make some sort of sense.

But still Sickert was adamant that his story must not be made public. He could see no benefit, only suffering, resulting from the publication of the truth so long after the event. Let them all bicker and squabble over their theories. What did it matter? He said he had even begun to think it was a mistake his having spoken in the first place. If he had kept quiet the story would have died with him, and 'the sins of the fathers would not have been visited on the sons', as he so enigmatically put it. The BBC team as well as Sickert's own closest friends, notably Jonas, set to work to show him that if he knew the truth it was his duty to speak out. His own Church, the Roman Catholic Church, rigorously opposed the concealment of any sin. Only good could come from the truth being known. After many weeks of coaxing, cajoling, reasoning and persuasion he came reluctantly to the conclusion that it would perhaps be best if his long-secret story were told. So on Friday 17th August 1973 Joseph Sickert appeared as a surprise witness in the final episode of the *Jack the Ripper* series.

I met Sickert the following month when I visited his Kentish Town home to interview him on behalf of the *East London Advertiser*. He had been chary on the phone, but agreed to see me after I pointed out that the *Advertiser* was the one surviving newspaper covering the area where the Whitechapel Murders had taken place, so had a sort of personal interest. He agreed that after his appearance on television he had nothing to lose by explaining his story more fully to the people of the East End. I found him a nervous little man, charming but withdrawn. His swept-back hair and elegant beard were silver-grey, and his face was rugged and aristocratic. He looked, I thought, like a delicate buccaneer. His voice was a self-contradiction, being at once genteel and rough. He pronounced words badly, but spoke them elegantly. He would say ' 'arsh' not as if it were 'harsh' and he was too lazy or untutored to pronounce the 'h', but as if ' 'arsh' were the correct pronunciation, and he spoke such diminutives with perfect diction. His friends knew him affectionately as Hobo. He did not seem eager to have any further publicity.

After several cups of coffee and a long dialogue on the ethics of speaking the truth at all costs, he seemed to warm to me, and said, 'I may have remained silent too long, I don't know. But the more time went by the more certain I became that no good would come of speaking out I confess I do feel less burdened now I have shared what I know.'

Then he told me the whole story. His mother had been a nervous woman whose fears and unhappiness were born in the dreadful isolation of a workhouse childhood. Congenitally deaf, she had started life at a disadvantage. The brutal treatment she had received during much of her early life had combined with her physical disability to make her unnaturally shy of contact with strangers. She was over-protective towards Joseph, and from his earliest days the boy was given the impression that some sinister memory haunted his mother's life. The odd unguarded word, snatches of conversation accidentally overheard, his mother's visible tenseness when a policeman came into sight—all this convinced the perceptive young Joseph that there was something in her past that threw a dark shadow over her present.

Years later, when he was about fourteen, his father, the famous Impressionist painter Walter Sickert, took him aside one day and in confidential tones recounted a tale the boy at first found impossible to believe. The story began, he said, subsiding into an armchair, in Victoria's Court in the early 1880s.

The Queen's grandson, Prince Eddy, later Duke of Clarence and Avondale, was a complex boy, and when he was twenty, in 1884, his mother, Princess Alexandra, became concerned about his personal development. His father Prince Edward, later King Edward VII, all but disowned his son. He did not like him, and took no pains to conceal the fact. To him the boy was a dunderhead, and about as fit to become King as one of his simpering college friends. To a devoted mother the restricted circles of the Court seemed a stifling environment in which to watch her boy grow up. If Eddy was to be King he must learn the realities of the people over whom he would one day rule. And as he was of an artistic rather than an academic turn of mind, Alexandra looked to the world of art as the one hope for Eddy's salvation. There he could be himself; his personality could grow; he could develop something of the noble Saxe-Coburg charisma which she had once loved so much in her husband, but which in him had become submerged in immorality, and in Eddy had never appeared at all. Above all, Eddy could escape the narrow confines of the Court and the damaging antipathy of his father.

In turning to the art world Alix's eyes could not fail to come to rest on the handsome young painter Walter Sickert. Four years Eddy's senior, he was a third-generation painter, both his father and his grandfather having been artists to the Royal Court of Denmark, whence Alix herself had come twenty years before. Alix wrote to Sickert and requested him to take Eddy under his artistic wing. The Princess was used to getting her own way, and the painter was always eager to further his own interests by ingratiating himself with the influential. He readily complied with the request, and also with the proviso that Eddy's ventures into the world of reality would not reach the ears of his father or grandmother.

'Mama would be troublesome', the wayward Alix told Sickert, who well knew the rage of Victoria was not to be dismissed lightly.

During this period, in the early days of his career after his premature exit from the Slade School of Art and his apprenticeship with the great American painter Whistler, Sickert rented rooms in a great red-brick terrace house at 15 Cleveland Street, the centre of an area that had become the Montmartre of London. Cleveland Street ran parallel with Tottenham Court Road. Its surrounding by-ways formed a little Bohemian village, a self-contained community of artists, writers and shopkeepers snuggling in self-satisfied oblivion between two of the busiest thoroughfares of the metropolis. The area attracted the young, the creative and the revolutionary. The mingling of their diverse characters, consistent only in their rejection of convention, produced a colony of upper-class beatniks that included William Morris and the young Bernard Shaw.

In his long vacations from Cambridge, and during illicit absences in term-time, the young Prince would pay secret visits to Sickert. Leaving the palace in a carriage emblazoned with the Royal Arms, he would change vehicles at a pre-determined spot and continue his journey to Sickert's in an ordinary coach, so forestalling by more than fifty years the system by which Edward VIII used to elude palace watchdogs when he was courting Mrs Simpson. Eddy's coachman on the second part of the journey was a likeable but ruthless young womanizer called John Netley, a man committed to carving a secure place in the service of the powerful, whatever the cost.

Eddy thrived in the relaxed atmosphere of the community, and eagerly urged Sickert to introduce him to as many varied people as the painter knew. Sickert's innate talent for seeing the good in others transcended class barriers, and he was accepted wherever he went, high or low. He was equally at ease with a fisherman or a king. Eddy grew to love him as a teacher and a friend, and grew ardently to identify himself with the *alias* he had assumed for his visits. As Sickert's younger brother Albert he had more freedom than he had ever tasted, and he relished the cloak-and-dagger touch of being referred to by his new acquaintances as 'young Mr S.'.

In the swelterng summer of 1884 Sickert introduced Eddy to a young shop-girl who frequently modelled for him. Her name was Annie Elizabeth Crook, also known as Cook. She worked in the tobacconist's at 22 Cleveland Street, clearly visible from the front windows of the studio. Though illiterate, the girl had an effusive charm. She was of Scottish descent, and had wound her way to London from her country village in the Midlands, her rustic imagination brimming with visions of fortune in the big city. The drabness of the town had at first disappointed her, but she was intelligent enough not to be too surprised to find the streets paved with stone. She was far from beautiful, but Eddy was immediately attracted to her because of the resemblance she bore in his eyes to his beloved mother. To say Eddy suffered from an Oedipus complex would be overstating the matter, but the relationship between him and Alix had always been one of great intimacy. The natural closeness of mother and son was intensified both by the alienation he suffered at the hands of his father, and the lack of outside stimulus inevitable for any member of a royal household. His less than healthy dependence upon her was exacerbated by her own possessive love.

Annie was flattered by the attention she received from her painter friend's younger brother. His air of sadness, which Sickert suspected Annie found romantic, and his overt appreciation of her own charms kindled an immediate response. Eddy later confided in Sickert that from their first meeting one side of him cried out for her while another, more entrenched and cautious, restrained him. Annie could have no notion of the pangs and longings which haunted Eddy endlessly during his happy visits to Cleveland Street, and which clouded his new-found contentment with bouts of depression. For all his adolescent longings for freedom, he knew he had but to look behind to see the spectral image of the throne, which was to pursue him unremittingly to his grave. That seat of majesty must be his only objective. All other ambition must be subordinated to the natural fulfilment of his destiny, kingship.

But with Annie he could deceive himself, and in her embrace be convinced by the cheering motto of Chaucer's prioress, 'Love Conquers All'. He presently gave himself over fully to his youthful passions, and half expected his responsibilities to melt under the advance of his burning love. Their emotions flared, and each helped convince the other they were deeply in love. Perhaps they were.

Annie became pregnant almost immediately, and at Marylebone Workhouse the following April she gave birth to a girl, Alice Margaret. The child underwent two baptisms, Anglican and Catholic. The affair between the couple was still a closely guarded secret between themselves and Sickert. Annie continued to live in the basement of No. 6 Cleveland Street and to serve in the shop. A girl she had worked with there, an Irish Catholic called Mary Kelly, was paid by Sickert to give up her job and move into the basement as the child's nanny. Kelly was eager to oblige because it had been Sickert who found her the position in the first place. The proprietor of the shop had been in need of assistance, and Sickert had approached one of his many friends, a lawyer who ran an East End refuge for poor working women. Within a matter of days the lawyer had brought Kelly to Cleveland Street and she started work in the shop.

The need for secrecy over Eddy and Annie's affair was impressed upon them all by Sickert, who had been warned by Alix not to allow her son to 'get himself into trouble'. They later went through a Catholic wedding ceremony at a St Saviour's private chapel, and Sickert and Kelly were the witnesses. Sickert himself was married to Ellen Cobden in 1885, and from then on travelled regularly to Dieppe, the Normandy port where he was to produce some of his finest paintings. When Eddy was away—which was often—Sickert would traipse contentedly back and forth from France with Annie and the child in tow. At least twice during the summer of 1886 Kelly went too. During her stay she developed an affection for the more romantic ring of the French language, and laughingly insisted ever after on being addressed as Marie Jeanette.

Eddy and Annie's union was doomed from the beginning. Too many had come to know Eddy's real identity, and even the friendliest tongues began to wag incorrigibly. When insidious rumour and garbled third-hand speculation finally filtered into the higher echelons of Whitehall the reaction was first disbelief, then amazement, finally horror. The Marquess of Salisbury, then Prime Minister, hardly needed the sharply worded note instructing him to deal with the situation which had been penned in a paroxysm of fury by the Queen as soon as she learned the news. But Salisbury's interests were at variance with those of the Queen, who merely wanted the affair brought to an end and Eddy's part in it hushed up.

For Salisbury the tidings from Cleveland Street represented more than a family scandal. Victoria was furious not because she expected Eddy's behaviour to rain destruction upon the throne, but because a member of her household had dared have private feelings and a mind of his own, and that a serious course of action had been taken without Her Imperial Majesty's leave. After her initial fit of rage she regarded the episode as hardly more than an eldest son's peccadilloes, worthy of a reprimand but little more. The discerning Salisbury, however, could see that Eddy had been sowing not only wild oats, but the seeds of revolution.

Many pundits already thought Victoria would be the last monarch. Socialism was claiming new devotees with alarming speed, and there was something in the intensely patriotic spirit of the British that had always nurtured a covert mistrust of its Teutonic Royal Family. This dormant resentment was played upon unashamedly by the republicans, and as the seventies became the eighties it frequently seemed clear that England was entering her last years as a sovereign state. Poverty and disease ravaged the lower classes no worse than they had in previous reigns, but now, thanks to the republicans, the poor had someone to blame—the idle rich. There was little love for their Queen left in the hearts of the poor; the Irish spoke of her disparagingly as the Famine Queen. Finally there were attempts to assassinate her. Her son Edward's involvement in divorce scandals and his insatiable sexual appetite made the situation drastically worse.

Eddy seemed the only hope of salvaging some last vestige of the common man's affection for his Royal Family. Young and attractive, he was popularly regarded as the one King who might make the throne secure again. If he too slid on to the downward path of immorality and dissipation, Salisbury feared, the end of the monarchy was surely nigh.

In his adventures at Cleveland Street Eddy had created a danger worse even than if he had followed in his father's mucky footprints. For he had courted and married a Catholic, and even fathered a child by her. The age was bedevilled with an anti-Catholic feeling so intense that even without the prevailing threat of socialism, Eddy's marriage could have precipitated a revolution. Salisbury's first troubled Administration had begun in 1885. The following year there were dynamite outrages in London, and rioters at Trafalgar Square clashed violently with the police and the Army in the Bloody Sunday conflict. Ireland had exploded with renewed fervour. Salisbury was in his most desperate situation since coming to power. But he was little concerned with his own regime; that was of small consequence at a time when the monarchy and the very structure of British politics seemed on the brink of collapse. Every titbit of information was used by the socialists and republicans to embarrass and disgrace the Crown and to discredit the Government. Salisbury could see with crystal clarity that Eddy's behaviour was enough at this perilous moment of history to fire the fuel of revolution.

To end the affair quickly, he staged a raid in Cleveland Street in 1888. Sickert later described the raid to his son. It was late afternoon as he wandered into the street from Maple Street and saw a gang of ruffians lounging against the wall near Howland Street. They were all strangers, an uncommon sight in that insular community. He sensed that there was something odd in their presence, but was too immersed in his own thoughts to isolate his suspicions. Later, too late, he realized the truth. They may have been dressed as ruffians, but in reality they were a trained body of men *imitating* the loafing classes.

Suddenly a shout went up and a street brawl began. Soon that end of the street was a morass of fighting bodies. They cried out and cursed, and the vulgar spectacle drew people from their homes and shops. Sickert still could not define his fears, but he vaguely felt the acid taste of impending misfortune when he looked up and saw the studio end of the street deserted. He made off at a brisk pace towards the studio to ensure all was well with Eddy, who was staying there at the time. Before he was half-way along the street two hansom cabs turned into the road from Tottenham Street. One drew up outside the studio, the other went directly to the corner and parked by Annie's basement at No. 6. Two men in brown tweed went into the studio, and a fat man and a woman went into the basement. Sickert knew then the meaning of the charade behind him, and he knew it was too late to do anything without bringing harm upon himself. The two men came out of the studio, leading Eddy between them.

'He knew what it was all about', said Sickert, 'I could see the fear written in his face. I stood in the shadows by the shop and looked on with an awareness of the absurd inevitability of tragedy, the same in life as on the stage. Nothing can alter the inevitable.'

The man and woman emerged almost immediately from the basement and brought Annie struggling to the street. The lovers caught a last desperate glimpse of each other as their captors bundled them into separate cabs. When Eddy saw her he reached into the void between them and howled lamentably. She remained silent, but his continued sobs, soon muffled under the covers of the cab, expressed the insupportable grief of them both. Then the cabs were rattling off towards Oxford Street, one turning right at the end, the other left. Sickert never saw Eddy again—and Annie once, possibly twice. But he never again saw the carefree Annie of Cleveland Street, just a hag. The raid was all over in a minute. As the last cab turned the corner the brawl behind him ended as quickly as it had begun and the charlatans dispersed. He went away and got drunk.

Eddy was returned to Court and placed under strict supervision. Annie was confined for a hundred and fifty-six days at

Guy's Hospital, and later at various workhouses and other
hospitals. She died thirty-two years later, insane. But Marie
Kelly escaped, Sickert knew not how, and fled back to the
East End, taking the child with her. Somehow, by a tortuous
route, the child was returned to Sickert, and he placed her in
the care of some poor relatives. It was not long, however, before
misfortune brought her into the care of the workhouse and a long
period in institutions followed. Later, about 1895, Sickert took
her to Dieppe, where she spent the rest of her childhood. Here his
own story ended, he reflected soberly, but he had come to know
details of what followed Kelly's flight.

In the event, removing Annie only compounded Salisbury's
dilemma, for Marie Kelly fell in with a gaggle of gin-sodden
East End harlots and shared her forbidden knowledge. Sickert
maintained he never really knew the details of the affair, but it
seemed that with the support of others, Kelly devised an
ambitious blackmail, which brought about their own destruction. Salisbury was now faced not only with the desperate need to
hush up Eddy's misdemeanours; but worse, he had to conceal the
ruthless way his bride had been institutionalized. A few stray but
vital pebbles kicked loose by Eddy had started to dislodge an
avalanche. Of one thing Salisbury was certain, said Sickert.
Kelly and her accomplices had to be silenced.

The man entrusted with the mission was Sir William Gull,
Physician in Ordinary to Queen Victoria, a noble and loyal
servant who had several times performed discreet abortions in
the marbled bedchambers of Windsor. The troublesome had
more than once been rendered harmless by Gull certifying
them insane. He had signed just such a bogus certificate in the
case of Annie. He was possessed of a bizarre sense of humour,
and an appetite for self-aggrandizement. He was also a Freemason of high standing. Sickert made the startling claim that
neither the Royal Family nor the Government was behind the
plot to silence Kelly, but at the instigation of Salisbury—one
of the country's most influential Freemasons—the operation
was carried out by and on behalf of the secret brotherhood.
For Masonry was the power behind the Throne and Government alike. If the Throne went, and Britain became a republic,
the Masons went too. Kelly and her cronies had to be silenced
if the reins of power were to remain firmly in Masonic hands,
but old Sickert thought it unlikely that Lord Salisbury ever
wanted anyone murdered, or imagined for a moment that Sir

William Gull would invent Jack the Ripper. It was more likely that he spoke with the rashness of Henry II over Becket and spat out angry words to the effect of, 'Will no one rid me of these meddling whores?'

It all sounded terribly unlikely.

CHAPTER TWO

The Sickert Story

I sat and looked at Joseph Sickert in silence. My mind was choked with a mass of questions so dense that to articulate any of them would instantly have obscured others. He had been speaking in his customary vague and disordered manner for nearly four hours. I was saturated with names and dates, and was having a hard job working out where facts ended and speculation began. I needed time to let it all sink in and to work out the real implication of his story. But despite my own confusion and the growing conviction that his story was not—could not be—true, I was sufficiently mesmerized by it to seek a further interview. Of one thing I was certain: Joseph Sickert may have been grossly misled, but he believed utterly in every syllable of his tale. If this was indeed the final solution, I told him, no amount of television programmes or newspaper articles like the one I was proposing to write could do justice to the story. A book was needed. The animated expression his rugged features had taken on as he became more involved in the telling of the tale seemed to recede behind a mask of stone, disappearing like a frightened bat in a sudden blaze of light. He reminded me that he had agreed to see me only in my role as reporter from the *East London Advertiser*. He was not seeking publicity, and had already turned down offers to have his story written by several well-known authors.

However, he did agree to see me again with a view to ironing out any details I was not clear about. He had lived with the story so long he could be forgiven for imagining that all I lacked were a few last pieces to the jigsaw. As far as I was concerned, at least, if his story was a jigsaw most of the pieces were missing and the rest lay face down. I was utterly befuddled.

I met him the following Sunday and we drove to Cleveland Street. As we toured the area where most of the early events in the Ripper saga were supposed to have taken place, he fed me extra details. Later, in between showers, we drove to the East End and walked around the grimy lanes and back alleys to the individual murder sites. I rifled his memory as we walked, and he seemed sufficiently at ease in my company by now to talk quite freely. As we wended our way through the rain-soaked streets, crowded with East Enders trudging to and from Petticoat Lane Market, and later in a tiny Commercial Street cafe over the strongest mug of tea I have ever tasted, understanding slowly dawned.

After the removal of Annie Elizabeth and the pacification of the ingenuous Eddy with a stern but paternal lecture from Lord Salisbury, the situation cooled somewhat. For the Queen, the problem was solved. It remained only for her to speak to her son the Prince of Wales in the strongest possible terms. Victoria's tirades rarely failed to wreak their desired influence on the bluff but not very tough Bertie. Reluctant but total obedience was the family tradition. This had even been the case with the christening of Bertie and Alix's eldest son; it was Victoria who chose Albert Victor Christian Edward for the infant Eddy; and it was Victoria who got her way, then as always. The anger she expended on her son over the Cleveland Street affair guaranteed that a strict discipline would be exerted upon the recalcitrant Eddy, at least for a few months.

Yet Salisbury was acutely conscious of the threat posed by the nanny, Marie Kelly. In a normal political climate the embarrassment she was capable of causing might have proved negligible. In 1888, though, her tale of the goings-on at Cleveland Street would have been seized with relish by the gossip-mongers of the republican and socialist movements. The dog-eat-dog political situation was creating some ferocious enemies for the Government and the Throne. If Kelly's scandalous morsel was picked up by these adversaries its scent would be followed back to Annie Elizabeth. The wicked treatment she had received, combined with Eddy's lamentable behaviour, would feed the revolutionary cause. The hateful spectre of a classless society loomed ever just below the horizon. The view was, admittedly, extreme, and had taken shape in

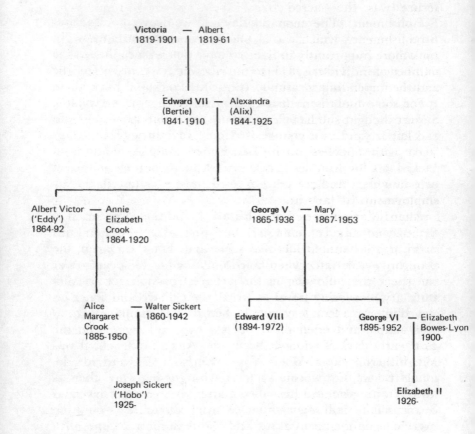

Victoria
1819-1901
—
Albert
1819-61

Edward VII
(Bertie)
1841-1910
—
Alexandra
(Alix)
1844-1925

Albert Victor
('Eddy')
1864-92
—
Annie
Elizabeth
Crook
1864-1920

George V
1865-1936
—
Mary
1867-1953

Alice
Margaret
Crook
1885-1950
—
Walter Sickert
1860-1942

Edward VIII
(1894-1972)

George VI
1895-1952
—
Elizabeth
Bowes-Lyon
1900-

Joseph Sickert
('Hobo')
1925-

Elizabeth II
1926-

Joseph Sickert's family tree as described by his father

the mind of a man who thought he saw his beloved motherland
with her back against the wall. In more stable times Salisbury
was as humane as his position allowed, but these were awkward
days, and the tension of the age was reflected in his policies.
The sort of democracy that favoured now the Liberals under
Gladstone, now the Conservatives under his own leadership,
was the only basis, he believed, for a healthy society. It was not
his own position as Premier, nor even the dominant role of the
Tories, that Salisbury felt it his duty to protect. Who played
the Administration and who the Opposition at any given

moment was of minor importance when Britain's entire political system seemed threatened. What had to be made secure was the sacred Tory-Liberal merry-go-round—the Establishment. The monarchy was the foundation of that Establishment—which, according to Sickert, had always to rank more importantly in Salisbury's list of priorities than any number of individuals. Hence the removal of Annie Elizabeth and the impending measures against Marie Kelly.

For some months nothing was heard of Kelly, and Walter Sickert thought she had fled back to her native Limerick. She had left Ireland as a young girl when her father, John Kelly, faced with hopeless unemployment beyond the Irish Sea, packed up his troubles, uprooted his family of six sons and two daughters and set sail for North Wales. There he found employment at an ironworks, and eventually became a foreman. Marie married a collier called Davies when she was sixteen, but any contentment she might have found in the harsh, death-haunted life of a miner's wife was curtailed less than three years later when he was killed in a mine explosion. She spent the following eight or nine months in a Cardiff infirmary recovering from an unspecified illness, and then she moved in with a female cousin living near by. Her life had ever been simple and often poor, but the poverty and squalor of those early days of widowhood were worse than anything she had hitherto experienced. Like so many underprivileged youngsters in the two and a half centuries since the fable of Dick Whittington and his cat had first beguiled the populace, she focused her still innocent mind's eye on London Town, that merry cluster of citizens at the end of the rainbow. She arrived in 1884 and never escaped. In a few short months she was rubbing shoulders with the dregs of humanity in London's East End, though she was still a cut above the degradation later to be imposed upon her by gin, fear and vital anonymity. Shortly after arriving in London she found her way to an East End convent which provided her with board and lodging in return for the coppers she earned doing domestic work. In 1885 she found a permanent position at the tobacconist's in Cleveland Street and left the East End, determined never to return. Only three years later, in the wake of the raid, circumstances washed her back to Whitechapel, where she went into hiding.

Salisbury's investigations showed she had not fled back to Ireland, where one of her brothers was thought to be serving with a battalion of the Scots Guards. Discreet inquiries were set in motion there, and also in Wales, and at all the known points on her journey to London where it was thought likely she may have fled. But little of her history was known by any except Sickert, whose show of ignorance forced the inquiry to grind to a fruitless halt. In the absence of fresh news it seemed that any hope of development was out of the question. The minnow had swum through the gap in the shark's teeth, and it was not going to be snapped up again with ease. In the weird, paradoxical style peculiar to politicians Salisbury regarded the failure as success. For Kelly to have evaded his net so completely she was remaining silent. As soon as she broke her silence with any degree of effect her whereabouts would be revealed, and she could be removed. If she was never heard of again it would only be because she had held her tongue. If she did that she would be harmless. And safe.

In late July or early August the inevitable and long-awaited clue arrived. A shoddy and unsophisticated attempt at blackmail was initiated. The old painter never revealed who had been the victim of the demand, but it was for a paltry—in other circumstances he might have said laughable—sum. It emanated from the East End. It seemed the blackmail was being practised only to pay protection money to a better-organized gang of blackmailers. Sickert was not familiar with the details, but it was discovered that Kelly was involved with three prostitutes, into whose class she had descended to fight off starvation, and at their instigation had resorted to the blackmail. It was a desperate act. She had seen enough of the Cleveland Street raid to enable her to predict her own fate if she were discovered. But fear is relative. It was easy to run the risk of a distant danger if the gamble delivered her from a close one. The perils at hand were death from starvation and the more sinister threats of the blackmail gang of which she had fallen foul. This was probably the Old Nichol Gang, which demanded money and dealt out violence and even death to the holder of an empty purse. Life was never cheaper than in Whitechapel in the eighties. Three women—Nichols, Chapman and Stride—were found to be involved in Kelly's pathetic coterie, and they had to be rendered harmless. On 31st August the operation began.

Sir William Gull was entrusted with the mission. In many ways an unlikely candidate, he was, in Salisbury's opinion, best qualified for the job for several reasons. Perhaps most significant, he was one of the country's most prominent

Freemasons, and had played a leading part in the select Masonic gatherings called by Salisbury to debate how best to handle the Cleveland Street case. As Sickert had impressed upon his son before, Freemasonry was the power behind the Government, and it was the unseen influence of the Masonic elders which dictated major policies, not the pleasing façade of Commons debate. As Gull was already deeply committed it was unnecessary to introduce an extra party. A loyal servant of Masonry who could see the value of the Crown to the secret brotherhood was essential for the task. Gull epitomized these qualities. Thanks to his ascension into the higher degrees of Masonry, he had, in 1871, been introduced to Princess Alexandra when her husband the Prince of Wales was struck down with typhoid. It had been only ten years since the death of the Prince's father, Prince Albert, of the same disease. It was therefore staggering at the time, and it has never been satisfactorily explained since, that the unknown Gull, son of a country barge-owner, should have been called in to attend the Prince, and that the Royal Physician, Sir William Jenner, should have been called merely as second opinion. Gull's supremacy as a Freemason explains his sudden promotion over the head of the greatest doctor in England. With Jenner's assistance he cured Bertie, but alone he reaped the rewards, receiving a baronetcy the following year. By 1888 he had repeatedly been made aware of the debt he owed to Freemasonry, and its subtle manipulation of those in power. He had already institutionalized Annie Elizabeth Crook with a bogus certificate of insanity, and no doubt Salisbury fully expected him to act in a similar way with Kelly and her associates.

What was not taken into account was Sir William's highly developed sense of the bizarre and his adamantine determination to proceed with a course of action entirely in his own way. He had always been hard-headed to the point that it was said his resemblance to Napoleon went beyond physical appearance. Since a minor stroke in 1887 his steadfastness in remaining faithful to any decision he may have made, however abstruse, was almost obsessional. He decided that capturing the whores and incarcerating them like Annie Elizabeth could have proved almost as unwise as allowing them to remain free. One poor woman shrieking for her truths to be heard and begging inspectors, doctors and visitors to believe she was the wife of a prince could easily have been dismissed as mad. But four apparent lunatics crying out the same tale, even though they were mere East End whores, would have produced a pattern many would have been eager to interpret. If to certify or imprison them was out of the question, and to leave them at large was clearly unthinkable, to kill them was the only practical alternative to Gull's ruthless mind.

He proceeded, said Sickert, to eliminate the women strictly according to Masonic ritual, and though Salisbury was disquieted by the embarrassment the murders caused his Cabinet, he was simultaneously pleased at the shameless display of Freemasonic supremacy it represented. Gull was conforming to a time-honoured Masonic rule, and nothing could be done to dissuade him from his course.

He was driven into the East End on several reconnaissance trips in the carriage of John Netley, chosen because he too was already deeply involved in the affair, having chauffered Eddy to and from Cleveland Street. Advance inquiries by Netley elicited the rough whereabouts of the victims, and Kelly herself was located with the aid of a picture. The third member of the Ripper party—and this seemed the most slender thread of Sickert's amazing story—was none other than the Assistant Commissioner of the Metropolitan Police and another high-ranking Freemason of the same lodge as Gull and Salisbury, Sir Robert Anderson. Gull had set aside a month for the whole operation to be completed. During that time he planned to kill the four women Nichols, Chapman, Stride and Kelly. In keeping with some weird Freemasonic principle, he contrived to spread a panic and terror that would be brought to a frightening climax with the final killing. But something went wrong, and for a reason Sickert never learned Catherine Eddowes was mistaken for Kelly and died in her place.

Because of the deliberately engineered panic which had a stranglehold on the East End after Eddowes's murder, it was out of the question to renew the quest for Kelly straight away. Thus Jack the Ripper lurked in the shadows for thirty-nine days, and many thought his day was done. But on 9th November, the morning of the Lord Mayor's Show, when most of the police force was absorbed with duties centred around that splendid event, Marie Kelly too was silenced. And Jack the Ripper dissolved into the nothingness from which he had so violently erupted only ten weeks before.

During the lull before the final murder Annie Elizabeth was removed from Guy's Hospital, said Sickert. Again his knowledge was vague, but he felt sure some vile operation had been

performed upon her, he suspected by Gull himself. Whether
this had been an attempt to erase dangerous memories from
her mind he could only guess; but on the one or two occasions
he saw her after that her personality had been transformed.
She seemed only half aware, and did not recognize him.
Unaccountably, she had also become subject to violent epileptic
fits. She spent almost the whole of the rest of her life confined in
workhouses, prisons and infirmaries. Whatever experiment may
have been carried out on her, however, she did not totally
forget her past. For on one occasion only she somehow managed
to escape from an institution, and by sheer determination
found Sickert's friends near Cleveland Street who were caring
for Alice Margaret. She was soon rearrested, and returned to
the workhouse.

'Audaces fortuna juvat—fortune favours the bold', said
Walter Sickert, succumbing to his weakness for expressing
himself in other languages. 'The Ripper crimes met with such
ghastly success because of the audacity with which they were
executed.'

He said the murderers located their victims, and in the
cases of Nichols, Chapman, Stride and Eddowes they offered
them a lift in their carriage. All but Stride were murdered
inside the vehicle as Netley jogged through the busy main
streets. The killers later allowed Netley to place the bodies
where they were found. Stride was too drunk to be reasoned
with, and she shambled off along the road when the carriage
came to a halt near her. Netley concealed the vehicle in a dark
thoroughfare south of Commercial Road, and Gull remained
inside. Anderson and Netley followed Stride to Berner Street,
and there she was accosted by Netley as Anderson kept watch,
said Sickert. The coachman overpowered her, threw her to the
ground and slashed her throat. They quickly made their way
back to the carriage where Gull awaited them and drove on to
Aldgate to murder the helpless tart they believed was Kelly.
One of the two younger men—Sickert did not say whether it
was Netley or Anderson—had learned Kelly was in custody at
Bishopsgate Police Station for drunkenness. They knew that at
any time after midnight she could be released, in keeping with
the humane and expedient policy of the City Police whose cells
were not adequate for them to retain all the drunks they
arrested in a night. Kelly was still at large, however, for the
Aldgate victim turned out to be Eddowes. Sickert never knew
how she was mistaken for Kelly. When she was finally run to

earth, Kelly, who alone of the victims had her own room, was murdered indoors.

'Only the undreamed of but simple truth that the murders of Nichols, Chapman and Eddowes did not take place where the bodies were found explains the impossible speed with which these elaborately brutal killings were executed, and the queer lack of blood on the ground near the bodies', Sickert explained.

The painter was induced to remain silent about the whole affair, he frankly confessed to his son, by fear for his own safety. He knew more than anyone else about Jack the Ripper, apart from the actual participators in the conspiracy. He felt relieved that he was allowed to remain in England, even though he did spend as much time as practical on the Continent to be away from the heart of the web. He even bought himself a house at Dieppe when he was toying with the idea of leaving England permanently. No actual threats were made but he did receive some strange, disconcerting warnings that he never fully described.

His silence was further guaranteed one day when he was working in his Dieppe studio. He was touching up a hurriedly painted river scene, a fishing-boat bobbing on a gentle swell. Suddenly and without warning the door opened and Lord Salisbury walked in. Without examining the picture on the easel, or even casting a glance at the rest of the canvases scattered about the room, he offered Sickert an immediate £500 for the picture. Sickert was surprised by the episode, but it did not take him long to work out the reason behind it. No mention had been made of Cleveland Street or the Whitechapel Murders, but he would have been a dullard not to have seen that the exorbitant fee was hush-money. At a time when he had to fight off a damaging sense of complacency if he received three pounds for a painting, the warning was almost welcome. As little would have been achieved by defiance, he accepted the bribe and remained silent until the day he felt compelled to tell all he knew to Joseph.

One violent and unexpected postscript was that the loathsome Netley, misguidedly believing he would find favour with the powerful, continued a lone campaign against Alice Margaret. If he killed her, he seemed to imagine, he would remove the final blemish from the future of his masters. Alice Margaret had at first been taken from Sickert and removed to Windsor, where she was to have been found somewhere to live and to have been cared for as befitted a royal child, however unwanted. Eventually the embarrassment of her presence became too acute, and, chiefly due to the machinations of those behind the Ripper murders, she was returned to Sickert. He passed her on to some poor relatives, and later had her looked after in Dieppe. Netley twice tried to murder the controversial infant by running her down with his cab—once in 1888 at the height of the Ripper's reign of terror and once in February 1892. On the first occasion he ran Alice Margaret down as she crossed either Fleet Street or the Strand with an elderly relative. When the cab struck her it passed right over her body. The driver was later described to Sickert by the relative, and he knew it could be none other than Netley. Sickert said that in the confusion after the second 'accident', in Drury Lane, Netley pushed through the crowd and fled to Westminster Bridge, pursued by several passers-by. He threw himself into the Thames and drowned. When Alice Margaret grew up she married a man called Gorman, who turned out to be impotent. Her relationship with Sickert had always been close, and the desperate loneliness that descended on her with growing deafness and a marriage devoid of physical love made the step from being Sickert's ward to being his mistress a natural one. She was his lover for more than twelve years, bore him a son, Joseph, and died in 1950. Sickert himself died in 1942.

As the years passed and the events of 1888 failed, like the rest of Sickert's memories, to fade into a uniform vagueness contrasted only by the odd pinnacle of clearly remembered detail, a strange effect manifested itself. He found himself, half willingly and half unconsciously, painting into his pictures cryptic references to the truth behind the Ripper murders. For many years, he said, it was his way of living with his ghastly knowledge and, in a perverse way, almost of setting the record straight.

CHAPTER THREE

The Truth and Nothing but the Truth?

In an article about Jack the Ripper in the *Pall Mall Gazette* in December 1888 the Earl of Crawford and Balcarres declared:

> In endeavouring to sift a mystery like this, one cannot afford to throw aside any theory, however extravagant, without careful examination, because the truth might, after all, lie in the most unlikely one.

Unlikely as Sickert's story was, it would have been irresponsible to dismiss it merely because it sounded absurd—it cried out to be investigated. To be fair, though, even absurd was an understatement. It sounded the most arrant, if entertaining, nonsense ever spun about Jack the Ripper, with the possible exception of the suggestion that the murderer was an escaped gorilla.

If the details of the road ahead were indistinct, at least its general direction was clear: every point in Walter Sickert's story had to be checked to see if any part of it was true. It could well have been a sensational fiction. It seemed significant that Walter offered no evidence to support his story. He had anxiously petitioned Joseph not to breathe a word, so he had clearly not expected it to reach the ears of the public. Perhaps this was why he produced no corroboration. Or perhaps the whole narrative was a pack of lies, and there *could* be no corroboration.

Admittedly a few facts were immediately apparent which began to establish Sickert's credentials. Hereditary deafness has blighted the Sickerts, just as it has the Royal Family. Princess Alexandra passed the disability on to her son Eddy. If Eddy had fathered a child as Sickert claimed it is almost certain she would have carried the trait. Alice Margaret Crook, the daughter Sickert ascribed to Eddy, was deaf. The registers of the St Pancras Board of Guardians, under whose care she came in 1902, make the terse comment: 'Stone deaf'. That the affliction was permanent is confirmed by a report made out by the Relieving Officer of the Westminster Union on 11th October 1905, on which date Alice Margaret applied for workhouse assistance because an injury to her foot was preventing her earning her own living. In a column headed, 'Cause of Distress, Temporary or Permanent', her deafness is once again noted. Her son Joseph is almost completely deaf in one ear, and his youngest daughter has no hearing at all. There is no evidence that Alice Margaret's mother Annie suffered any form of deafness, so the disability is almost certain to have been inherited from her father. Photographs of Joseph Sickert's three daughters as young children bear a certain similarity to a portrait of Eddy's three sisters, painted in 1883 by S. P. Hall, now hanging in the National Portrait Gallery. Joseph himself is the image of Walter Sickert, and appears to bear no physical resemblance to members of the Royal Family. A photograph of Alice Margaret, however, shows a marked similarity between her features and those of Princess Alexandra. Most noticeable are the widely spaced eyes, small mouth and firm, rounded chin. The story of Walter Sickert's fear for his own safety in the years succeeding the murders makes sense of a bewildering aspect of his life that even his friends were at a loss to explain—his frequent unexpected trips to the Continent. One of his closest friends, Marjorie Lilly, recalled his odd restlessness, his unpredictable departures for Dieppe and his equally unexpected returns. These disappearances were all the more difficult to account for because they damaged his influence on the development of new styles in painting. He could and should have wrought enormous changes in England's artistic policies. Instead he would return after long absences to an England where he would be dismissed as 'dated'.

These scattered facts which were emerging from the complicated Sickert saga were not evidence, however. The first task was to investigate Walter Sickert himself and to discover, for instance, if he was even remotely likely to have been chosen by Alix to befriend her son. It seemed inconceivable.

But Sickert was not, as I had always imagined, a down-at-heel artist whose penetrating paintings of low life reflected his own sordid background. He did have connections with royalty. He was born at Munich on 31st May 1860, the eldest son of Oswald Adalbert Sickert. Paint ran in their veins. Notable artistry first appeared in the family with Johann Jürgen Sickert, Walter's Danish grandfather, who was born at Flensborg in Schleswig-Holstein in 1803. Walter wrote of him:

> He was at the same time a painter of easel pictures and head of a firm of decorators, who were employed in the royal palaces by Christian VIII of Denmark. He lived and carried on his business in Altona.

Johann Jürgen was one of the earliest lithographers, and he sent his son Oswald, Walter's father, to study at Paris. Oswald, who was born at Altona in 1828, came to the attention of King Christian VIII through his father, who was in close contact with the Royal Family in the course of his work at the palace. Christian was so impressed with the talent of the young Oswald, which first manifested itself, according to Walter, in 'an astonishing portrait of himself at the age of sixteen', that he conferred on him a travelling purse to Copenhagen where he is said to have become a royal painter. Here it is quite likely that he came to know the whole Royal Family on a personal level, a connection which would have lapsed in 1848 with the death of Christian and the succession of the gluttonous Philistine Frederick VII. In his time at the palace Sickert would have become familiar with all branches of the Royal Family and probably made trips to the Yellow Palace, a summer castle nestling among beech groves at Bernstorff. This was the home of the Heir Apparent, Prince Christian of Schleswig-Holstein-Sonderburg-Glücksburg, later King Christian IX, and his wife Louise of Hesse. In 1844 their daughter Alexandra—Alix—was born.

Alix came to England and married Edward, Prince of Wales—Bertie—in 1863, when she was nineteen. Five years later Oswald Sickert arrived in London with his family and made Britain his permanent home, becoming a frequent exhibitor at the Royal Academy. He continued to paint until his death in 1885, and there is no reason to assume that any friendship that may have existed in Denmark between himself and Alexandra was in any way forgotten when she became Princess of Wales and future Queen. Quite the reverse: Alix, though remarkably popular with the people, was ever an outsider with the British Royal Family, and she never fully overcame her deep nostalgia for her beloved homeland. She went out of her way to be accepted as a member of Victoria's impressive dynasty, but she also clung dearly to her few old friends still within reach. Oswald Sickert and his talented son Walter are likely to have been among that privileged group.

Indeed, there is reason to suspect from the Court gossip of the day that a close bond existed between Walter and the beautiful Alix. One writer describes her fondness for a young painter who perfumed himself and wore his hair in ringlets. Though no names are mentioned, anyone who knew Sickert would realize that the object of her affection could have been none other than he. In the late 1870s he spent four years training for the stage, and eventually joined Henry Irving's company at the Lyceum. He was so proficient at the art of make-up that he successfully defied his own mother to pick him out from a crowd of actors on the stage. His disguise as a gnarled and toothless old man quite deceived her. The influence of the theatre never left Sickert, and even after he had turned his back on acting he would live the life of the artiste rather than the artist. He would change his appearance almost as frequently as his old cronies who still trod the boards at the Lyceum in a different role every night. One day his light brown hair would cascade in floods of curls over his shoulders and he would parade in flamboyant, cavalier clothes. The next day he would have cropped his hair *en brosse* and would go about for weeks in stern greys and blacks.

In later years Sickert was so firmly ensconced in the Royal circle that his second wife, Christine Drummond-Angus, was given the honour of embroidering a vestment of Sickert's design for use on State occasions. The garment, known as the Blue Tunicle, is kept at Westminster Abbey and has been used at every coronation, royal wedding and funeral since it was donated in 1920.

Ennui, one of Sickert's paintings which he told his son contained a veiled reference to the truth behind the Ripper crimes, was at one time owned by Queen Elizabeth, the Queen Mother.

Sickert has been charged with spreading many contradictory stories about the identity of the Whitechapel Murderer, and though this accusation is false, it is easy to see how it evolved. Until his story about Eddy and Annie Elizabeth, which he

shared with no one but his son, Sickert told only one story about
the Ripper. But he told it so regularly and to so many people
that at second and third hand it suffered inevitable distortion.
Sickert thus became the source of an imbroglio of conflicting
tales, despite the fact that he had told only one.

Marjorie Lilly, who died in 1976, remembered Sickert as 'a
strange, compelling and complicated man'.

She said, 'He had a passion for conversation and naturally
took centre stage at any gathering without realizing he did so.
His fascination with the Ripper case was intense and I thought
perhaps he knew the truth.'

The story he repeatedly regaled her with during their
twenty-five-year friendship was always the same. And she
maintained it was the same version he told everyone else. Sickert
himself told his son that he invented this story deliberately. His
knowledge about the Ripper burned inside him like a torch,
and he could not prevent his conversation drifting on to the
subject of the murders. Revealing the truth, he believed, would
have put him in danger. His invented 'solution' served two
purposes: it satisfied his unending need to chatter on about the
Ripper, and over many years it provided him with an entertaining after-dinner yarn that automatically made him the
most magnetic person in any group, a position he delighted in
occupying.

It is fortunate that Osbert Sitwell was sufficiently stimulated
by Sickert's apparent fixation with the Ripper to record the
bogus account. He recalled it in his introduction to *A Free
House!*, an anthology of Sickert's writings. Sitwell wrote:

> Some years after the murders he had taken a room in a
> London suburb. An old couple looked after the house and
> when he had been there some months the woman, with whom
> he used often to talk, asked him one day, as she was dusting
> the room, if he knew who had occupied it before him. When
> he said "No", she had waited a moment and then replied,
> "Jack the Ripper?" . . .
> Her story was that his predecessor had been a veterinary
> student. After he had been a month or two in London, this
> delicate-looking young man—he was consumptive—took to
> occasionally staying out all night. His landlord and landlady
> would hear him come in about six in the morning and then
> walk about in his room for an hour or two, until the first
> edition of the morning paper was on sale, when he would
> creep lightly downstairs and run to the corner to buy one.

Quietly he would return and go to bed. But an hour later, when the old man called him, he would notice, by the traces in the fireplace, that his lodger had burnt the suit he had been wearing the previous evening. For the rest of the day the millions of people in London would be discussing the terrible new murder, plainly belonging to the same series, that had been committed in the small hours. Only the student seemed never to mention them: but then he knew no one and talked to no one, though he did not seem lonely . . . the old couple did not know what to make of it: daily his health grew worse and it seemed improbable that this gentle, ailing, silent youth should be responsible for such crimes. They could hardly credit their own senses and then, before they could make up their minds whether to warn the police or not, the lodger's health had suddenly grown much worse and his mother, a widow who was devoted to him, had come to fetch him back to Bournemouth where she lived. . . . From that moment the murders stopped. He died three months later.

The story has had a remarkable effect: firstly it inspired Marie Belloc Lowndes to write her best-selling novel *The Lodger*. By way of Mrs Lowndes, Sickert has inspired two plays, at least five films, including *The Man In The Attic* and *The Phantom Fiend*, and a two-act opera by Phyllis Tate also called *The Lodger*.

It has even been suggested that a serious theory about the Ripper's identity, hailed by many as the closest we are likely to get to the truth, can also be traced back to Sickert. The assertion, which unfortunately is not substantiated by any documentary evidence, is made by Donald McCormick in his book *The Identity of Jack the Ripper*. It concerns the theory about Montague John Druitt, who has been the prime suspect in the case since the publication in 1965 of Tom Cullen's *Autumn of Terror* and Daniel Farson's *Jack the Ripper* in 1972. The starting-point of their investigations was a paragraph in the private notes of Sir Melville Macnaghten, a hurried draft of his official notes in the Scotland Yard file. These were shown to the two authors by Sir Melville's daughter, Lady Christabel Aberconway, who died in August 1974.

The combined researches of Cullen and Farson produced what on the surface looks like a plausible case against Druitt, a failed barrister who drifted into the teaching profession. In fact the case against Druitt is non-existent, as will be shown in Chapter 8.

McCormick says that he traced a London doctor who knew Sickert, and whose father was at Oxford with Druitt. This doctor maintained that Sickert repeated his 'lodger' yarn to Sir Melville Macnaghten one day at the Garrick Club. Sir Melville latched on to the story because, like the veterinary student, Druitt also had a widowed mother living at Bournemouth. The argument runs that the inclusion of Druitt's name on Macnaghten's list of suspects was a direct result of hearing Sickert's tale and coupling the obviously fictitious student with the man whose body was dragged from the Thames on the last day of 1888.

Until McCormick can produce the name of his London doctor, however, his suggestion is no more than an interesting possibility.

Whether or not Sickert was responsible for Druitt's nomination as a Ripper candidate we may never know, but Druitt did play a part in the rambling saga the painter expounded to his son. Sickert said that from the very beginning Druitt had been a scapegoat, though he had no idea how he had been selected or how the shady arrangements had been made.

The answer to that one would have confounded even Sickert.

CHAPTER FOUR

The Murders

A murder story rarely loses anything in the telling. When the tale is as compelling and ghastly as the Whitechapel Murders it cannot fail to be embellished and distorted beyond measure. Jack the Ripper rapidly became absorbed into the folklore of East London, and no one would reproach the working folk whose possession he has become for adding their own spice to the much-told tale. The cockney granddad, sitting by the hearth surrounded by his eager brood, can be forgiven for adding a dash of romance, or somehow writing himself into the story. The same understandable weakness in his forebears transformed Robin Hood from a mean criminal into the noblest of England's folk-heroes.

It is one of the tasks of the historian to pare away the interpolations of later years, to part fact from legend without demolishing either, for both are valuable when properly set in context. It is a sombre reflection that in the case of Jack the Ripper several so-called serious historians have betrayed their responsibility and set down in print their own invented details and baseless speculation as definite fact. Their stories, perpetuated in print, were not the transient bedtime tales of the common folk, the once-heard fairy tale spoken in hushed tones in the flickering firelight and then gone for ever. Their dishonesty has done more to hinder the search for truth than all the hundreds of honestly concocted fables that have spilled from almost every front parlour and public bar in the East End. Even senior policemen of the day, notably Sir Robert Anderson, fabricated details about the Ripper to inject new, if bogus, life into their memoirs. Numerous authors in journals and full-length books have followed their example, to imbue with apparent logic often completely misguided arguments. The most extreme offender, it seems, was a romancer called Leonard Matters. His book *The Mystery of Jack the Ripper*, published in 1929, is based on unsupported and palpably false statements, developing along a ragged tangent of wild speculation masquerading as fact. Even the smallest act of dishonesty on the part of an author is reprehensible, for while appearing to clarify it obscures the already fading threads of truth.

Is it possible, then, after nearly ninety years of conjecture and deception, to get back to basics? The only documentary records likely to be free of exaggeration and romance are the notes of the policemen directly engaged on investigating the case at the time. In his *Jack the Ripper in Fact and Fiction*, pubblished in 1965, Robin Odell complained:

> It is a pity . . . that Inspector Abberline, who was in charge of the murder hunt, never took up the pen. Of all the persons who played a part in the search for the murderer, none was more actively in touch with events than the inspector.

But though he never wrote a book, Inspector Frederick George Abberline did take up the pen. Abberline's writings on the Ripper, and those of his fellow-inspectors engaged on the case, were not sensational flannel for otherwise drab autobiographies, but were handwritten Special Reports written on the spot at the time of the killings. They contain no extraneous detail and are direct and to the point, if quaintly punctuated. They are the most accurate and valuable writings on the Whitechapel Murders, and the reason they have never before been published is that since 1888 they have been kept in the secret files of Scotland Yard and the Home Office.

Though the closed files at the Yard were not to have been opened to the public until 1992, I was granted permission to see them, and spent four days in July 1974 copying their contents verbatim. They are stored in a grubby cardboard box and comprise three bulging manila folders, each stamped with a code number and the words *Closed Until 1992*. They are known for convenience as the *Victims*, *Suspects* and *Letters* files, the latter containing hundreds of letters received from cranks the world over, many of them written in red ink and some in blood, and the majority of them signed 'Jack the Ripper'.

Between 1888 and 1891 all papers and reports concerning murders in the vicinity of Whitechapel were consigned to the *Victims* file. In 1892 the file was closed, and two years later Sir Melville Macnaghten inserted his own notes in the vain hope of making the rest clear. The *Victims* folder, neatly tied with pink tape, contains individual case files marked thus:

EMMA ELIZABETH SMITH, aged 45, murdered on 3rd April 1888.
MARTHA TABRAM alias TURNER, aged 35 to 40, murdered on 7th August 1888.
MARY ANN NICHOLLS [sic] murdered on 31st August 1888.
ANNIE SIFFEY alias CHAPMAN, murdered on 8th September 1888.
ELIZABETH STRIDE, murdered on 29th September 1888.
CATHERINE BEDDOWES [sic], murdered 29th September 1888.
MARIE JEANETTE KELLY, murdered on 9th November 1888.
ROSE MYLETT alias LIZZIE DAVIS, murdered on 26th December 1888.
ALICE McKENZIE, murdered on 17th July 1889.
TRUNK OF A FEMALE, found on 10th September 1889.
FRANCES COLES, murdered on 13th February 1891.

Only those I have indicated by bold type were victims of the Ripper, as will be shown presently. The reports in the individual files tell much of the story. Mary Ann Nichols, the first victim, was found in Bucks Row—now Durward Street— a dark thoroughfare running parallel with and close to the day and night bustle of Whitechapel Road. Inspector J. Spratling of J Division takes up the story in his Special Report written only a few hours after the murder:

P.C. 97J Neil reports at 3.45 a.m., 31st inst. [August], he found the dead body of a woman lying on her back with her clothes a little above her knees, with her throat cut from ear to ear on a yard crossing at Bucks Row, Whitechapel. P.C. obtained the assistance of P.C.'s 55H Mizen and 96J Thain. The latter called Dr Llewellyn, No. 152 Whitechapel Road. He arrived quickly and pronounced life to be extinct, apparently but a few minutes. He directed her removal to the Mortuary, stating he would make a further examination there, which was done on the ambulance.

Upon my arrival there and taking a description I found that she had been disembowelled, and at once sent to inform the doctor of it. He arrived quickly and on further examination stated that her throat had been cut from left to right, two distinct cuts being on the left side. The windpipe, gullet and spinal cord being cut through, a bruise apparently of a thumb being on the right lower jaw, also one on left cheek. The abdomen had been cut open from centre of bottom of ribs on right side, under pelvis to left of the stomach; there the wound was jagged. The omentum or coating of the stomach was also cut in several places, and two small stabs on private parts appeared done with a strong bladed knife, supposed to have been done by some left handed person, death being almost instantaneous.

Description: age about 45; length 5 ft 2 or 3; complexion dark; hair dark brown turning grey; eyes brown; bruise on lower right jaw and left cheek, slight laceration of tongue; one tooth deficient front of upper jaw, two on left of lower.

Dress: brown ulster, 7 large brass buttons (figure of a female riding a horse and man at side thereon), brown linsey frock, grey woollen petticoat, flannel drawers, white chest flannel, brown stays, black ribbed woollen stockings, men's spring-sided boots, cut on uppers, tips on heels, black straw bonnet, trimmed black velvet.

I made enquiries and was informed by Mrs Emma Green, a widow, New Cottage adjoining, and Mr Walter Purkis, Eagle Wharf, opposite, also of William Louis, night watchman to Messrs Brown & Eagle at wharf near, none of whom heard any screams during the night, or anything to lead them to believe that the murder had been committed there.

The stations and premises of the East London and District Railways, also the wharves and enclosures in the vicinity have been searched but no trace of any weapon could be found there.

P.C. states he passed through the Row at 3.15 a.m. and P.S. 10 Kirley about the same time, but the woman was not there then and is not known to them.

A more complete account written in the strong, attractive copperplate of Abberline himself once the inquiry had got under way, says:

About 3.40 a.m. 31st ult. as Charles Cross, carman of 22 Doveton Street, Cambridge Road, Bethnal Green, was passing through Bucks Row, Whitechapel (on his way to work) he noticed a woman lying on her back on the footway (against some gates leading into a stable yard). He stopped to look at the woman when another carman (also on his way to work) named Robert Paul of 30 Fosters Street, Bethnal Green came up and Cross called his attention to the woman, but being dark they did not notice any blood, and passed on with the intention of informing the first constable they met. On arriving at the corner of Hanbury Street and Old Montague Street they met P.C. 55H Mizen and acquainted him of what they had seen, and on the constable proceeding towards the spot he found that P.C. 97J Neil (who was on the beat) had found the woman, and was calling for assistance.

P.C. Neil had turned on his light and discovered that the woman's throat was severely cut. P.C. 96J Thain was also called and sent at once for Dr Llewellyn of 152 Whitechapel Road who quickly arrived on the scene and pronounced life extinct and ordered the removal of the body to the Mortuary. In the meantime P.C. Mizen had been sent for the ambulance and assistance from Bethnal Green station, and on Inspector Spratling and other officers arriving, the body was removed to the Mortuary. On arriving there the inspector made a further examination and found that the abdomen had also been severely cut in several places, exposing the intestines. The inspector acquainted Dr Llewellyn who afterwards made a more minute examination and found that the wounds in the abdomen were in themselves sufficient to cause instant death, and he expressed an opinion that they were inflicted before the throat was cut.

The body was not then identified. On the clothing being carefully examined by Inspector Helston he found some of the underclothing bore the mark of Lambeth Workhouse which led to the body being identified as that of a former inmate named Mary Ann Nichols, and by that means we were able to trace the relatives and complete the identity. It was found she was the wife of William Nichols of 37 Coburg Street, Old Kent Road, a printer in the employ of Messrs Perkins, Bacon and Co., Whitefriars Street, City, from whom she had been separated about nine years through her drunken and immoral habits, and that for several years past she had from time to time been an inmate of various workhouses. In May of this year she left Lambeth Workhouse and entered the service of Mr Cowdry, Ingleside, Rose Hill Road, Wandsworth. She remained there until the 12th July when she absconded stealing various articles of wearing apparel. A day or two after she became a lodger at 18 Thrawl Street, Spitalfields, a common lodging house, and at another com-

CENTRAL OFFICER'S
SPECIAL REPORT.

SUBJECT *The Murder in Whitechapel*

REFERENCE TO PAPERS
5 2 9 8 3

CRIMINAL INVESTIGATION DEPARTMENT,

SCOTLAND YARD,

19th day of Sept. 1888

With reference to the subject named in margin. I beg to report that about 3.40. am 31st Ulto as Charles Cross, carman of 22 Doveton Street, Cambridge Road, Bethnal Green was passing through Buck's Row, Whitechapel (on his way to work) he noticed a woman lying on her back on the footway (against some gates leading into a stable Yard) he stopped to look at the woman when another carman (also on his way to work) named Robert Paul of 30 Foster St. Bethnal Green came up, and Cross called his attention to the woman, but being dark they did not notice any blood, and passed on with the intention of informing the first constable they met, and on arriving at the corner of Hanbury St. and Old Montague St. they met P.C. 55 H. Mizen and acquainted

(1)

The first page of Inspector Abberline's report

mon lodging house at 56 Flower & Dean Street up to the night of the murder.

About 1.40 a.m. that morning she was seen in the kitchen at 18 Thrawl Street when she informed the deputy of the lodging house that she had no money to pay her lodgings. She requested that her bed might be kept for her and left stating that she would soon get the money. At this time she was drunk. She was next seen at 2.30 a.m. at the corner of Osborn Street and Whitechapel Road by Ellen Holland, a lodger in the same house, who seeing she was very drunk requested her to return with her to the lodging house. She however refused, remarking that she would soon be back and walked away down the Whitechapel Road in the direction of the place where the body was found. There can be no doubt with regard to the time because the Whitechapel church clock chimed 2.30 and Holland called the attention of the deceased to the time.

We have been unable to find any person who saw her alive after Holland left her. The distance from Osborn Street to Bucks Row would be about half a mile. Inquiries were made in every conceivable quarter with a view to trace the murderer but not the slightest clue can at present be obtained.

Eight days later the killer struck again. As yet he had not been baptized by the unknown crank who, towards the end of September, would send a letter signed 'Jack the Ripper' to the Central News Office. For the moment he was still known only as the Whitechapel Murderer; faceless, elusive, and somehow, even after only two killings, already more frightening than any villain to have emerged from the deeply villainous East End.

At 6.10 on the morning of 8th September Inspector Joseph Chandler was on duty at Commercial Street Police Station, Spitalfields, when he received information that another woman had been murdered. The crime had taken place in Hanbury Street, a long, narrow thoroughfare running east from Commercial Street. It was named after the local firm of brewers, Truman, Hanbury & Buxton, and today the concrete bulk of Truman's Brewery occupies most of one end of the street— including the site of the Ripper's second murder.

In 1888 the road had no feature to distinguish it from any of the mean streets of dilapidated four-storey brick houses, crumbling and rat-infested, that scarred the landscape in every direction. These buildings—no stretch of the imagination will allow 'homes'—were the scab which concealed a festering sore: humanity at its most degraded and corrupt. Most of the houses in Hanbury Street were built in the second quarter of the eighteenth century, when the inhabitants of Spitalfields were prosperous Huguenot silk-weavers and when, in spring-time, countless window-boxes would create a blaze of red and yellow beauty in every street. Never did prosperity tumble on to the helter-skelter of misfortune with such dire results. John Stow's *Survey of London*, published in 1598, describes the area as it had been before the relentless expansion of the capital swallowed it whole:

> On all sides without the houses of the suburb are the citizens' gardens and orchards, planted with trees both large and sightly and adjoining together. On the north side are the pastures and plain meadows, with brooks running through them, turning water-mills with a pleasant noise. Not far is a great forest, a well-wooded chace, having good covert for harts, bucks, does, boars and wild bulls. The corn-fields are not of a hungry, sandy mould, but as the fruitful fields of Asia, yielding plentyful increase, and filling the barns with corn.

But urbanization in itself had not brought poverty. In the late 1500s, when the area was first seriously developed, it was nothing if not fashionable. The half-starved wretches who haunted Hanbury Street in the 1880s could have no conception that the squalid tenements directly opposite where the new murder had taken place had at one time been a fine orchard, or that at Easter 1559 it had been no condescension but an honour for Queen Elizabeth I to attend with more than a thousand escorts a joyful service at St Mary's Spital, when there had been morris dancers and a festive accompaniment of trumpets, flutes and drums. But since those days, when Piccadilly itself was a ploughed field overlooking a broad sweep of meadows and rooftops to the sailing barges of the Thames, perhaps any transformation was possible. In 1649, the year of King Charles I's execution, property at the western end of Hanbury Street included three houses, a yard, two sheds, a cowhouse and a garden as well as the orchard already mentioned.

The golden days of the Huguenots were brought to an abrupt end with the first stirrings of the Industrial Revolution. Steam-power soon gave birth to the steam loom. The silk-weavers who had operated their hand looms at home were sucked into the factories. The human element vanished, and what had been a well-organized craft took on the sweat and drudge of mass production. The fortunes of the area and its people simply disintegrated. And it was to a decaying, grimy and disease-ridden slum that Inspector Chandler turned his steps that cold September morning.

I at once proceeded to No. 29 Hanbury Street and in the back yard found a woman lying on her back, dead, left arm resting on left breast, legs drawn up, abducted, small intestines and flap of the abdomen lying on right side above right shoulder, attached by a cord with the rest of the intestines inside the body; two flaps of skin from the lower part of the abdomen lying in a large quantity of blood above the left shoulder; throat cut deeply from left and back in a jagged manner right around the throat.

I at once sent for Dr Phillips, divisional surgeon, and to the station for the ambulance and assistance. The doctor pronounced life extinct and stated the woman had been dead at least two hours. The body was then removed on the police ambulance to the Whitechapel Mortuary.

On examining the yard I found on the back wall of the house (at the head of the body) and about 18 inches from the ground about six patches of blood varying in size from a sixpenny piece to a point, and on the wooden pailing on left of the body near the head patches and smears of blood about 14 inches from the ground.

The woman has been identified by Timothy Donovan, deputy of Crossinghams lodging house at 35 Dorset Street, Spitalfields, who states he has known her about 16 months as a prostitute, and for past 4 months she had lodged at above house. At 1.45 a.m. 8th instant she was in the kitchen, the worse for liquor and eating potatoes. He (Donovan) sent to her for the money for her bed, which she said she had not got and asked him to trust her, which he declined to do. She then left stating that she would not be long gone. He saw no man in her company.

Description: Annie Siffey, age 45; length 5 ft; complexion fair; hair wavy, dark brown; eyes blue; two teeth deficient in lower jaw, large thick nose.

Dress: black figured jacket, brown bodice, black skirt, lace boots, all old and dirty.

A description of the woman has been circulated by wire to all stations and a special enquiry called for at lodging houses etc., to ascertain if any men of a suspicious character or having blood on their clothing entered after 2 a.m. 8th inst.

In a detailed fifteen-page report on the first two murders, Abberline recorded that there was 'no doubt that the same person committed both murders'. He went on:

The identification in this case has also been clearly established. She was the widow of a coachman named Chapman who died at Windsor some 18 months since from whom she had been separated several years previously through her drunken habits, and who up to the time of his death made her an allowance of 10/– per week. For some years past she has been a frequenter of common lodging houses in the neighbourhood of Spitalfields, and for some time previous to her death she had resided at 35 Dorset Street where she was last seen alive at 2 a.m. on the morning of the murder . . . From then until her body was found no reliable information can be obtained as to her movements.

The murderer withdrew into the shadows and left a disorganized police force and dumbfounded Press and public to confuse themselves still further in an excited chase into every conceivable blind alley, both actual and figurative. For three weeks nothing happened. But it was the calm before the storm. On 29th September he reappeared for a veritable orgy of violence, and perpetrated his notorious 'double event', two killings in one night. The first was Elizabeth Stride, forty-five years old, a gangling Swede known as Long Liz. The second was Catherine Eddowes, two years younger, a pathetic little woman who through drink and years as a street-walker looked nearer sixty, as mortuary photographs of her show. From comments about her at her inquest, though, it seems she somehow managed to maintain a chirrupy sauciness.

It is surprising that, after the wealth of written notes in the Yard files relating to Nichols and Chapman, those on the remaining Ripper victims are almost empty. In the case of Eddowes this is understandable. As she was murdered in City Police territory Scotland Yard were not in charge of the investigation into her death, as they were with all the other victims. But the dearth of information in the Stride file is less easy to understand. It contains no direct report of the murder or of police inquiries. And Kelly's file, which any reasonable investigator would expect to find crammed with reports, statements, maps and copious other material, is the sparsest of them all. The fourteen pages of notes relating to Stride do, however, contain some new and important evidence which will be examined in depth in a later chapter. But for information about the murder itself we are presented solely with a clipping from the *Daily News* of 6th October, which is the first document in the file. Even this does not deal so much with the murder as with the inquest. In the Home Office file, however, there is a report on the actual murder by Chief Inspector Donald Swanson. Before examining Swanson's report, another important Ripper document that has never before been published, let *The Times* of Monday, 1st October, set the scene:

> The scene of the first crime is a narrow court in Berners- [*sic*] street, a quiet thoroughfare running from Commercial- road down to the London, Tilbury and Southend Railway. At the entrance to the court are a pair of large wooden gates, in one of which is a small wicket for use when the gates are closed. At the hour when the murderer accomplished his purpose these gates were open; indeed, according to the testimony of those living near, the entrance to the court is seldom closed. For a distance of 18ft or 20ft from the street there is a dead wall on each side of the court, the effect of which is to enshroud the intervening space in absolute dark- ness after sunset. Further back some light is thrown into the court from the windows of a workmen's club, which occu- pies the whole length of the court on the right, and from a number of cottages occupied mainly by tailors and cigarette makers on the left. At the time when the murder was committed, however, the lights in all of the dwelling-houses in question had been extinguished, while such illumination as came from the club, being from the upper story, would fall on the cottages opposite and would only serve to intensify the gloom of the rest of the court.

Swanson's Home Office report, dated 19th October, says:

> I beg to report that the following are the particulars respecting the murder of Elizabeth Stride on the morning of 30th September 1888.—
>
> 1 a.m. 30th Sept. A body of a woman was found with the throat cut, but not otherwise mutilated, by Louis Diem- schutz (secretary to the Socialist Club) inside the gates of Dutfield's Yard in Berner Street, Commercial Road East, who gave information to the police. P.C. 252 Lamb pro- ceeded with him to the spot and sent for Drs Blackwell and Phillips.

1.10 a.m. Body examined by the doctors mentioned who pronounced life extinct, the position of the body was as follows:—lying on left side, left arm extended from elbow, cachous lying in hand, right arm over stomach, back of hand and inner surface of wrist dotted with blood, legs drawn up, knees fixed, feet close to wall, body still warm, silk handkerchief round throat, slightly torn corresponding to the angle of right jaw, throat deeply gashed and below the right angle apparent abrasion of skin about an inch and a quarter in diameter.

Search was made in the yard but no instrument found.

The central section of this report contains a previously un-known piece of evidence that becomes crucial when viewed in the light of the Sickert version of the murders. The evidence will be fully examined later. The last part of the report says:

The body was identified as that of Elizabeth Stride, a prostitute, and it may be shortly stated that the enquiry into her history did not disclose the slightest pretext for a motive on behalf of friends or associates or anybody who had known her. The action of police besides being continued in the directions mentioned in the report respecting the murder of Annie Chapman was as follows.

A. Immediately after the police were on the spot the whole of the members who were in the Socialist Club were searched, their clothes examined and their statements taken.

B. Extended enquiries were made in Berner Street to ascertain if any person was seen with the woman.

C. Leaflets were printed and distributed in H Division asking the occupiers of homes to give information to police of any suspicious persons lodging in their houses.

D. The numerous statements made to police were en-quired into and the persons (of whom there were many) were required to account for their presence at the time of the murders and every care taken as far as possible to verify the statements.

Concurrently with enquiry under head A the yard where the body was found was searched but no instrument was found . . .

Under head C. 80,000 pamphlets to occupiers were issued and a house to house enquiry made not only involving the result of enquiries from the occupiers but also a search by police and with a few exceptions—but not such as to convey suspicion—covered the area bounded by the City Police boundary on the one hand, Lamb St., Commercial St.,

Great Eastern Railway and Buxton St., then by Albert St., Dunk St., Chicksand St. and Great Garden St. to Whitechapel Road and then to the City boundary. Under this head also Common Lodging Houses were visited and over 2,000 lodgers were examined.

Enquiry was also made by Thames Police as to sailors on board ships in Docks or river and extended enquiry as to Asiatics present in London. About 80 persons have been detained at the different police stations in the Metropolis and their statements taken and verified by police and enquiry has been made into the movements of a number of persons estimated at upwards of 300 respecting whom communications were received by police and such enquiries are being continued.

Seventy-six butchers and slaughterers have been visited and the characters of the men employed enquired into, this embraces all servants who have been employed for the past six months.

Enquiries have also been made as to the alleged presence in London of Greek Gipsies, but it was found that they had not been in London during the times of the various murders.

Three of the persons calling themselves Cowboys who belonged to the American Exhibition were traced and satisfactorily accounted for themselves.

Up to date although the number of letters daily is considerably lessened, the other enquiries respecting alleged suspicious persons continues as numerous.

As previously explained, the second murder of the night was that of Catherine Eddowes in Mitre Square, Aldgate. Enemy action during the Second World War so badly damaged the stations of the City Police, under whose jurisdiction the murder fell, that few of their extant documents predate the 1940s. The papers relating to the killing of Catherine Eddowes were among those destroyed in the Blitz. As the Scotland Yard file on Eddowes contains only some horrid photographs of her body taken at the mortuary and an irrelevant extract from the *Philadelphia Times* of Monday, 3rd December 1888, it seemed there was no surviving contemporary report of the murder written by a man actually connected with the case. But in February 1975 when I was granted access to the Home Office files I found a plethora of notes, some actually written by a City policeman engaged on the case. But the eight-page report written by Inspector James McWilliam of the City of London Police Detective Department leaves many questions unanswered. As Henry Matthews, the Home Secretary, scribbled on a sheet of paper attached to McWilliam's report, 'The printed report of the inquest contains much more information than this. They evidently want to tell us nothing.'

A far more complete report of the murder, which is also in the file, was compiled, ironically, by the Metropolitan Police. On 6th November Swanson wrote:

> I beg to report that the facts concerning the murder in Mitre Square which came to the knowledge of the Metropolitan Police are as follows:—
>
> 1.45 a.m. 30th Sept Police Constable Watkins of the City Police discovered in Mitre Square the body of a woman, with her face mutilated almost beyond identity, portion of the nose being cut off, the lobe of the right ear nearly severed, the face cut, the throat cut, and disembowelled. The P.C. called to his assistance a Mr Morris, a night watchman and pensioner from Metropolitan Police, from premises looking on the Square, and surgical aid was subsequently called in, short details of which will be given further on in this report.
>
> The City Police having been made acquainted with the facts by P.C. Watkins the following are the results of their enquiries so far as known to Met. Police:—
>
> 1.30 a.m. the P.C. passed the spot where the body was found at 1.45 a.m. and there was nothing to be seen there at that time.
>
> 1.35 a.m. Three Jews, one of whom is named Mr Lewin[1] saw a man talking to a woman in Church Passage which leads directly to Mitre Square. The other two took but little notice and state that they could not identify the man or woman, and even Mr Lawende states that he could not identify the man; but as the woman stood with her back to him, with her hand on the man's breast, he could not identify the body mutilated as it was, as that of the woman whose back he had seen, but to the best of his belief the clothing of the deceased, which was black, was similar to that worn by the woman whom he had seen, and that was the full extent of his identity.
>
> 2.20 a.m. P.C. 245A Long (the P.C. was drafted from A Division temporarily to assist "H" Division) stated that at the hour mentioned he visited Goldstone [Goulston] Street Buildings, and there was nothing there at that time, but at
>
> 2.55 a.m. he found in the bottom of a common stairs

[1] This man's name was in fact Joseph Lawende. Interestingly, Swanson spells his name correctly only a few lines on.

leading to No. 108 to 119 Goldstone Street Buildings a piece of a bloodstained apron, and above it written in chalk, the words, "The Juwes are the men who will not be blamed for nothing", which he reported, and the City Police were subsequently acquainted at the earliest moment, when it was found that beyond doubt the piece of apron found corresponded exactly with the part missing from the body of the murdered woman.

The surgeon, Dr Brown, called by the City Police, and Dr Phillips who had been called by the Metropolitan Police in the cases of Hanbury Street and Berner Street, having made a post mortem examination of the body reported that there were missing the left kidney and the uterus, and that the mutilation so far gave no evidence of anatomical knowledge in the sense that it evidenced the hand of a qualified surgeon, so that the police could narrow their enquiries into certain classes of persons. On the other hand as in the Metropolitan Police cases, the medical evidence shewed that the murder could have been committed by a person who had been a hunter, a butcher, a slaughterman, as well as a student in surgery or a properly qualified surgeon.

The result of the City Police enquiries were as follows:— beside the body were found some pawn tickets in a tin box, but upon tracing them, they were found to relate to pledges made by the deceased, who was separated from her husband, and was living in adultery with a man named John Kelly, respecting whom enquiry was at once made by Metropolitan and City Police, the result of which was to shew clearly that he was not the murderer. Further it shewed that the deceased's name was Catherine Eddowes, or Conway who had been locked up for drunkenness at Bishopsgate Street Police Station at 8.45 p.m. 29th and being sober was discharged at 1 a.m. 30th. Enquiry was also made by the City and Metropolitan Police conjointly into her antecedents, and it was found that there did not exist amongst her relations or friends the slightest pretext for a motive to commit the murder.

At the Goldston [*sic*] Street buildings where the portion of the blood-stained apron was found the City Police made enquiry, but unsuccessfully and their subsequent enquiries into matters affecting persons suspected by correspondence or by statements of individuals at Police Stations, as yet without success, have been carried on with the knowledge of the Metropolitan Police, who on the other hand have daily acquainted the City Police with the subjects and natures of their enquiries.

Upon the discovery of the blurred chalk writing on the

wall, written—although mis-spelled in the second word—in
an ordinary hand in the midst of a locality principally
inhabited by Jews of all nationalities as well as English, and
upon the wall of a common stairs leading to a number of
tenements occupied almost exclusively by Jews, and the
purport of the writing [being] to throw blame upon the
Jews, the Commissioner deemed it advisable to have them
rubbed out. Apart from this there was the fact that during
police enquiries into the Bucks Row and Hanbury Street
murders a certain section of the Press cast a great amount of
suspicion upon a Jew named John Pizer, alias "Leather
Apron", as having been the murderer, whose movements at
the dates and hours of those murders had been satisfactorily
enquired into by Met. Police, clearing him of any connection,
there was also the fact that on the same morning another
murder had been committed in the immediate vicinity of a
socialist club in Berner Street frequented by Jews—con-
siderations which, weighed in the balance with the evidence
of chalk writing on the wall to bring home guilt to any
person, were deemed the weightier of the two. To those
police officers who saw the chalk writing, the handwriting
of the now notorious letters to a newspaper agency bears no
resemblance at all.

Rewards were offered by the City Police and by Mr
Montagu [the M.P. for Whitechapel] and a Vigilance Committee formed, presided over by Mr Lusk of Alderney Road,
Mile End, and it is to be regretted that the combined result
has been that no information leading to the murderer has
been forthcoming. On the 18th Oct. Mr Lusk brought a
parcel which had been addressed to him to Leman Street
[police station]. The parcel contained what appeared to be a
portion of a kidney. He received it on 15th Oct. and submitted
it for examination eventually to Dr Openshaw, curator of
London Hospital Museum, who pronounced it to be a human
kidney. The kidney was at once handed over to the City
Police, and the result of the combined medical opinion they
have taken upon it is that it is the kidney of a human adult, not
charged with fluid, as it would have been in the case of a body
handed over for purposes of dissection to an hospital, but
rather as it would be in a case where it was taken from the
body not so destined. In other words similar kidneys might
and could be obtained from any dead person upon whom a
post mortem had been made from any cause, by students or
dissecting room porter. The kidney, or rather portion of the
kidney, was accompanied by a letter couched as follows:—

From Hell

Mr Lusk
   Sir
       I send you half the
Kidne I took from one women
prasarved it for you tother piece I
fried and ate it was very nise. I
may send you the bloody knif that
took it out if you only wate a whil
longer
    signed   Catch me when
           you can
        Mishter Lusk

The postmarks upon the parcel are so indistinct that it cannot be said whether the parcel was posted in the E. or E.C. districts, and there is no envelope to the letter, and the City Police are therefore unable to prosecute any enquiries upon it.

The remaining enquiries of the City Police are merged into those of the Metropolitan Police, each force cordially communicating to the other daily the nature and subject of their enquiries.

The foregoing are the facts so far as known to Metropolitan Police, relating to the murder in Mitre Square.

An exquisite cunning that surpassed even the diabolical success of the early murders was in evidence in the killing of Catherine Eddowes. No scream or sound of a scuffle was heard; if the murder indeed took place in the Square it was committed less than fifteen minutes before the discovery of the body, and the killer's timing was uncannily precise, for P.C. Watkins had passed through on his beat only a quarter of an hour before and seen nothing. In that brief space of time the murderer had apparently not only performed in total silence the elaborate butchery described in Swanson's report, he had also carried out the delicate surgical operation involved in removing one of the woman's kidneys. The kidney is one of the most difficult organs to locate, as it is secreted deep inside the body and concealed in a mass of fatty tissue. Yet the remains of Eddowes were found in the darkest corner of Mitre Square. No theorist has yet been able to explain how the Ripper worked with such silent skill and swiftness, his efficiency unimpaired by the impenetrable gloom.

The mad confidence of the Ripper seemed to have reached a climax, breaking through the limits of his self-control. Since his first frenzied appearance he had left no clues. Now he appeared to lay them deliberately. An irrational sense of invincibility has frequently been the downfall of arrogant murderers. Not so Jack the Ripper. What looked like his act of supreme defiance—the writing on the wall—only created worse confusion among his hunters.

After the double murder, the newspapers disclosed that a letter written in red ink and signed 'Jack the Ripper' had been received by the Central News Office, having been posted in the London E.C. area two days before the murder. A day after the murder, a postcard was received bearing the same signature. The name needed to be published only once. Within hours of the appearance of the first issues of the newspapers containing the texts of the two messages the indelible name Jack the Ripper had seared itself into the minds of East Enders.

Panic descended on the East End. Centenarian William Ifland is one of the few people left who know exactly what it was like living in Whitechapel through the grim autumn of 1888. He was born in Russia in 1873. At the age of thirteen he fled the persecution and poverty of life under the Tsars, and after tramping half-way across Europe with his aged aunt and baby sister he found a ship that was sailing for England—a country where, as far as he knew, a Jew could live free of the fear of pogroms. The ship docked at Tilbury in 1886, and in a matter of days the three penniless immigrants, without a word of English between them, had been mercifully absorbed into the Russian quarter of the East End. They eventually found drab lodgings in Gun Street, Whitechapel. At the end of 1888, shortly after the Ripper committed his final atrocity, William —now nearly sixteen—set off on his own for Canada.

At the age of a hundred and one, in September 1974, he caught his first glimpse of England in eighty-six years. After a lifetime beyond the Atlantic he wanted to see Europe again before he died.

I met the diminutive Ifland in his room at the Kensington Hilton on the last day of his stay in London. He was due that morning to fly to Rome, where he was to begin an exhaustive tour of Europe's capitals. In the previous week he had been reunited with his sister Lena, a toddler when he had last seen her, at her home in Sidney Street, Whitechapel.

'I am one of the few who remember life in the heart of the

place where Jack the Ripper was on the loose', he said in a voice
that was still thickly overlaid with Russian inflections.

'A lot of people still living were alive then, but not many
were old enough to understand what was happening. But I was
fifteen. I understood all right.'

He recalled the nervousness and tension evinced by nearly
everyone he knew, and though it had been nearly ninety years
before, and precise details had faded from his mind or become
buried in generations of later experience, he said he could
picture clearly 'the terrible quiet'.

'It was not a loud shouting panic that came upon us people
of the East End but a long silence. Everyone was tense and
quiet and I remember the agitated whispers, "Jack the Ripper
has struck again", "The Ripper's been at work".'

A story in *The Times* of 12th November 1888 provides a
good example of the mutual suspicion and high state of
nervousness that Ifland remembers:

> Shortly after 10 o'clock last night as a woman named
> Humphreys was passing George-Yard, Whitechapel, she
> met in the darkness and almost on the identical spot where
> Martha Tabram was murdered, a powerful-looking man
> wearing large spectacles. Trembling with agitation she
> asked, "What do you want?" The man made no answer, but
> laughed and made a hasty retreat. The woman shouted
> "Murder" several times and soon alarmed the neighbours.
> Uniformed policemen and detectives ran to the yard from
> all directions. They entered a house into which the man had
> retreated, and he was apprehended. A crowd of people
> quickly collected, who exhibited an almost unanimous
> inclination to lynch the mysterious person, but the police
> were fortunately able to protect him. Being taken to Leman
> Street Police Station, he accounted for his presence in the
> yard by the fact that he was paying a visit to a friend who
> is an inhabitant of it. He referred the police to a well-known
> gentleman at the London Hospital, and in the result he was
> set at liberty.

So it came to Kelly's turn. 'ANOTHER WHITECHAPEL
HORROR, MORE REVOLTING MUTILATION THAN
EVER', screamed the *Illustrated Police News*, which devoted its
entire front page to an artist's impressions of events surrounding
the final killing.

No report of Kelly's death appears in either the Scotland

Yard file or the Home Office file. A scribbled note by Commissioner Sir Charles Warren, merely recording that another Whitechapel Murder had been reported and was in the hands of the Assistant Commissioner, is all the Home Office file yields. By this time the East End was in a lather of fury and terror, and the hysteria was reflected in the Press. For a balanced view of the situation the newspapers must at this stage be used sparingly: they simply cannot be relied upon. Despite the barrenness of the three major sources of information, however, an official record of events surrounding Kelly's murder does exist. The Middlesex County Records Office contains a batch of previously unpublished documents, the original statements of witnesses, made to police on the morning of the murder. All but one are in the handwriting of Abberline himself:

Statement of Thomas Bowyer, 37 Dorset Street, Spitalfields, in the employ of John McCarthy, lodging house keeper, Dorset Street.

Says that at 10.45 a.m. 9th instant, he was sent by his employer to number 13 room, Millers [*sic*] Court, Dorset Street for the rent. He knocked at the door, but not getting any answer he threw the blinds back and looked through the window, which was broken, and saw the body of deceased woman whom he knew as Mary Jane. Seeing that there was a quantity of blood on her person and that she had been apparently murdered, he immediately went and informed his employer Mr McCarthy, who also looked into the room and at once despatched Bowyer to the police station, Commercial Street, and informed the Inspector on duty (Insp. Beck) who returned with him and his employer who had also followed to the station. He knew the deceased and also a man named Joe, who had occupied the room for some months past.

Statement of John McCarthy, Lodging House Keeper, 27 Dorset Street, Spitalfields.

I sent my man Thomas Bowyer to No. 13 room, Millers Court, Dorset Street owned by me for the rent. Bowyer came back and called me, telling me what he had seen. I went with him back and looked through the broken window, where I saw the mutilated remains of deceased whom I knew as Mary Jane Kelly. I then despatched Bowyer to the Police Station, Commercial Street (following myself) to acquaint the police. The Inspector on duty returned with us to the scene at Millers Court. I let the room about ten months ago to the deceased and a man named Joe, who I believed to be her husband. It was a furnished room at 4/6 per week. I sent for the rent because for some time past they had not kept their payments regularly. I have since heard the man Joe was not her husband and that he had recently left her.

Statement of Joseph Barnett, now residing at 24 and 25 New Street, Bishopsgate (a common lodging house).

I am a porter in Billingsgate Market, but have been out of employment for the past 3 or 4 months. I have been living with Marie Jeanette Kelly who occupied No. 13 room, Millers Court. I have lived with her altogether about 18 months, for the last eight months in Millers Court, until last Tuesday week (30 Ulto) when in consequence of not earning sufficient money to give her and her resorting to prostitution, I resolved on leaving her, but I was friendly with her and called to see her between seven and eight p.m. Thursday (8th) and told her I was very sorry I had no work and that I could not give her any money. I left her about 8 o'clock same evening and that was the last time I saw her alive.

There was a woman in the room when I called. The deceased told me on one occasion that her father, named John Kelly, was a foreman of some iron works and lived at Carmarthen or Carnarvon, that she had a brother named Henry serving in 2nd Battn. Scots Guards, and known amongst his comrades as John too, and I believe the Regiment is now in Ireland. She also told me that she had obtained her livelihood as a prostitute for some considerable time before I took her from the streets, and that she left her home about 4 years ago, and that she was married to a collier, who was killed through some explosion. I think she said her husband's name was Davis or Davies.

Statement of Mary Ann Cox, No. 5 Room, Millers Court, Dorset Street, Spitalfields.

I am a widow and an unfortunate.[1] I have known the female occupying No. 13 room, Millers Court about 8 months. I knew her by the name of Mary Jane. About a quarter to twelve last night I came into Dorset Street from Commercial Street, and I saw walking in front of me Mary Jane with a man. They turned into the court and as I entered the court they went indoors. As they were going into her room, I said good night Mary Jane. She was very drunk and could scarcely answer me, but said good night. The man was

---

[1] The Victorian euphemism for 'prostitute'.

carrying a quart can of beer. I shortly afterwards heard her
singing. I went out shortly after twelve and returned about
one o'clock and she was still singing in her room. I went out
again shortly after one o'clock and returned at 3 o'clock.
There was no light in her room then and all was quiet, and I
heard no noise all night.

The man whom I saw was about 36 years old, about 5ft
5 in. high, complexion fresh and I believe he had blotches
on his face, small side whiskers and a thick carroty moustache,
dressed in shabby dark clothes, dark overcoat and black
felt hat.[1]

Mary Jane was dressed I think, last night when I saw her,
in a linsey frock, red knitted cross-over around shoulders,
had no hat or bonnet on.

The following statement is the only one of the batch not written
out personally by Abberline:

*Elizabeth Prater, wife of William Prater of No. 20 room, 27
Dorset Street, states as follows:—*
I went out about 9 p.m. on the 8th and returned about
1 a.m. 9th and stood at the bottom of Millers Court until
about 1.30. I was speaking for a short time to a Mr McCarthy
who keeps a chandler's shop at the corner of the court. I
then went up to bed. About 3.30 or 4 a.m. I was awakened
by a kitten walking across my neck, and just then I heard
screams of murder about two or three times in a female
voice. I did not take much notice of the cries as I frequently
hear such cries from the back of the lodging-house where the
windows look into Millers Court. From 1 a.m. to 1.30 a.m.
no one passed up the court, if they did I should have seen
them. I was up again and downstairs in the court at 5.30 a.m.
but saw no one except two or three carmen harnessing their
horses in Dorset Street. I went to the "Ten Bells" P.H. at the
corner of Church Street and had some rum. I then returned
and went to bed again without undressing and slept until
about 11 a.m.

*Statement of Caroline Maxwell, 14 Dorset Street, Spitalfields, the
wife of Henry Maxwell, a lodging house deputy.*
I have known deceased woman during the past 4 months,
she was known as Mary Jane and that since Joe Barnett left
her she has obtained her living as an unfortunate. I was on

---

[1] The man with the carroty moustache was cleared of suspicion because
Kelly was seen with another man later.

speaking terms with her although I had not seen her for 3 weeks until Friday morning 9th instant about half past 8 o'clock. She was then standing at the corner of Millers Court in Dorset Street. I said to her, what brings you up so early. She said, I have the horrors of drink upon me as I have been drinking for some days past. I said why don't you go to Mrs Ringer's (meaning the public house at the corner of Dorset Street called the Britannia) and have ½ pint of beer. She said, I have been there and had it, but I have brought it all up again. At the same time she pointed to some vomit in the roadway. I then passed on, and went to Bishopsgate on an errand, and returned to Dorset Street about 9 a.m. I then noticed deceased standing outside Ringers public house. She was talking to a man, age I think about 30, height about 5ft 5in, stout, dressed as a Market Porter. I was some distance away and am doubtful whether I could identify him. The deceased wore a dark dress, black velvet body, and coloured wrapper round her neck.

Mrs Maxwell's assertion that she saw Kelly at nine o'clock when medical evidence shows she had been dead five or six hours when her body was found at 10.45, is one of the enduring mysteries concerning the Ripper case. Whether Mrs Maxwell was lying, mistaken or drunk has never been explained. The only certainty is that she was wrong.

Statement of Sarah Lewis, No. 24 Great Pearl Street, Spitalfields, a laundress.
Between 2 and 3 o'clock this morning I came to stop with the Keylers at No. 2 Millers Court as I had had a few words with my husband. When I came up the court there was a man standing over against the lodging house on the opposite side in Dorset Street but I cannot describe him. Shortly before 4 o'clock I heard a scream like that of a young woman, and seemed to be not far away. She screamed out murder. I only heard it once. I did not look out of the window. I did not know the deceased.
Sarah Lewis further said that when in company with another female on Wednesday evening last at Bethnal Green, a suspicious man accosted her. He carried a black bag.

Statement of Julia Venturney
I occupy No. 1 room, Millers Court. I am a widow but now living with a man named Harry Owen. I was awake all night and could not sleep. I have known the person occupying No. 13 room opposite mine for about 4 months. I knew the man

who I saw down stairs (Joe Barnett) he is called Joe, he
lived with her until quite recently. I have heard him say that
he did not like her going out on the streets. He frequently
gave her money. He was very kind to her. He said he would
not live with her while she led that course of life. She used
to get tipsey occasionally. She broke the windows a few
weeks ago whilst she was drunk. She told me she was very
fond of another man named Joe, and he had often illused her
because she cohabited with Joe (Barnett). I saw her last
yesterday, Thursday about 10 a.m.

Statement of Maria Harvey of 3 New Court, Dorset Street.
    I slept two nights with Mary Jane Kelly, Monday and
Tuesday last. I then took a room at the above house. I saw
her last about five minutes to seven last night in her own
room, when Barnett called. I then left. They seemed to be on
the best of terms. I left an overcoat, two dirty cotton shirts,
a boy's shirt and a girl's white petticoat and black crape
bonnet in the room. The overcoat shown me by police is the
one I left there.

The statements are accompanied by the following note:

> Inspector Walter Beck, 'H' Division, who
> was first called, together with the
> constables on the beat will attend at the
> Inquest, also myself who will speak of
> contents of room &c if necessary.
>   [signed] F. G. Abberline, Inspector.

Marie Kelly was so horribly mutilated she hardly seemed any
longer in human form. With her death Jack the Ripper
disappeared from the face of the earth. It was as if the insane,
motiveless lone killer for whom everyone was searching had
never existed. Sickert, of course, maintained he never had.

CHAPTER FIVE

The Mad Pork Butcher

Between the beginning of September and a week after the death of Kelly, more than a hundred and sixty men were arrested on suspicion of being connected with the Whitechapel Murders. A study of the contemporary Press, both national and local, puts the number somewhere between a hundred and thirty and a hundred and fifty in London alone. Though newspaper references do not always name the men arrested, the number tallies closely with the multitudinous reports of arrests in the Scotland Yard file, so can be relied upon. In January 1889 the Yard sent a directive to all stations in the Metropolitan area, calling for reports on all arrests in connection with the Whitechapel Murders to be sent to headquarters. The *Suspects* file bulges with weird and wonderful suggestions about the identity of Jack the Ripper.

The papers create a strong impression that the police were playing some sort of game. They certainly had a fixed idea about the killer's class, if not his precise identity. A suspect had only to give some indication that he was not a complete lay-about to be released. Merely showing to the arresting officer's satisfaction that he had an address was enough to obtain freedom. On no occasion was an alibi for the nights of the murders given and, what is stranger, none was asked for. A story related in a letter to the *Daily Express* of 16th March 1931 provides a typical example of the curious policy adopted by the police. Under the heading *I Caught Jack the Ripper*, former P.C. Robert Spicer of Woodford Green, Essex, claimed that he was on duty in the East End about two hours after the double

murder on the night of 29th–30th September. Suddenly he
came upon a man sitting with a prostitute on a brick dustbin.
The man, well dressed and carrying a black bag, had blood on
his cuffs. He evaded Spicer's questions and was promptly
arrested. Certain he had caught the Ripper, the twenty-two-
year-old constable marched his suspect along to Commercial
Street Police Station. There, under cursory questioning from
the station officer, the suspect claimed he was a respectable
doctor living at Brixton. Immediately he had imparted this
uncorroborated piece of information he was released, without
being asked to open his bag. The suspect was not even required
to explain what a respectable Brixton doctor had been doing
talking to a prostitute in an East End alleyway at three o'clock
in the morning.

This singular preoccupation with the addresses of suspects
is well illustrated in the following reports selected from the
Suspects file. The first was written by Inspector D. Fairey of
Rochester Row Police Station:

> At about 12.40 p.m., 21st inst. [November] Mrs Fanny
> Drake (Conservative Club), 15 Clerkenwell Green, came to
> Rochester Row Station and stated she had put the police on
> the Whitechapel Murderer and had now called to know the
> result. She was walking over Westminster Bridge when a man
> answering the description of the murderer met her, and as he
> passed, gave such a grin, as she should always remember.
> She at once retraced her steps and followed him until oppo-
> site Westminster Abbey, when meeting a mounted Inspector
> she told him of her suspicion, pointed out the man, and came
> to this station, the inspector following and watching the man.
> About 5 minutes afterwards Inspr Walsh came in and stated
> that the gentleman referred to had been followed by him to
> the Army and Navy Stores, Victoria Street, Westminster,
> and had now come to the station to see the lady. I interviewed
> him in the charge room, when he at once produced a
> number of letters and business cards proving himself beyond
> doubt to be Mr Douglas Cow of Cow & Co., India-Rubber
> Merchants, 70 Cheapside, and 8 Kempshott Road, Streat-
> ham Common. This information I at once imparted to the
> lady when she at once apologized to Mr Cow for having
> caused him inconvenience, and both parties then left the
> station.

This report displays not only the widely held belief that no one 'respectable' could have been the Ripper, but also the panic that held London in its grip—a tension so extreme it compelled a woman to denounce a man as a murderer because of the way he grinned.

The 'correctness' of a man's address is once more seen as an unassailable character reference in another report in the file. Inspector J. Bird of A Division wrote:

> I beg to report that at 9.40 p.m., 22nd November 1888, James Connell of 408 New Cross Road, draper & clothier age 36, height 5ft 9in, complexion fresh, long dark brown moustache, dress: brown check suit, ulster with cape, red socks, Oxford shoes, soft felt hat, an Irishman was brought to this (Hyde Park) Station by P.C. 271A Fountain under the following circumstances. Martha Spencer of 30 Sherborne Street, Blandford Square, married, stated that he spoke to her near the Marble Arch, they walked together in the park and he began to talk about "Jack the Ripper" and Lunatic Asylums and said that no doubt, when he was caught, he would turn out to be a lunatic. In consequence of this conversation she became alarmed and spoke to the P.C. who accompanied them to the station. A telegram was then sent to Greenwich Station for enquiry as to the correctness of his address and his respectability, a satisfactory reply having been received he was then allowed to go, as nothing further suspicious transpired.

Of all the suspects arrested none was thought more likely to have been the Ripper than the Mad Pork Butcher who was arrested in Holloway on 12th September, four days after the second murder. Had the real Ripper retired after killing Chapman, no doubt Joseph Isenschmid would have gone down in history as the Whitechapel Murderer. As it later turned out, the Ripper's worst atrocities were carried out after Isenschmid was safely under lock and key.

Isenschmid's fate was sealed very early in the Ripper investigation, when a rumour that the murderer was a man known as Leather Apron gained wide belief. Inspector Abberline wrote in his long Special Report on the murder of Nichols:

> In the course of our inquiries amongst numerous women of the same class as the deceased it was ascertained that a feeling of terror existed against a man known as Leather Apron, who it appeared has for a considerable time past been levying blackmail and illusing them if his demands were not

complied with, although there was no evidence to connect
him with the murder. It was however thought desirable to
find him and interrogate him as to his movements on the
night in question, and with that view searching enquiries
were made at all common lodging houses in various parts of
the metropolis but through the publicity given in the 'Star'
and other newspapers the man was made acquainted with
the fact that he was being sought for and it was not until the
10th instant [September] that he was discovered when it was
found that he had been concealed by his relatives. On his
being interrogated he was able however to give such a
satisfactory account of his movements as to prove conclusively that the suspicions were groundless.

In an annexed report, Inspector Helston pointed out that
Leather Apron was a man called Jack Pizer. Panic over the
Leather Apron rumour had created a climate with all the
mad fervour of a witch-hunt, and when finally poor Pizer, a
boot-finisher whose house rendered up five sharp knives, was
arrested and taken to Leman Street Police Station for questioning public feeling ran so high that a huge mob gathered in the
street outside, calling for his blood. Even after he was exonerated the police dared not release him, and kept him in a cell for
twenty-four hours lest the revenge-hungry crowd should lynch
him. Shy and nervous as he was, Pizer was sufficiently enraged
at the injustice he had suffered to sue several newspapers for
rashly stating on his arrest that he was the killer. He won his
case, and was awarded substantial damages.

Even when the story of his innocence had circulated the
scandalized East Enders still would not rest. They had sunk
their teeth in the Leather Apron rumour and they would not
let go. If Pizer was innocent *he* was not Leather Apron, was the
twisted logic of the hunt. This was Isenschmid's downfall. A
loquacious publicity-seeker called Mrs Fiddymont, landlady of
the Prince Albert pub in Brushfield Street, less than a quarter
of a mile from Hanbury Street, took advantage of the packs of
hungry newshounds who appeared so promptly from Fleet
Street after the murder of Annie Chapman. Mrs Fiddymont
spun the yarn to several reporters that she had seen a fearful-
looking stranger in her pub at seven o'clock on the morning of
the murder. According to Mrs Fiddymont, the interloper wore a
stiff brown hat, a dark coat and no waistcoat. There was blood
on his right hand and on his face, and his shirt was torn. His
eyes, she said, were as wild as a hawk's.

As was so often the case, the police arrived to interview Mrs Fiddymont after the gentlemen of the Press had already bled her of information. Nevertheless, her testimony was taken down, and in the strained atmosphere of the murder hunt possibly more attention was paid to it than it might have earned in more rational times. Only three days later, a report from Holloway Police Station was received by officers at Whitechapel. It did not take long for the figment of Mrs Fiddymont's imagination to be connected with the subject of that report. Contained in the ten Special Reports in the Yard file on Chapman, it says:

METROPOLITAN POLICE
Y Division
Holloway, 11th Sept 1888

I beg to report that at 10 p.m., 11th inst., Dr Cowan, 10 Landseer Road and Dr Crabb of Holloway Road came to station and stated that Joseph Isenschmid, a butcher and a lunatic, a lodger at No. 60 Milford Road, and he having left his lodgings on several occasions at various times, it was thought that he might be connected with the recent murders at Whitechapel. In company of Sub Inspr Rose and Sergt Sealey, C.I.D., I went to the above address and saw George Tyler, occupier, who stated that at 11 p.m., 5th inst. he met Isenschmid in Hornsey Road, who asked him if he would accommodate him with a lodging.

He took him home and he left the house at 1 a.m. 6th, returned at 9 p.m. 6th, left again at 1 a.m. 7th, returned at 9 p.m., left again at 6 a.m. 9th inst., returned at 6 p.m., stayed in house about 30 minutes. He then left to go to Tottenham, returned at 1 a.m. 10th, left again at 2 a.m., returned at 9 p.m. and left again at 1 a.m. 11th and has not yet returned.

I then proceeded to No. 97 Duncombe Road and saw Mrs Isenschmid, his wife, who stated that she had not seen her husband during past two months, but he visited the above premises during her absence on 9th inst. and took away some clothing. She further stated that he was in the habit of carrying large butcher's knives about with him and did not know how he obtained his livelihood. His movements being suspicious, I directed P.C. 376 Cracknell to keep observation on the house and to bring Isenschmid to station, should he return, for enquiries. I also directed observation to be kept on 97 Duncombe Road, Upper Holloway. I respectfully suggest that further enquiries be made by C.I.Department.

No description of man could be obtained sufficient to circulate at present.

                                        Jn Styles, D. Inspr.

Inspector Styles's suggestion was heeded and C.I.D. officers took over the case. In a report dated 13th September, Acting Superintendent J. West of H Division (Whitechapel) wrote:

. . . no new facts have been brought to the notice of police excepting that a man has been detained at Holloway Station on suspicion, since removed to the Infirmary, Fairfield Road, Bow, having been certified as a dangerous lunatic. Sergeant Thick has examined the man's clothing but failed to find any trace of blood upon any of it. Enquiries are being made as to the man's whereabouts on the night in question.

This man's name is Joseph Isenschmid, is a butcher by trade but failed in business about 12 months since. His arrest was brought about through information received from Drs Cowan & Crabb of Holloway, their attention having been called to him by a man named Tyler of 60 Milford Road, Holloway, who stated that Isenschmid, who was his lodger, had frequently been absent from home at early morning.

Detective Sergeant William Thick carried out investigations and on 17th September he wrote:

I beg to report that I called several times at 60 Milford Road, Upper Holloway, with a view of interviewing Mr Tyler re the movements of Joseph Isenschmid, but failed, and I am also unable to ascertain where he is employed. On calling again yesterday I saw a boy named Briggs who informed me that Mr Tyler had removed early that morning, and he did not know where to. The boy was the only person in the house and stated that several gentlemen had called there for Mr Tyler during the last few days. He could say no more. I called on Mrs Geringher, the person referred to in wife's statement, who stated that she did not know the man I referred to and that no person but the regular customers had visited her house, a public house. I have made careful enquiries amongst Germans whom I know in this neighbourhood, but failed to find any trace of "Isenschmid" having been seen in this neighbourhood.

I called at Fairfield Road, Bow, Infirmary Asylum where "Isenschmid" is still detained. I saw the Medical Superintendent who informed me that "Isenschmid" had told him that the girls at Holloway had called him "Leather Apron" and that he had said to them in the way of chaff, I am "Leather Apron", and he supposed they had informed the police. He was a "butcher" by trade but had failed in business. He had a few words with his wife and he left her. He was now getting his living by going to the Market early in the morning, buying sheep's heads, kidneys and sheep's feet, taking them home to his lodgings and dressing them, then taking them to Restaurants and Coffee Houses in the West End of the town, and selling them, and that that was the cause of him being up so early in the morning, and that was the only way open to him to get his livelihood.

The Superintendent would like for police to give instructions what he was to do with Isenschmid. I beg to add that further and careful enquiries are being made with a view of tracing the whereabouts of Mr Tyler to obtain further particulars from him. Also other persons who are likely to give further details of Isenschmid's movements on dates of the recent murders.

The following day, the 18th, Inspector Abberline put pen to paper over the Isenschmid inquiries. He wrote:

I beg to report that inquiries have been continued relative to the various matters in connection with the murders, including the lunatic who was detained by police at Holloway on 12th Inst., and handed over to the parochial authorities same day.

He gives the name of Joseph Isenschmid, and his occupation has been that of a butcher. He is now detained at Bow Infirmary asylum, Fairfield Road, Bow, and from his description he is believed to be identical with the man seen in the Prince Albert P.H., Brushfield Street, Spitalfields, with blood on his hands at 7 a.m. on the morning of the murder of Annie Chapman. Dr Mickle, the medical officer of the Institution, has been consulted with a view to Isenschmid being seen by Mrs Fiddymont and the other witnesses. The doctor is of opinion this cannot be done at present with safety to his patient. It has been ascertained that this man has been wandering about and away from his home for several weeks past, and when he left his home he took with him two butchers knives. He has been previously confined in an asylum, and is said to be at times very violent. Although at present we are unable to procure any evidence to connect him with the murders he appears to be the most likely person that has come under our notice to

have committed the crimes, and every effort will be made to
account for his movements on the dates in question.

In an H Division Special Report dated 19th September
Sergeant Thick recorded the statement of Isenschmid's wife,
perhaps the most incriminating of all the comments about the
lunatic:

> I beg to report that on 12th inst. I called at the Islington
> Workhouse and found that Joseph Isenschmid had been
> removed from there to Fairfield Road, Bow, Infirmary
> Asylum. I then saw Mrs Isenschmid, his wife, at 97 Dun-
> combe Road, Upper Holloway, who stated that they had
> been married twenty one years.
> He is a "Swiss" and was at that time employed as a
> journeyman butcher. They then went into business as Pork-
> butchers at 59 Elthone Road, Upper Holloway, but even-
> tually failed. Her husband then began to get very much
> depressed and repeatedly stopped away from his home at
> night and remained away for several days. He has been in
> Colney Hatch Lunatic Asylum for ten weeks and was dis-
> charged from there about the middle of last December and
> came home supposed to be quite well. He then got employ-
> ment as journeyman butcher at a Mr Marlett's, High Street,
> Marylebone, and stopped there till Whitsuntide. He then
> left and has done nothing since to her knowledge. He pro-
> fessed to have had work but did not bring home any money.
> He has not slept at home for quite two months. About three
> or four weeks ago he was found in a house in Caledonian
> Road and was charged. He was taken to Clerkenwell Police
> Court and remanded for enquiries to be made about him. He
> was eventually discharged. He then came home again and
> changed his underclothing and left again. I did not see him
> again.
>   She then added, "I went away into the country to visit my
> friends last Sunday week (1st Inst.) and returned again on
> Monday following. I was then informed by my daughters
> that my husband had been home and took his shirts and
> collars away. Mr Tyler, 60 Milford Road, Upper Holloway,
> had called during my absence and left a message for me to
> call on him. I went there on Tuesday morning. I did not see
> my husband. When he left he had two bone knives and his
> butcher's clothes with him. I don't know what has become of
> them. I do not think my husband would injure anyone but
> me. I think he would kill me if he had the chance. He is fond
> of other women. He used to frequent a public house kept by a

'German' named Geringher in Wentworth Street, White-chapel. He is known as the mad butcher."

Observation was kept on Isenschmid as he languished in the asylum, Dr Mickle ready at a moment's notice to contact Inspector Stilson if he learned anything incriminating from the lunatic. Stilson's visits to the asylum became less and less frequent as each proved more fruitless than the last. And finally Jack the Ripper struck again and the pathetic Mad Pork Butcher of Holloway was left to rot in his cell, drowning in his own insanity.

CHAPTER SIX

The Motive

In a letter to Gladstone, then Prime Minister, from her widowhood retreat at Osborne House on the Isle of Wight, written on 11th February 1886 Queen Victoria said, 'The Queen cannot sufficiently express her <u>indignation</u> at the monstrous riot which took place the other day in London, and which risked people's lives and was a <u>momentary</u> triumph of socialism and disgrace to the capital'.

She was referring to the unexpected outcome of a meeting of the unemployed—who, it has been estimated, formed nearly 10 per cent of the working population that year—in Trafalgar Square on 8th February. It was the first and in some ways the least disturbing of the episodes of violence which were part of the social backcloth of the period in which Walter Sickert set his unlikely story.

It has already been shown that Sickert mixed with the highest and the most humble, and in the words of Osbert Sitwell was a friend of 'prize-fighters, jockeys, painters, music-hall comedians, statesmen, washerwomen and fishwives'. He certainly mixed in the right circles to share in the intimate gossip of the Court. Though there is no available *documentary* proof that he was a friend of Princess Alexandra, he was certainly a friend of her husband the Prince of Wales. The painter was a leading figure in the raffish cliques in which Bertie throve, and they met constantly at such gatherings as the wild parties thrown by Oscar Wilde. But this does not make the story true. It merely lends the teller a little more credibility.

In any murder investigation the motive is the foundation on

which the case is built, unless the crimes in question are those of a lunatic, and hence motiveless. It has been generally concluded that the latter was true of the Jack the Ripper murders. Sickert, however, claimed there was a precise motive for the East End killings, and that those behind the crimes were trying to conceal the wayward behaviour of a highly placed member of the Royal Family. For a mass of reasons England was in turmoil, revolution seemed only a step away and the monarchy was already unpopular. The conspirators believed they were hushing up a scandal that was likely to topple the throne from its crumbling dais.

Whether or not the Heir Presumptive to the throne did father a bastard and marry an illiterate Catholic, the first essential was to discover whether such conduct would even have been considered important. Was there really a threat of revolution? Were the Royal Family unpopular to the extent that many thought the monarchy would end with the death of Victoria? These were the vital questions.

Several diverse political influences were coming to a head in the mid-eighties. Separately, they would undoubtedly have been troublesome. Combined as they were, they formed a positive danger to the established order.

Revolutionary feeling was reaching a new pitch. Discontent was spreading among the poorly paid working-class and the growing numbers of unemployed. Successive Governments were rocked by the Home Rule controversy which had inspired a civil conflict so savage in Ireland that, as George Earle Buckle, editor of *The Times*, wrote, 'the contagion of lawlessness spread to England'. European and Asian immigrants were flooding into all the major cities, especially the squalid environs of the docklands, where almost without exception a passing Englishman would feel an alien in his own land. The experience was new and dangerous. The proud patriotism engendered during eight hundred years of freedom from foreign invasion was under threat. The jingoistic spirit conjured up by Disraeli in the 1870s had somehow insinuated itself into the make-up of even the lowliest Briton. As men had dominion over the earth, so the English had dominion over men. The jealous possessor of an imaginary Divine Right to conquer and annex, to rule over and lead to enlightenment, the Englishman never more strongly regarded his homeland as his castle. When foreigners began spilling in such profusion into the very heart of his home cities, the resentment was bitter and prolonged. Nor did the hatred end there. Mutual suspicion and mistrust grew up between the various racial types. Through language difficulties and a fear of integration, this degenerated into the establishment of impenetrable ghettos. Race fights became commonplace. And as each aggressive, insecure community became increasingly insular for fear of murder or rape, the hatred deepened and the violence grew worse.

The tide of another power, socialism, which had been subject to a steady ebb and flow for thirty years, looked set by the mid-eighties to flood England and parts of Europe. Since 1849, when Karl Marx had settled in London, the focus of socialist thinking had shifted to England. Marx continued to live and write in London until his death. And though the father of Communism died in 1883, his influence lived on, expanded and propagated by his daughter Eleanor and his close friend and collaborator Friedrich Engels. In 1885, the year the royal bastard is supposed to have been born, socialism received a potent shot in the arm with the publication of the second volume of Marx's great work, *Capital*. Robert Cecil, third Marquess of Salisbury, Britain's Prime Minister during the period of the Whitechapel Murders and the man named by Sickert as the chief conspirator, was shrewdly aware of the danger he and his class faced from the disciples of Marx. Writing of events fifteen years later, the historian James Joll said:

> Karl Marx prophesied the impending destruction of the existing social order and the total re-organization of society in favour of the workers. For Marx's followers in 1900, the days of Salisbury and his kind were numbered.

On Black Monday—8th February 1886—angry crowds in Trafalgar Square heard violent speeches from the socialists John Burns and Henry Champion, and from the Marxist founder of the Social Democratic Federation, H. M. Hyndman. After the rally broke up, a militant section inflamed by the vehemence of the speakers marched through Pall Mall, St James's Street and Piccadilly to Mayfair and Hyde Park, breaking the windows of the Conservative Club, other club houses and private homes. Waving red flags and brandishing cudgels and stones, the 2 000-strong crowd swept forward, wrecking and robbing shops and causing damage and loss worth £50 000. Owing to a mistake a reserve force of police went to The Mall instead of Pall Mall. In the right place they might at least have been able to dilute the rioters' venom. Two days later in a thick fog a rumour was circulated that another mob was gathering, and in sheer panic that the 'brutal violence and infamous rapine' was to repeated many West End shopkeepers barricaded themselves in. No major incident occurred but the threat of riot in the capital was so alarming that a special committee was set up to consider the problem. It sat for nine days, with the Home Secretary himself taking the chair, and as a result of its report, which contained references to the 'grave mistakes' committed by the police, Sir Edmund Henderson, the Chief Commissioner, resigned. This did nothing to help matters. His successor, General Charles Warren, used military tactics in the vain hope of quelling the anger of the working classes who clamoured for justice—and who were incited by socialist agitators and the pangs of hunger and cold to resort to the only strength they knew, violence. Warren confronted the poor with his new-style military police force and kept them at bay all through the winter of 1886 to 1887 only with the unuttered but unmistakable threat that any breach of the peace would result in direct and bloody conflict. Consequently the unemployed proceeded to draw attention to themselves with demonstrations outside fashionable churches, which to all outward appearances were peaceful, banner-waving affairs, but which camouflaged a smouldering resentment. Such a situation could not last.

The Press began seriously discussing the possibility of a working-class uprising, and in October 1887 the prospect of further riots looked so close that Salisbury suggested Trafalgar Square be railed off. Warren had already banned public meetings as it had become a forum for agitators. But before the Prime Minister's plan could be implemented a new conflict erupted on 13th November, Bloody Sunday. Nearly a hundred thousand unemployed converged on Trafalgar Square from all sides. Among them were Eleanor Marx and members of the socialist Fabian Society, including George Bernard Shaw, the brilliant speaker Annie Besant and the artist and poet William Morris, who had declared himself a socialist and a revolutionary. The furious crowds, urged on by the socialists and radicals in their midst, and armed to the teeth with knives, sticks, pokers and iron bars, surged forward to the Square, to be met by four thousand policemen. Warren had lined the Square with

three hundred Life Guards and the same number of Grenadier
Guards, all armed with loaded muskets and bayonets. In the
ensuing struggle one person was killed and more than a hundred
and fifty injured. All was quiet by midnight, but the clash
caused irreparable damage to relations between police and
public, feeding the fires not only of socialism but of anarchy.
In *London*, a history of the capital and its people, Felix Barker
and Peter Jackson describe the period 1886–9 as 'three violent
years':

> It began with the tinkle of glass as stones smashed the
> windows of clubs in Pall Mall; it ended with a hoarse roar of
> victory by East End dockers when they were granted a basic
> rate of 6d. an hour. In the three years that separated these
> events, London became a violent battleground.

The other great political upheaval of the day was the
increasingly bitter struggle over the question of Home Rule for
Ireland. On this issue, 'the whole political world was in
convulsion', according to one contemporary chronicler.
Home Rule had become the burning issue since 1885. In June
of that year the Liberals under Gladstone were defeated in the
Commons after five years in office because the Irish members
voted with the Opposition. The defeat demonstrated for the
first time the influence of one Charles Stewart Parnell, leader
of the Irish Nationalists. Though he had only 85 members he
held the balance of power between the Liberals and the
Conservatives. After Gladstone's defeat, Lord Salisbury
formed a minority Conservative government, but six months
later Gladstone was back with a majority over the Conservatives of 86. By this time the Grand Old Man had undergone a dramatic conversion to the idea of Home Rule, but the
subsequent Bill he introduced with the intention of bringing it
about was rejected by the Commons. Gladstone immediately
dissolved Parliament and fought the new election of mid-1886
purely on the Irish issue. The result was a decisive victory for
Salisbury's Conservatives, who gained 316 seats. Their sup-
porters over Home Rule, the Liberal Unionists, gained 78.
The Gladstonians won only 191 seats and the Parnellites 85.
    The struggle for Irish independence had for years brought
terror and violence to dwellers on both sides of the Irish Sea,
bombings and shootings finally culminating in 1882 in the

cold-blooded murder in Phoenix Park, Dublin, of the new Irish Chief Secretary, Lord Frederick Cavendish, and his Under-Secretary Thomas Burke. The Fenians, launched specifically for the purpose of promoting revolution and over-throwing the English government in Ireland, continued with dynamite outrages at major buildings and monuments in London and the provinces. At last they made an audacious attempt at blowing up Scotland Yard itself. The Fenian threat had reached such alarming proportions by 1884 that the Special Irish Branch, the forerunner of the Special Branch, was set up to bring the problem under control.

The world forgives heinous crimes in its favourites and castigates the tiniest transgression in those it hates. It is fair to say the process hardly ever works in reverse. It is therefore difficult to see how a popular figure could be so viciously lampooned over a trivial error of judgement as was Edward, Prince of Wales, over the patently unimportant Tranby Croft 'scandal' of 1891. The simple answer is, that despite the eulogies of several biographers, he was *not* popular. Even the prudish, hypocritical values of late Victorian England would hardly have allowed one negligible incident to turn a whole country against a beloved prince. In fact Bertie was the possessor of an odious reputation until shortly before his accession to the throne in 1901. The gloom of dishonour and unpopularity had occasionally lessened in the forty years since he first fell seriously from public favour, but generally he was despised. And despite the rapturous appreciation of the masses at the jubilee of his ageing mother, Queen Victoria, she too suffered definite, if less prolonged, bouts of disfavour.

Tranby Croft brought the Prince into the witness box of a public court of law for the second time in his profligate life. It was arguably the least serious of all his many mistakes, but it had an incalculable effect in plunging his name still deeper into the bog of notoriety. Finally, during a visit to Brussels in 1900, an anarchist fired a pistol through the open window of a train in which the Prince sat. The bullet missed its mark, but the would-be assassination was a realization of what many had pondered with a voodoo-like malice over many years. It was the culmination of public resentment and the natural consequence of several previous displays of antipathy, such as a demonstration against him when he visited Cork with Princess Alexandra in 1885. The

crowd hissed and booed the royal couple, and even pelted them
with onions. His notoriety spread beyond British shores, and in
1898 he was hissed and mercilessly caricatured during a visit to
Paris.

Exactly how unpopular the Prince was can be gauged by the
events of the Tranby Croft affair and its aftermath. In September 1890 the Prince was staying along with other guests at
Tranby Croft, the Yorkshire country home of his friend Arthur
Wilson, a wealthy shipowner. During a game of baccarat several
guests noted that one of the players, Sir William Gordon-
Cumming, was cheating. The next evening they watched his
play more carefully in order to confirm their suspicions, and later
reported their observations to the Prince. Foolishly, he compelled the fraud to sign an undertaking that because he had
cheated he would renounce gambling for ever. Gordon-
Cumming agreed in exchange for a promise that the incident
would never be mentioned again. Unfortunately, the secret was
shared by too many, and one of the guests betrayed him to an
outsider. Fashionable society grasped the sordid titbit with
customary greed. His reputation thus publicly besmirched,
Gordon-Cumming sued Mr and Mrs Arthur Wilson—and other
guests who had accused him of cheating—for slander. In the
subsequent court hearing the Prince of Wales was treated with
scant respect, and though Gordon-Cumming lost his suit, the
Prince was hissed by the crowds that lined his route from court.
In her biography of Princess Alexandra, Georgina Battiscombe
quotes a coachman who spoke of Bertie after the 'Baccarat Case'.
His words, she says, reflected the feeling of many ordinary folk.
'God will never allow such a wicked man to come to the throne'.

It was alleged by the prosecution that the Prince habitually
encouraged baccarat, an illegal game, that he had decided
Gordon-Cumming was a cheat on the flimsiest of evidence and
that he had acted improperly in not immediately reporting the
charge to Gordon-Cumming's commanding officer instead of
summarily dealing with it himself. Not pleasant allegations, but
the most ductile imagination cannot admit they were the acts of
a *wicked* man whom God would never allow to come to the
throne. Such a denunciation would surely never have been
uttered if the Prince had been even vaguely popular.

A comment made during the trial by Gordon-Cumming's
counsel, Sir Edward Clarke, is interesting support of Sickert's
claim that the monarchy was dangerously weak. Alleging the

Prince hushed up the initial charges against Gordon-Cumming
in order to save his own honour, Clarke said there had been
other examples of men ready 'to sacrifice themselves to support
a tottering throne or prop a falling dynasty'. (My italics.) The words
were plainly intended to mean that the Prince's own dynasty
was perilously unsound. An advocate of Clarke's undisputed
competence would not have clouded his addresses with the
preposterous or irrelevant: there was something rotten in the
state of England. Bertie later wrote that because of Tranby
Croft he was subjected to a 'torrent of abuse . . . not only by
the Press, but by the Low Church and especially the Non-
conformists'.

His reputation had first suffered seriously in 1869 when he
appeared in court over the Mordaunt divorce case. In *Clarence*,
his biography of Eddy, Michael Harrison wrote:

> It was the indiscreet practice of the Prince of Wales to pay
> social calls on young married women, and to spend a con-
> siderable time with them alone, after the footman had been
> instructed not to disturb the *tête-à-tête*. What made the
> indiscretion even more noticeable was that His Royal
> Highness neglected to cultivate the acquaintance of the
> ladies' husbands—or even to express a wish to meet them.

In the Mordaunt case, the Prince was named as one of Lady
Mordaunt's lovers after she calmly announced that her new-
born child was not her husband's but Lord Cole's. Cole was
only one of a pride of well-born rakes the promiscuous Lady
Mordaunt entertained. Even though the Prince was treated
with great courtesy in court, and denied any improper famili-
arity with the lady, and despite the fact that on this occasion he
was cheered as he left the Divorce Court, still the first serious
blow to his reputation had been struck. Soon the popular Press
was calling into question his fitness to become King, and public
opinion turned against him. Princess Alexandra was always
remarkably popular with the people, and in his treatment of her
Bertie's reputation suffered further damage. Privacy has no
real meaning for most of the silver spoon breed, especially those
whose spoons bear the crest of the Lion and the Unicorn.
It soon became clear to Bertie that he could not conceal his
infidelity. His amorous affairs rapidly became a subject of
nation-wide gossip. That he had half expected. But what he
could not have foreseen was the vehemence of public reaction.

The covertly sentimental British had taken Alix well and truly into their hearts, and one night when she appeared in the Royal Box at the opera the audience rose to their feet and cheered. When Bertie appeared moments later he was hissed.

Pleasure-seeking and unashamed debauchery, it seemed to the country, were the Prince's sole purposes in life. Lambasting the degenerate Heir Apparent became a favourite pastime for the self-righteous hypocrites of the drawing-room and the denizens of the gutter Press—a practice rendered doubly stimulating by the dual morality and holier-than-thou philosophy that epitomized the Victorians. One publication collected all the basest tales of the Prince's immorality from the underworlds of Paris and London and presented them in the form of a pastiche of Tennyson's *Idylls of the King*, under the crude punning title, *The Coming K—*.

Yet another divorce scandal broke in 1876. This time it seems the Prince of Wales played, uncharacteristically, an almost guiltless role, his one misdemeanour amounting to writing some compromising letters to Lady Aylesford, who was being divorced by her husband on the grounds of her adultery with Lord Blandford, elder brother of Lord Randolph Churchill. Churchill obtained a packet of letters written by the Prince to Lady Aylesford which Lord Randolph described as of 'the most compromising character', adding that if they were published they would ensure the Prince 'would never sit upon the Throne of England'. As a result the Prince challenged Churchill to a duel but was curtly refused.

In 1888, the year of the Ripper murders, the name of the Prince of Wales had become so reviled that even his own nephew, the German Kaiser, threatened to cancel a visit to Austria unless the Prince, who was staying in Vienna, departed first.

Despite the blaze of glory into which Queen Victoria emerged at her Golden Jubilee, she too suffered unpopularity during much of her reign. In her early years as Queen she had been hissed on public occasions, notably during one visit to Ascot, and seven separate attempts were made on her life. In one incident she was hit over the head and knocked unconscious by a retired lieutenant of the 10th Hussars.

The obsessional mourning she affected after the death in 1861 of her beloved consort Albert did much to damage her popularity. The country became irritated by her prolonged seclusion, and outraged by her obstinate refusals to take part in

public events. A campaign against her social hibernation led
eventually to a monarchy crisis. Sir Henry Ponsonby, her
private secretary, declared in 1871 that if Victoria had been a
man she would have been turned off the throne. Resentment
against her seclusion spread quickly, and in a scurrilous
pamphlet called *What Does She Do With It?* she was accused
of hoarding £200,000 of her constitutional allowance every
year. The accusation succeeded in turning the greater part of
the working-classes against her. They could not abide a miserly
monarch. Events came to a head when *Reynolds' Newspaper*
announced that she planned to abdicate. The idea was unfounded, but it finally gave public expression to the fact
that abdication seemed the only solution to the crisis. On 6th
November 1871 she was bitterly attacked by Sir Charles Dilke,
a radical M.P. who, referring to her seclusion, accused her of
dereliction of duty. He urged his audience to depose Victoria,
eliminate the monarchy entirely and set up a Republic. It was
just the sort of event momentarily to deflect the Queen from her
utter determination to live as she pleased. She jealously
guarded her sovereignty, and the fear of revolution haunted her
all through life. Since the mid-sixties she had been nervously
aware of the possibility of what she termed 'a new French
Revolution' in England, brought about by the vast gulf
between the lower and upper classes. But still she lived the
life of a regal hermit, and in 1872 a sixth attempt was made to
kill her. After the seventh and final attempt at regicide in 1882,
the Queen's popularity measurably increased. Alone, she
might then have been able to take the monarchy forward to a
more stable situation. But with the Prince of Wales on the
rampage all over England there was no hope of dragging the
name of the Royal Family out of the mire. And by the mid-
eighties the Royal Family, especially Prince Eddy, had a new
enemy—Henry Labouchere, editor of the magazine *Truth*. He
hated the monarchy, and he especially hated Eddy. He
rigorously opposed the moves to grant an official allowance to
the Prince of Wales's children and ruthlessly pilloried the
Royal Family, both as individuals and as an institution, in the
controversial pages of his journal.

At the outset, Sickert's evaluation of the importance of Eddy's
behaviour had not seemed to bear the gloss of truth. The gloss
had been dulled by the murky antics of Eddy's father. If the
Prince of Wales was corrupt what would one more regal

reprobate matter? In studying the political and social climates, though, one can see that purely because of the fabled immorality of his father, Eddy's conduct was immensely important: he was the bright hope for the future. If he was involved in the sort of affair Sickert attributed to him the camel's back would have well and truly cracked. The inveterate enemies of the Crown, including Dilke and Labouchere, would certainly have conspired—and probably succeeded—to bring about the downfall of Britain's eight-hundred-year-old monarchy.

One aspect of the motive has not yet been examined: the apparent threat of Catholicism and the related danger of a marriage between Prince Eddy and a Catholic. The constitutional perils contained in the alleged alliance between Eddy and Annie Elizabeth Crook can be measured precisely. For in 1890 the question of Eddy's official marriage arose and a crisis developed when he chose as his bride Princess Hélène d'Orléans, daughter of the Comte de Paris, who, much to everyone's horror, was a Roman Catholic.

A fierce and irrational hatred of Catholics still existed in the hearts of many English Protestants, even into the early part of the twentieth century, and the cry of 'No Popery!' could still be heard in the eighties and nineties. As recently as 1850 anti-Catholic demonstrations took place in London, an effigy of Cardinal Wiseman was burnt in the streets of Bethnal Green and crowds heaping loud abuse on the Pope broke the windows of Catholic churches and attacked priests. The Church of England dominated the country, and any deviation from Protestantism was regarded with the deepest suspicion. Some years after the Bethnal Green episode an Anglican vicar in East London was pelted with bread pudding for taking such a minute step in the direction of Rome as placing candles on his altar and decking his choirboys in surplices. Even as late as 1910 Edward VII was strongly criticized in the Press for attending a service at St James's Roman Catholic Church at Spanish Place in West London.

As far as the Establishment was concerned, Eddy becoming involved with a Catholic was one of the worst things that could have happened in the mid-eighties. Over the question of his proposed marriage to Hélène in 1890, Queen Victoria wrote a strong letter warning him off her. His marriage to a Catholic, she predicted, would have 'the very worst effect possible'. At a time of such unrest, when the throne was already in danger, those extreme words of warning could mean only one thing: Victoria foresaw an uprising that would end the monarchy.

Lord Salisbury was also frightened of that possibility. According to Sir Philip Magnus in his *King Edward the Seventh*, Salisbury's pronouncement on the subject was in unmistakable terms. When the Prince of Wales asked him if it was possible for Eddy to marry Hélène and she remain a Catholic, Salisbury warned him that 'the anger of the middle and lower classes might endanger the throne if it became known that he had advanced or even contemplated it'.

It has been suggested that one of the greatest flaws in Sickert's story was that the Royal Marriages Act and the Act of Settlement were still on the statute book at the time Eddy is alleged to have married Annie Elizabeth Crook. Donald Rumbelow points out in his *Complete Jack the Ripper* that, under the Royal Marriages Act, Eddy's marriage to Annie Elizabeth could have been set aside as illegal because he was under twenty-five at the time of the marriage and he had married without the Queen's consent. The Act of Settlement excluded anyone married to a Roman Catholic from inheriting the Crown. All this is true, but whether or not Eddy's marriage to Annie Elizabeth would have been valid in law would not affect the reaction of the populace at the news of such an alliance. Salisbury and Lord Halsbury, the Lord Chancellor, were obviously aware of the two Acts when, according to Magnus, they composed elaborate memoranda on the political and legal aspects of Eddy's betrothal to Hélène—yet Salisbury still envisaged revolution as a result of the proposed marriage.

In her letter to Eddy, Victoria told him a marriage to a Catholic would mean he would lose all his rights. A. J. Balfour, Salisbury's nephew and a Conservative M.P., though he could see the romance of the affair, wrote, 'We shall have a great deal of trouble over it all'.

When the Prince of Wales wanted to visit the Pope in 1903 he was told by the Cabinet that such a course could cause great unrest among Protestants, who still regarded Rome as a threat.

'This is absurd', wrote Balfour. 'But the people we have to deal with are absurd also!'

Balfour's opinion sums up the impotence of Rumbelow's argument: the law may have appeared a safeguard against Eddy's irresponsibility, but the law could not control the illogical emotions of the middle and lower classes.

If Eddy had indeed not only married a Catholic but also fathered her child—a child conceived out of wedlock—it is easy to see that Salisbury and the Royal Family would have regarded the affair as crucial. To Victoria, wrote Elizabeth Longford, 'in her state of nervous tension all unwelcome news assumed immense proportions'.

If Eddy's conduct was not sufficient to cause chaos, Salisbury could hardly be blamed for thinking it was. If Sickert's story of the clandestine wedding and birth turned out to be true, it would be perfectly credible that Salisbury would have tried to cover up the affair by institutionalizing Annie Elizabeth Crook. But removing her would only have compounded the difficulty, for Sickert said Marie Kelly escaped to tell the tale. If that was the case, Salisbury not only had to cover up the initial scandal but also the brutal treatment he had meted out to Eddy's paramour.

The circumstances were right and the stage was set for Sickert's drama. It remained only to see if the curtain ever rose.

CHAPTER SEVEN

Cleveland Street

Cleveland Street, W.1., is a long, narrow road running approximately north-west to south-east between Euston Road and Goodge Street. One entire block has been demolished since the days of Jack the Ripper, and the site is now occupied by a much enlarged Middlesex Hospital, whose nineteenth-century predecessor in Cleveland Street was important but considerably smaller. Apart from this one change the street is pretty much as it was then, and is dominated by sombre three-storey houses, some of whose ground floors serve as shops or offices.

When Cleveland Street and the events Sickert alleged went on there were investigated the painter began to earn some real credibility. Much of what he said became provable fact, and there were several peripheral factors which suggested he could not have been lying.

Of all the questions jockeying for first consideration, one was of overriding importance: did the main characters in Sickert's story even exist? It had been Sickert who had drawn up the dramatis personae, and if his story had been false it was more than likely the less illustrious characters of the tale would have been fictitious too. Clearly Prince Eddy, the Prime Minister and Sir William Gull were real people, but John Netley, Annie Elizabeth Crook and her daughter Alice Margaret were another matter. Chapter 12 describes the search for John Netley, so little need be said of him here. Of paramount importance at this stage in the investigation were the two lowly females whose behaviour and, in the case of the child, whose very existence is supposed to have set off such an appalling chain-reaction.

The electoral register for Cleveland Street in the 1880s produced no names that were helpful. This was not surprising, as Annie Crook, being a woman, would not have had the vote and the only other relevant resident, Sickert himself, had so many rooms around London that he never bothered with such trivia as registering his occupation. Robert Emmons pointed out in his *Life and Opinions of Walter Richard Sickert* that the painter concerned himself little with money matters and behaved with quite reckless generosity. According to Marjorie Lilly, he rarely thought about money until it was no longer there. This had two effects: considering money a mere formality, he behaved even more contemptuously towards the worldly demands of bureaucracy, such as filling in forms. Secondly, he rarely had much cash to spare, and when it ran out altogether (which it often did in those early days), remaining unregistered and elusive helped if he had to bolt one night without paying the rent.

The *Post Office Directory of London* between 1885 and 1888 was no more useful in checking hard facts. What it did confirm, however, was that the 'community' picture of the area painted in Sickert's story was accurate. There were shopkeepers in plenty—Henry Fletcher, greengrocer; Henry Mowbray, hairdresser; Isaac Lyons, linen-draper; George Endersby, bookseller; Mrs Sarah Winslow, Chandler's Shop—and so on in a seemingly endless stream, all traders in that one narrow thoroughfare. In a day when skilled crafts were a living part of the social system, there was still room for Thomas Walter Cadwallader, Locksmith, and William Leader, Umbrella Maker. In addition there were chair-makers, boot-makers, cabinet-makers, coach-body makers, woodcarvers, saddlers, hatters, bookbinders, engravers, silver-chasers, French polishers and craftsmen of every kind. One can see at a glance that the area would have been ideally suited to the young artist. Within sight of his rooms at No. 15 there were gathered a picture-liner, an artist's colourman and further along Henry Landsbert, a dealer in works of art. There was no more likely place in London for Sickert to have had a studio. It had for many years been the favourite centre for young artists at the beginning of their careers. As William Gaunt recorded in *The Pre-Raphaelite Tragedy*, Holman Hunt had his studios in Cleveland Street and it was the birthplace and nursery of the renowned Pre-Raphaelite brotherhood, associates of which included Millais, the Rossettis, Ford Madox Brown and Hunt himself.

Cleveland Street was liberally sprinkled with Coffee Rooms, such as those of Henry Lindner or Mrs Ann Storey, where the men of the 'village' could forsake their womenfolk and the cares or creations of the day and in time-honoured manner, perpetuated now by the male population of France—gather for a long and often intense midday discussion. In the evening similar relaxation could be had in finer style over a glass of ale in the George and Dragon, the City of Hereford or The Crown.

But of Annie Elizabeth Crook, tobacconist's shop assistant of No. 6, basement, there seemed no trace until BBC researcher Karen de Groot made a search of the Rate Books for the two boroughs into which Cleveland Street cut, Marylebone and St Pancras. The 1888 Rate Book for the street records:

Number 6   Elizabeth Cook (Basement).

It was close. Sickert said the basement of No. 6 was inhabited by Annie Elizabeth Crook. The Rate Book showed the name Elizabeth *Cook*. This was consistent with Sickert's story that Annie's surname was often rendered as Cook. Her existence was finally proved when another document was checked. This was the birth certificate of her daughter. The certificate was obtained from Somerset House in order to check Sickert's basic claims, which were:

(1) Annie Elizabeth Crook was a tobacconist's assistant in Cleveland Street in the eighties.
(2) In April 1885 she gave birth to an illegitimate child.
(3) The birth took place at Marylebone Workhouse.
(4) The father of the child was Prince Eddy.
(5) The child's name was Alice Margaret Crook.

The birth certificate confirms four of these five points. It is dated 18th April 1885 and records:

SEX:	Girl
NAME:	Alice Margaret Crook
PLACE OF BIRTH:	Marylebone Workhouse
NAME OF MOTHER:	Annie Elizabeth Crook, confectionery assistant from Cleveland Street
NAME OF FATHER:	Blank
OCCUPATION OF FATHER:	Blank

The birth certificate is marked with a cross by which is written, 'The mark of Annie Elizabeth Crook, Mother, 6 Cleveland Street, Fitzroy Square'. The address shows that the Elizabeth Cook of the Rate Book and Annie Elizabeth Crook were one and the same. And the cross confirms another part of Sickert's story, that Annie was illiterate.

Three years after the birth of Alice Margaret, in April 1888, a police raid took place in Cleveland Street and both Eddy and Annie Elizabeth were taken away, Sickert claimed. Annie, he said, was certified insane and spent a hundred and

The birth certificate
of Alice Margaret
Crook

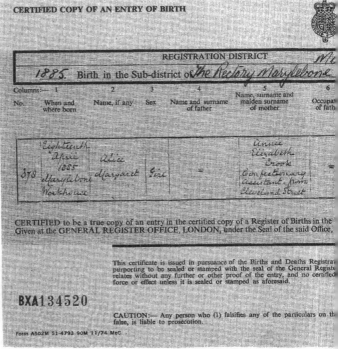

fifty-six days at Guy's Hospital. During this time he believed she underwent some sort of operation that was contrived to destroy her memory of events in Cleveland Street, for on the one or two occasions he saw her after that she was a different person and no longer recognized him. Sir William Gull himself, Sickert thought, had performed the operation, which not only affected her memory but made her epileptic. After Guy's she spent months confined in various workhouses, and eventually, when it was realized she no longer possessed any dangerous knowledge, she was released—a harmless wreck, broken in body and spirit, abandoned in the streets from which she had so recently been snatched a normal healthy woman. But she was unable to support herself, nor could she survive at all on her own. After drifting in and out of workhouses for months in a vague search for shelter, she was eventually apprehended once more and confined for the rest of her life in prisons, hospitals and workhouses. She died in 1920 at 367 Fulham Road. By then she was hopelessly insane.

Guy's Hospital do have records of patients in the nineteenth century but they are incomplete. The register of patients for 1888 is missing, so it is not possible to check if Annie Elizabeth

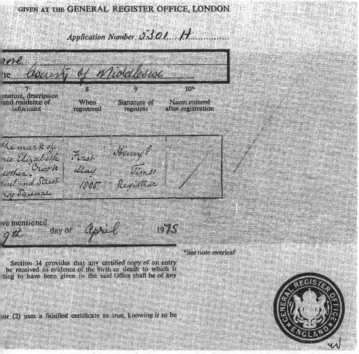

was confined there as Sickert said. There are, however, independent facts which at least make the story credible. Sir William Gull maintained close connections with Guy's all his life and, significantly, was at one time in charge of an asylum for twenty insane women at the hospital. According to Michael Harrison, Gull's very presence in the Royal Household is in need of explanation, for rather than being an expert in disease generally, he specialized in paraplegia, diseases of the spinal cord and abscess of the brain. This specialization and his association with the asylum for women at Guy's are not only consistent with the story of Annie Elizabeth's incarceration—

they also support Sickert's assertion that he had many times been of invaluable service in removing the troublesome by certifying them insane. He not only had the ability to perform the sort of operation that Sickert thought Annie Elizabeth had undergone, he also had the place to do it.

As to her movements after Guy's, Mr Alan Neate, keeper of the Greater London Record Office, was extremely helpful. Wading through the hundreds of registers in his custody, he found scattered but useful records of her movements between 1885 and her death. The earliest mention of her name was in the papers of St Marylebone Workhouse, which showed she entered the institution on 18th April 1885 (the day her child was born) and left on 5th May.

No further record of Annie Elizabeth can be found until 22nd January 1889, when she spent one day at St Giles Workhouse in Endell Street, High Holborn. There is then no mention of her name until 1903, when she became an inmate of institutions under the care of the St Pancras Board of Guardians. Mr Neate carefully compiled exact details of her movements between February 1903 and March 1913, with only a few months here and there untraceable. She was almost solidly in workhouses and hospitals during this decade, as is borne out in the GLC records:

Apr 18th 1885–May 6th 1885	St Marylebone Workhouse
Jan 22nd 1889 (one day)	St Giles Workhouse, Endell Street
Feb 7th 1903–Feb 23rd 1903	St Pancras Workhouse
Mar 12th 1903–Mar 27th 1903	St Pancras Workhouse
Oct 28th 1903–Nov 13th 1903	St Pancras Hospital
Nov 13th 1903–May 13th 1904	St Pancras Workhouse
May 13th 1904–Nov 11th 1904	Highgate Hospital
Nov 11th 1904–Nov 14th 1904	St Pancras Workhouse

On 14th November 1904 she was transferred from St Pancras Workhouse to Poland Street Workhouse, and from that point on was chargeable to St James's Parish of the Westminster Board of Guardians:

Nov 14th 1904–Aug 7th 1906	Poland Street Workhouse
Nov 11th 1906–Apr 3rd 1907	Poland Street Workhouse
Apr 3rd 1907–Jun 11th 1907	*Cleveland Street Infirmary*
Jun 11th 1907–Oct 31st 1907	Hendon Infirmary, Colindale

Oct 31st 1907–Mar 12th 1913   *Cleveland Street Infirmary*
Mar 12th 1913– ?   Hendon Infirmary
Feb 19th 1920–
Feb 23rd 1920   Fulham Road Workhouse

After that coincidental return to Cleveland Street and spending five and a half years in the infirmary there—her longest recorded stay anywhere—she was admitted to Hendon Infirmary in March 1913, and there is no record of her ever having been released. Her name next appears in the registers of Fulham Road Workhouse in 1920, four days before her death. She died in the hospital next door to the workhouse. Its address, as Sickert said, was 367 Fulham Road.

At last some positive information was forthcoming, but was it necessarily proving Sickert's story true? Admittedly he was right about her being an inmate of various institutions almost solidly until her death, and was correct about the address where she died. But it was hard to imagine that a person confined as a lunatic would have been kept in workhouses. My knowledge of these institutions was vague. I knew that under the old poor laws of England there was a workhouse in each parish where indigent, vagrant and idle people were set to work and supplied with food and clothing, or what was termed indoor relief. What I did not know was that some workhouses were used as places of confinement for rogues and vagabonds. Bishop Atterbury (1662–1732) wrote:

Hast thou suffered at any time by vagabonds and pilferers? Esteem and promote those useful charities which remove such pests into prisons and workhouses.

Before the Poor Law Amendment Act of 1834 the workhouses gained a reputation as nurseries of idleness, ignorance and vice. But the Act united parishes to improve the management of workhouses. This gave rise to the Poor Law Unions which had control of workhouses containing from a hundred to five hundred inmates. Circulars published by the Lunacy Commission between 1890 and 1912, now at the Public Record Office in London, show that not only was it common practice for lunatics to be detained in workhouses, but that no records were required to be kept of them. It was consequently quite possible for a perfectly normal person to have been confined as insane in a workhouse. If this is what happened to Annie

Elizabeth Crook there would have been no hope of appeal or protection because no one would have known of her incarceration. Many workhouses even had padded rooms, and not until 1910 were local boards of guardians required to keep records of inmates confined in them.

Suddenly it became clear. The workhouses would have been the ideal place to have confined Annie Elizabeth. Had she been put in an asylum, proper records would have to have been kept, and she would have received regular visits and checks from Lunacy Commission inspectors. Whereas in a padded cell at a workhouse she could be confined without even the approval of a doctor, and no questions would have been asked once she was committed.

Despite Mr Neate's exhaustive research, however, there were still gaps in the list of Annie Elizabeth's movements. There is no trace of any records explaining her whereabouts between her removal from Guy's, about September or October 1888, and 22nd January 1889 when she was at St Giles Workhouse for one day. Then there is another gap until 1903. The only other record discovered shows that on 29th April 1894 the child Alice Margaret was admitted to St Giles Workhouse. It was stated on her admission papers that her mother was in prison, which tallies with Sickert's account of Annie Elizabeth's fate.

The record of medical treatment Annie Elizabeth received at 367 Fulham Road in the few days prior to her death confirms Sickert's testimony that she died insane. The doctor attending the Lunacy Observation Ward where she was confined wrote:

20.2.20   Confused—sometimes noisy and hilarious, at other times almost stuporous—has delusions that she is being tortured—takes no interest in her surroundings.
23.2.20   Sudden attack of cardiac failure which ended in death at 12.40 a.m.

Records of her admission to several workhouses and hospitals state she was epileptic, which again confirmed Sickert's story. All at once, everything the painter said about the fate of Annie Elizabeth was turning out to be true. Her delusions of being tortured would seem hardly surprising if the whole of his story was accurate.

It is hard to explain how or why Annie Elizabeth was moved

from the custody of one Board of Guardians to another, and from workhouse to workhouse, with such apparent ease. Rules were extremely rigid and paupers were interrogated closely about their movements in previous years before they were allowed into any workhouse. Before a pauper could receive indoor relief in an area he or she had to establish what was called a 'settlement' there by three years' continuous residence or by birth. If a pauper turned up at a parish where he had no settlement he would be returned to his own parish forthwith. There was provision for the removal of paupers from one area to another, by orders made by magistrates. But the process was long and complicated and rigorously discouraged. No such procedure was invoked with Annie Elizabeth Crook. She moved from area to area, and no questions were asked. This was extraordinary. She was treated unlike all the other workhouse inmates of her time, and all rules went by the board when she came to be dealt with.

In response to a request for further information on this unusual treatment, Mr Neate wrote saying that it was surprising but not *necessarily* irregular. 'Cases often occurred', he said, 'of a transfer made amicably between all concerned *to avoid the legal formalities.*' (My italics.)

This raises several questions: why was Annie Elizabeth Crook considered important enough to have rigid rules waived so that she could be moved from place to place more expeditiously? What made her different from all the other workhouse inmates? Why did no one want to draw attention to her by going through the regular procedure? And who arranged the short cuts?

Sickert's account of her marriage to Eddy and the events which followed answers all questions but the last. And as for that, I did not learn until later the remarkable importance of a gentleman by the name of the Rev. Henry Luke Paget.

And so the facts build up, stripping Sickert's story of its fantastic garb and showing, detail by detail, that at least the basis of his narrative is true. There is documentary proof that Annie Elizabeth Crook did exist; she did live in Cleveland Street; she did work in a tobacconist's shop there; she did give birth to a daughter when and where Sickert claimed; she did disappear from Cleveland Street and her steady job in the shop for no apparent reason (the birth of her child cannot explain her fall from being well enough off to be a ratepayer in her own home to the poverty of life in a workhouse); she did become an

inmate of institutions that contained padded cells almost
solidly until her death (and during that time, an age of strict
convention, was treated in a puzzlingly unconventional
manner); she did become an epileptic; she did die at 367
Fulham Road in 1920; and she was insane at the time.

But none of this connects her with Prince Albert Victor or
even suggests Eddy knew Cleveland Street. Interestingly,
Eddy's name was linked with Cleveland Street in *Their Good
Names* by H. Montgomery Hyde, published in 1970. Hyde
noted that Eddy had been a rumoured frequenter of a male
brothel in Cleveland Street. Two years later when Michael
Harrison published *Clarence*, his biography of the Prince, he
went even further. Though he had never heard of Sickert's
story, Harrison claimed that Eddy was very much tied up with
goings-on at Cleveland Street. He said that in 1889, the year
after the Ripper murders, Eddy was not only a frequenter but
the central participant in a scandal which erupted at the male
brothel. The brothel was at No. 19 Cleveland Street, immediately opposite the shop where Annie Elizabeth Crook worked
until 1888, and only two doors away from Sickert's studio.

Eddy was bisexual, as Harrison showed. His amorphous
sexuality conspired with an utter disregard for decorum—or
rather, perhaps, a total *inability* to act as he ought—to thrust
him in and out of love with entirely unsuitable women, men
and boys. He could be in love with several people at once, as he
later showed when, apparently deeply committed to Princess
Hélène d'Orléans, he was simultaneously writing love-letters
to the pretty Lady Sybil St Clair Erskine.

It is no surprise, then, that Eddy should have allowed himself to be drawn into the brothel, not because he was desperately homosexual but because he allowed himself *to fall in love*
with his closest friends, be they male or female. There was no
ungovernable lust in Eddy; at least there is no evidence to
show there was; but he was weak, enormously soft-hearted and
sufficiently unsophisticated to allow one smile or tender word
to intoxicate him emotionally and lead him into desperate
affairs he was powerless to control. Such had been the nature of
his romance with Annie Elizabeth Crook. His presence in the
Cleveland Street brothel scandal makes much greater sense in
the light of his affair with Annie Elizabeth. He had been to
Cleveland Street before, made many friends of all kinds, and
yearned to return. In so doing he was led into the vices of No.
19.

There is totally independent evidence that Eddy was associated with Annie Elizabeth. Aleister Crowley—magician, poet, painter, chess-master and lecher, the man who called himself 'The Great Beast'—claimed in his book *The World's Tragedy*, published in Paris in 1910, that he had some compromising letters from Eddy to a boy called Morgan who lived in Cleveland Street. At first glance this claim appears only to strengthen the evidence that Eddy was associated with the street itself. But the real value of Crowley's alleged letters becomes apparent when one discovers that the boy Morgan was the son of Mrs Morgan *who ran the very shop at No. 22 Cleveland Street in which Annie Elizabeth worked.* This brings Eddy even closer to Annie Elizabeth. Harrison showed he went as far as No. 19, opposite Annie's shop. Crowley connected him with the actual shop, a place he must surely have visited regularly if he struck up a close enough relationship with Morgan to write him letters.

And that word 'compromising', what exactly did it mean? Knowing Eddy's bisexual nature, they could have been love letters to the boy. Or equally likely, they may have been letters mentioning some compromising detail of his affair with Annie Elizabeth, the sort of imprecise but scandalous detail that later led a Cleveland Street wag to pen these words:

> Jack and Jill went out to kill
> For things they couldn't alter
> Jack fell down and lost his crown
> And left a baby daughter.

Despite all this there is no concrete proof of a marriage between Annie Elizabeth and the Prince—Chapter 8 describes the elaborate cover-up which was set in motion to destroy such evidence. Sickert claimed the wedding took place at a St Saviour's Infirmary Chapel. For some time it looked as if this were the first point in his story in which he must have been wrong: no St Saviour's Infirmary could be found, let alone one that contained a chapel. But finally Ian Sharp of the BBC found records of just such an institution in Osnaburgh Street, within a stone's throw of Cleveland Street. The infirmary, now St Saviour's Hospital, has long since removed to Hythe in Kent, and it was some job tracing it. The Reverend Mother in charge admits the wedding could have taken place at the chapel of the old infirmary, but no records of the institution have survived. A search of the indexes at St Catherine's House in London, the new home of the births, marriages and deaths records, for every quarter between January 1884 and December 1889 proved fruitless. The names Coburg, Cook, Cooke, Crook, Crooke, Saxe, Saxe-Coburg (the surname of the Royal Family) and Sickert were all checked and double-checked, but to no avail. Royal weddings are not normally registered with the public marriages, but there was always the chance that Eddy had married under an assumed name, most likely of all his pseudonym Albert Sickert. But all trace of such a marriage, if it ever reached the registry, has long since been obliterated. The one real hope had been the Infirmary itself, and its records were gone for ever.

Still no baby. The most hopeless part of the quest, it seemed, was the bastard story. The existence of Annie Elizabeth Crook of Cleveland Street and *her* bastard child was established. It seems undeniable that Eddy frequented the very shop where Annie Elizabeth worked. But connecting Annie Elizabeth's child with Eddy proved another matter.

Before Joseph Sickert revealed his father's story in 1973 no one had suggested Eddy fathered a child, and Buckingham Palace still deny all knowledge of any offspring of the prince. Despite this, after months of fruitless research, I received a copy of a letter containing a statement, written in all innocence, about a child of the Duke of Clarence! It will be remembered that Eddy was created Duke of Clarence and Avondale in 1890. The letter had been written by a Mr Frederick Bratton of Harlesden to Lady Dowding, from whom I received the copy by a circuitous route. It was an ordinary conversational letter, but I was particularly struck by one paragraph which said:

> I was especially interested in particulars of the Duke of Clarence. My grandmother was 'commanded' to court to foster feed a child of the Duke's. She was selected from a number of 'possibles' after countless tests and interviews. At the last moment her uncle, Dr J. Bratton (Mayor of Shrewsbury etc) put his heavy foot down and sent regrets on her behalf. He told the family that Court life was 'frivolous' and that she might get into trouble, whatever that might mean.

I wrote to Mr Bratton, who replied with a charming letter but was unfortunately not able to help with documentary evidence. He emphasized that the whole affair had been 'very hush-hush', which was certainly consistent with Sickert's tale.

He was quite positive that the child his grandmother was to have foster fed was the issue of Prince Albert Victor, Duke of Clarence—Eddy. The story appeared in a published history of the Bratton family. This was against everything anybody else had said, except Walter Sickert.

To sum up: Annie Elizabeth Crook did exist. She did live where and when Sickert said. She gave birth to an illegitimate child exactly when Sickert said. There are completely independent claims that Eddy fathered a child, and that he was not only a frequenter of Cleveland Street but of the very shop where Annie Elizabeth worked.

One further point: in his article in *The Criminologist*, suggesting by implication that Eddy was Jack the Ripper, Dr Thomas Stowell referred to him as 'S'. There has not been a satisfactory explanation as to why he did this. It seems beyond coincidence that more than thirty years ago Walter Sickert claimed Eddy used to pose as his younger brother and pass himself off as 'Albert Sickert' or 'S'. So, in a roundabout way, another aspect of Sickert's story is confirmed.

CHAPTER EIGHT

Cover-up

A great deal is at stake if the Establishment considers it necessary to operate a full-scale cover-up. For the truth of the Jack the Ripper affair to have been painstakingly concealed can mean nothing less than that State security was at risk, or that someone high in the Government or the Royal Family was involved. Walter Sickert said it happened for both reasons, and it has already been shown that the political situation of the day was explosive, that Eddy did frequent Cleveland Street and that he almost certainly fathered Annie Elizabeth Crook's child. But has there been a cover-up? At first glance the idea might sound too bizarre or melodramatic to be given much thought. But there can be no doubt that tracks were covered at an alarming rate, which in itself proves there was something of the magnitude of the events in Sickert's story that needed hiding. That a cover-up has occurred is certain. The bulk of the evidence to show this appears in this chapter, but the ramifications of the cover-up spread throughout the rest of the book.

A vital side-issue of the cover-up is that it destroys every theory as to the identity of the murderer yet forwarded, except one which is so tenuous and fraught with inconsistency that it cannot be taken seriously—the notion that Prince Eddy himself was the killer. If Donald McCormick had been right in saying the Whitechapel Murders were committed by a mad

Russian doctor called Pedachenko, sponsored by the Russian police to bring disgrace upon anarchists in Britain, the English authorities would hardly have gone to great lengths to hush up the truth of the case. On the contrary, they would have blazoned the truth to the world in order to remove the disgrace they had earned in failing to lay the Ripper by the heels. This applies equally to every other theory except Sickert's story. There would be no need to hide the fact that Jack the Ripper was a vengeful midwife, as William Stewart proclaimed; a Jewish slaughterman, as averred by Robin Odell; that he was the poisoner Thomas Neill Cream; the wife-murderer George Chapman; a mad social reformer; a deranged surgeon re-venging the death of his son, who had contracted syphilis from a whore; or even that he was James Kenneth Stephen, the tutor of Prince Eddy, as suggested by Michael Harrison. There would certainly have been no cause for a cover-up if the Ripper had been the failed barrister Montague John Druitt, accused by both Daniel Farson and Tom Cullen in their books on the murders. Druitt, however, is a special case, and is very much involved in the cover-up, as will be seen. The final part of this chapter is devoted to proving Druitt's innocence and describing his true part in the case. Thus, though all previous theories fall down through individual weaknesses, they are all destroyed by the one fact that a cover-up has taken place.

Perhaps until the blowing open of the gigantic Watergate conspiracy, many would have dismissed any suggestion of a Government cover-up as preposterous. Now no one can deny that the concept of concealment is an integral part of govern-ment today. It is a mistake to imagine the idea is new.

The Ripper cover-up has been divided into several distinct parts, one of which has already been noticed but not properly recognized:

(1) Vital evidence was suppressed at the Ripper inquests.

(2) When Eddy returned to Cleveland Street in 1889 and became involved in the male brothel scandal there, an elaborate cover-up was mounted by the most powerful men in England. This was to hide not his bisexual nature (which was well known by then anyway), but his connection with that particular street. The course of justice was deliberately perverted to continue the cover-up that had begun with the removal of Eddy's Catholic wife and snowballed into the Whitechapel Murders. Despite the enormous amount of time and effort put

into concealing the Cleveland Street brothel case, however, one man threatened to reveal everything. The ruthlessness of the conspirators was once more displayed when this man was tried on trumped-up charges and jailed for a year to keep him silent.

(3) A plausible scapegoat was set up in case it became necessary to announce that the Ripper had been caught, and to satisfy anyone who happened to investigate the case in later years.

(4) Documents that contained the truth about the Ripper were destroyed.

Facts were hidden from the beginning, even in open court. The first part of the cover-up started at the inquest of Annie Chapman.

The hearing was opened by Coroner Wynne E. Baxter at the Working Lads' Institute in Whitechapel Road on Monday, 10th September 1888. Baxter already had the unfinished inquest of 'Polly' Nichols on his hands when Chapman was murdered.

On Thursday the 13th the medical evidence was given. After the most superficial description of Chapman's injuries, divisional police surgeon George Bagster Phillips said, 'I think I had better not go into further detail of these mutilations which can only be painful to the feelings of the jury and the public'.

The coroner allowed Phillips to withhold his evidence for that day, but at the resumed hearing Baxter demanded the full truth. Even though the coroner was only ensuring that normal procedure be adhered to, Phillips behaved in an odd and suspicious manner, trying until the last moment to break the law and suppress vital evidence. The dialogue proceeded thus:

CORONER   Dr Phillips, whatever may be your opinion and objections, it appears to me necessary that all the evidence that you ascertained from the post-mortem examination should be on the records of the court for various reasons which I need not enumerate. However painful it may be, it is necessary in the interests of justice.

PHILLIPS   I have not had notice of that. I should have been glad if notice had been given me because I should have been better prepared to give the evidence; however, I will do my best.

CORONER   Would you like to postpone it?

PHILLIPS   Oh no. I will do my best.

CORONER   Can you give any indication of how long it would take to perform the incisions found on the body?

PHILLIPS   I think I can guide you by saying that I myself could not have performed all the injuries I saw on that woman, and effect them, even without a struggle, under a quarter of an hour. *I still think it is a very great pity to make this evidence public.* These details are fit only for yourself, sir, and the jury.

CORONER   We are here in the interests of justice and must have all the evidence before us. I see, however, that there are several ladies and boys in the room, and I think that they might retire.

Even after the women and children had left, Dr Phillips persisted in his reluctance to give evidence, so his motive for suppressing information was not to save the feelings of the public present, as he had implied. After the court had cleared he said:

PHILLIPS   *I still feel that in giving these details to the public you are thwarting the ends of justice.*

CORONER   We are bound to take all the evidence in the case and whether it is made public or not is a matter for the responsibility of the Press.

FOREMAN   We are of the opinion that the evidence the doctor on the last occasion wished to keep back should be heard.

CORONER   I have carefully considered the matter and have never before heard of any evidence requested being kept back.

PHILLIPS   I have not kept it back. I have only suggested whether it should be given or not.

CORONER   We have delayed taking this evidence as long as possible, because you said the interests of justice might be served by keeping it back; but it is now a fortnight since this occurred and I do not see why it should be kept back from the jury any longer.

PHILLIPS   I am of the opinion that what I am about to describe took place after death, so that it could not affect the cause of death, which you are inquiring into.

CORONER   That is only your opinion and might be repudiated by other medical opinion.

PHILLIPS   Very well. I will give you the results of my post-
mortem examination.

For all his squirming and defiance Dr Phillips could not
deflect Baxter from following the course of justice. What is to be
deduced from this irregular behaviour? Phillips knew the law
as well as the coroner. He was well used to testifying at inquests, he knew that the doctor giving evidence of a post-
mortem examination was required to furnish the court with all
his facts, and there is ample evidence in the contemporary
East London press and in reports of other inquests that he was
not averse to describing gruesome injuries in public. It was the
first time, certainly in the Whitechapel district, that a doctor
had made a request that he be allowed to suppress evidence, as
Wynne Baxter was quick to inform him. In the case of the
Whitechapel Murders, Dr Phillips had stumbled across something it was necessary for him to hide. He claimed that his
reticence was in the interests of justice, but even two weeks
after the murder, when further delay on such a pretext was
patently useless, he still wished to remain silent. Plainly he
wanted the inquest to be brought to a close without his evidence being heard, in which case it would have remained secret
for all time. Even today the description of the injuries he was
finally compelled to make has a peculiar and sinister significance to a particular group of people. This significance will be
examined in detail in Chapter 10.

The first part of the cover-up reached full swing at the
inquest on the final victim, Marie Kelly. First, the inquest was
illegally wrested from the hands of Coroner Baxter and then
carried out in an illegal fashion by another coroner who
deliberately withheld vital information. The murder had taken
place in Baxter's territory, the Whitechapel district, but the
inquest was finally held at Shoreditch Town Hall. This was an
unprecedented deviation, and inspired one juror to take the
new coroner to task.

'I do not see why we should have the inquest thrown on our
shoulders when the murder did not happen in our district, but
in Whitechapel', he said.

Mr Hammond, the Coroner's Officer, replied, 'It did not
happen in Whitechapel'.

The coroner broke in severely, 'Do you think that we do not
know what we are doing here? The jury are summoned in the
ordinary way, and they have no business to object. If they

persist in their objection I shall know how to deal with them. Does any juror persist in objecting?'

The dissident would not be quietened by threats. 'We are summoned for the Shoreditch district', he said. 'This affair happened in Spitalfields.'

'It happened within *my* district,' lied the exasperated coroner.

But another juryman came to the rescue of the first and declared, 'This is not my district. I come from Whitechapel, and Mr Baxter is my coroner.'

The coroner managed to get the last word on the subject by saying, 'I am not going to discuss the subject with the jurymen at all. If any juryman says he distinctly objects, let him say so.'

Pausing more to observe the effect of his threatening tone than for any retort, he went on, 'I may tell the jurymen that jurisdiction lies where the body lies, not where it was found', which appeared to contradict his previous statement about the murder having happened in his district. At all costs he was determined to preside over this particular inquest. Why?

It might have been possible to sympathize with Coroner Roderick MacDonald had he then proceeded to conduct the inquest in a proper manner. But he was out to conceal evidence. This undisputed fact, combined with the irregular method by which he gained jurisdiction over the hearing in the first place, shows that MacDonald was a major character in the cover-up operation. Wynne Baxter would certainly have sifted every ounce of evidence from this hearing, as he had shown by his determination in the previous Ripper inquests. He would have brooked no opposition from characters like Dr Bagster Phillips who wanted to conceal vital testimony. And this is why Coroner Baxter was not given the chance of running the Kelly inquest. Too much had to be hidden, as is borne out by the fact that this was the most sensational murder of the nineteenth century, yet the Scotland Yard file on it is considerably smaller than that of any of the other Ripper cases—and positively insignificant when compared to several other unsolved murder files of the same year.

MacDonald abruptly terminated the inquest after less than a day and recorded the jury's verdict of 'wilful murder against some person or persons unknown'. He had not asked the police surgeon—once again Dr Phillips—if any portions of the body were missing. He had not tried to establish the nature of the murder weapon. He had not established the time of death, which was a vital omission because two witnesses claimed to

have seen Kelly in the street after daylight on the morning her
body was found.

As Tom Cullen pointed out in his *Autumn of Terror*, British
common law since Edward I has required that 'all the injuries
of the body, also all the wounds, ought to be viewed; and the
length; breadth and deepness, with what weapon, and in what
part of the body the wound or hurt is . . . all which things must
be enrolled in the roll of the coroner'. As a police surgeon well
used to testifying at inquests himself, MacDonald knew this.
'*Yet he chose deliberately to suppress this evidence*', wrote Cullen.

> "There is other evidence which I do not propose to call," he
> announced rather grandly at the close of the inquest, "for if
> we at once make public every fact brought forward in
> connection with this terrible murder the ends of justice might
> be retarded." What did he mean by this extraordinary
> statement? Was he being guided by Scotland Yard, which
> had been so anxious to get the inquest out of Coroner Wynne
> Baxter's hands? *What were the police trying to hide?*

Even Cullen, who was trying to prove Montague Druitt was the
murderer, was struck by the obvious cover-up which was in
progress.

Coroner MacDonald not only broke the law in suppressing
evidence, but was under instructions to do so, for no Government action was taken to correct the situation, despite indignant leaders in the national newspapers, like that of the *Daily
Telegraph* which said:

> Much surprise is expressed that the inquest should have
> been closed before an opportunity was given to the relatives
> of the deceased to identify the body. As they are believed to
> reside in Ireland there was some delay to be expected in
> finding them.
> It is in the power of the Attorney General to apply to the
> High Court of Justice to hold a new inquest, if he is satisfied
> that there has been rejection of evidence, irregularity of
> proceedings, or insufficiency of inquiry. This course is
> improbable as it is stated that Dr Phillips, the divisional
> surgeon of police, with whom the coroner consulted in
> private, has had a commission from the Home Office for
> some time and he does not consider himself a 'free agent';
> but it is pointed out that by hurriedly closing the inquest the
> opportunity has been lost of putting on record statements
> made on oath and when the memory of witnesses is fresh. It

is not improbable that a long interval may elapse before a prisoner is charged at the police court.

Once more the strange Dr Phillips expedites the cover-up by providing a reason for serious irregularities being tolerated. Firstly he succeeded at the Kelly inquest in his determination to withhold evidence and consulted with the coroner only in private (which Baxter had rightly refused to allow). Secondly he alone was the reason for the inquest not being reopened, as it most certainly should have been. At least, he allowed himself to be used as the excuse for the Kelly hearing not being revived. That he had a Home Office commission would hardly have stopped him testifying at so important a hearing. On the contrary, in normal circumstances the Home Office would have been eager for justice to be done. But with Jack the Ripper they were not. The authorities clearly wanted the murder of Marie Kelly swept under the carpet as efficiently as they were later to conceal once again Eddy's connection with Cleveland Street. It was part of the same dubious operation.

The indecent haste with which the inquest was handled meant also that a crucial statement made by a man named Hutchinson was not heard. Hutchinson gave a remarkably detailed description of a man he claimed to have seen with Kelly shortly before her murder. Afterwards there were dogged attempts by the police to undermine Hutchinson's certainty about the man. But he would not be tripped up on details, nor would he have his evidence altered. He even put himself in danger of being implicated by insisting he was one of the last people to see Kelly alive, probably *the* last apart from her murderer. It is possible that had Hutchinson been properly examined in a court of law, his testimony could have proved flawed or false. He may not have seen the Ripper, but an innocent 'client' of Kelly's who disappeared before the killer arrived. But there is nothing in police records, public or secret, which suggest Hutchinson was unreliable. Quite the reverse: in the Scotland Yard file, Inspector Abberline described Hutchinson's statement as 'important', and expressed the opinion that it was true. It was therefore essential that his evidence be given in open court. He was the only man to give a good description of the person most likely to have been Jack the Ripper. Yet he was not even called to give evidence.

Hutchinson's statement is written in thick black copperplate on blue Special Report sheets headed *Commercial Street*:

METROPOLITAN POLICE
Re Murder   H Division
12th November 1888

At 6 p.m. 12th George Hutchinson of the Victoria Home, Commercial Street came to this station and made the following statement.

"About 2 a.m. 9th I was coming by Thrawl Street, Commercial Street, and just before I got to Flower and Dean Street, I met the murdered woman Kelly and she said to me, Hutchinson will you lend me sixpence. I said I can't I have spent all my money going down to Romford, she said good morning I must go and find some money. She went away toward Thrawl Street. A man coming in the opposite direction to Kelly tapped her on the shoulder and said something to her, they both burst out laughing. I heard her say alright to him and the man said you will be alright for what I have told you. He then placed his right hand around her shoulders. He also had a kind of a small parcel in his left hand with a kind of strap round it. I stood against the lamp of the Queens Head Public House and watched him. They both then came past me and the man hung down his head with his hat over his eyes. I stooped down and looked him in the face. He looked at me stern. They both went into Dorset Street I followed them. They both stood at the corner of the court for about 3 minutes. He said something to her. She said alright my dear come along you will be comfortable. He then placed his arm on her shoulder and [she] gave him a kiss. She said she had lost her handkerchief. He then pulled his handkerchief a red one out and gave it to her. They both then went up the Court together. I then went to the court to see if I could see them but could not. I stood there for about three quarters of an hour to see if they came out. They did not so I went away.

Beneath the statement has been written:

Circulated to A.S. [All Stations].
Description, age about 34 or 35, height 5 ft 6, complexion pale. Dark eyes and eye lashes. Slight moustache curled up each end and hair dark. Very surley looking. Dress, long dark coat, collar and cuffs trimmed astrakhan and a dark jacket under, light waistcoat, dark trousers, dark felt hat turned down in the middle, button boots and gaiters with white buttons, wore a very thick gold chain with linen collar, black tie with horse shoe pin, respectable appearance, walked very sharp, Jewish appearance. Can be identified.

George Hutchinson

No. 6.

Metropolitan Police.

Special Report.

H Division.

12th November 1888

Reference to Papers.

Re murder

At 6 p.m. 12th George Hutchinson of the
Victoria Home Commercial Street Came
to this Station and made the following
Statement

About 2 am 9th I was coming by Thrawl
Street. Commercial Street. and Just before I
got to Flower and Dean Street. I met the
murdered woman Kelly. and she said
to me Hutchinson will you lend me
sixpence. I said I can't I have spent
all my money going down to Romford
she said good morning I must go and
find some money. she went away toward
Thrawl Street. a Man comeing in the opposite
direction to Kelly. tapped her on the shoulder
and said something to her they both
burst out laughing. I heard her say
alright to him. and the man said you
will be alright. for what I have told
you. he then placed his right hand around
her shoulders. He also had a kind of
a small parcel in his left hand. with a
kind of a strap round it. I stood
against the lamp of the Queens Head Public
House and watched him. They both
then came past me and the man hu
down his head. with his hat over his
eyes. I stooped down and looked
him in the face. He looked at me

George Hutchinson

Part of Hutchinson's statement
This bore his signature at the foot of each page of the statement.

In his book *Clarence*, Michael Harrison claimed there was an elaborate cover-up mounted to keep Eddy's name well away from anything to do with Cleveland Street. This was not, as Harrison imagined, purely to hide Eddy's involvement in activities at the male brothel. It was to remove any possibility of his previous, and more dangerous, escapades in Cleveland Street coming to light. In the brothel affair, wrote Harrison,

> Eddy was the central participant. It is hardly surprising, therefore that the Establishment conspired elaborately to conceal the truth, and that, until now, this process has not been fully recognized. On account of the publicity that the official enquiries had attracted, it was necessary to mount the whole pantomime performance of a criminal trial, with contracted judge, counsels, witnesses, and plaintiff.

This was informed guesswork on Harrison's part, and he produced no evidence to back up the opinion. But the official papers relating to the Cleveland Street case, which have been deposited with the Director of Public Prosecutions since 1889, were opened to the public in 1975, and it is now possible to say with certainty that Harrison was correct.

The papers show that the scandal began in July 1889 when a delivery boy called Swinscow was questioned by police because he appeared to have more spending money than his meagre wages would have allowed. He revealed that another boy, a Post Office clerk called Newlove, had asked him along to No. 19 Cleveland Street to take part in homosexual activities. Under questioning Newlove broke down and later told police about a pseudo-clergyman called Veck, in reality another Post Office worker, who was a prime mover in the 'crimes'. A trap was set, and on 9th July a police constable overheard Veck offer Newlove money to defend himself against any court action over the offences.

Already the cover-up was taking shape, for it rapidly became obvious to the senior police officers in charge of the investigation that Eddy was a regular caller at the brothel. Papers in the D.P.P. file name Eddy ('P.A.V.'—Prince Albert Victor) as an alleged patron of the house. Inspector Abberline, the man in charge of the Ripper inquiries in East London, suddenly turned up in the West End to head the Cleveland Street scandal case.

Evidence was secured against Veck, as already stated, on 9th

July. *But it was not until six weeks later, on 20th August, that he was arrested.* This long delay was entirely the responsibility of Abberline, so far the one definite link between the Ripper murders and Cleveland Street. The purpose of the delay was to allow the chief offenders to escape, and so dilute the danger of any publicity arising from a trial. Abberline's men kept watch on the house after the evidence was secured against Veck, and on 9th July P.C. Sladden saw a number of men entering and leaving the house. The following day the furniture belonging to the proprietor of the brothel, Charles Hammond, was taken out, but nothing was done to arrest either Veck or anyone else connected with the brothel. It later transpired that Hammond had escaped to France and had taken his furniture with him— and all this had happened while Abberline's men were keeping watch.

As Foreign Secretary as well as Prime Minister, Lord Salisbury played an active part in the cover-up, as the D.P.P. file shows. A regular customer at No. 19 was Lord Arthur Somerset, Extra Equerry and Superintendent of the Stables to the Prince of Wales. In a letter contained in the file, the Prince of Wales expressed his satisfaction that Salisbury had allowed Somerset to leave the country before he could be arrested. If Somerset had been brought to trial Eddy's name would certainly have become linked publicly with Cleveland Street.

Salisbury was also responsible for making sure Hammond was not brought back to England. He would have been the chief prosecution witness, and could have named every person, including Eddy, who had patronized his house. In July, when the Home Secretary wrote asking Salisbury if Hammond should be extradited from France, Salisbury made quite certain the villain remained at large. On 24th July he informed the Home Secretary that he did not 'consider this to be a case in which any official application could justifiably be made to the French government for assistance in surrendering the fugitive to this country'. The only reason the French Government would not have been approached to assist in the extradition of an offender would have been if the offence were a petty one. But if that were true, why is the D.P.P. file crammed with hundreds of letters and memoranda from all the most eminent men in the land—the Prince of Wales, the Prime Minister, the Lord Chancellor, the Home Secretary, the Attorney-General, the Chief Commissioner of the Metropolitan Police and the Director of Public Prosecutions? This was no unimportant case: there is at least four times as much documentation connected with the Cleveland Street affair as there is in the combined records of the Home Office and Scotland Yard on all the Whitechapel Murders. Most of this mass of correspondence deals with ways of hushing up the scandal, as is shown by the following memorandum from the Director of Public Prosecutions, dated 24th August 1889. It refers to the chief prosecution witness, a boy called Algernon Alleys, who claimed to have compromising letters from a Mr Brown, clearly established in the file as the pseudonym of Lord Arthur Somerset:

> It is proposed to call on Tuesday if possible only witnesses whose evidence implicates Newlove and Veck—and Hammond who is not yet in custody—and to avoid if possible putting any witness into the box who refers to "Mr Brown".

Eventually Veck and Newlove were tried for having committed unnatural offences with male persons and with having induced others to do the same. They pleaded guilty. It was a period when convicted homosexuals were dealt harsh punishments, life imprisonment not unknown. But Veck was jailed for four months and Newlove for nine months. This was an appalling travesty of justice. Veck, the worst offender in the case and the man who had corrupted the young boys, received less than half the punishment of one of his victims.

The job of co-ordinating the cover-up was in the hands of the Treasury. With the help of a solicitor called Arthur Newton they made attempts to bribe Alleys, the only important witness still in England, to leave the country. They were even prepared to pay for his keep if he sailed for America, as well as all his travelling expenses. The Government was desperate to hush up the events in Cleveland Street. The vastness of the D.P.P. file on the case and the involvement of so many eminent men in trying to cover-up the scandal makes it certain that it was not Lord Arthur Somerset's name they were protecting, but Eddy's.

The Queen herself was involved. Though the Court Circular for 7th October 1889 recorded that the Lord Chancellor, Lord Halsbury, was received by Her Majesty for a social gathering at Balmoral, it is clear that he visited the Queen that day mainly to discuss the scandal with her. For the D.P.P. file contains a long, deeply thought out legal opinion by Halsbury on whether the charges against certain people connected with the brothel should be proceeded with. It is written on Balmoral paper, so it was an urgent matter. Had it been anything but of paramount importance he would surely have waited until he returned to London the next day to put pen to paper.

The file provides sound evidence that the Government was desperate to hush up Eddy's alleged part in the scandal. This would not have been the case if it had been only a matter of homosexuality, though that was serious enough. Only a scandal that would have threatened the Throne would have necessitated the involvement in the cover-up of so many notable men. But by 1889 it was common knowledge that if Eddy was not completely homosexual, he was certainly bisexual. Yet this knowledge did not bring about an empire-rocking scandal. It was not homosexuality that was being covered up, but Eddy's involvement with Cleveland Street, and the truth about Jack the Ripper.

The cover-up did not end with the perversion of justice carried out by the highest in the land in allowing Somerset and Hammond to go free. The ruthlessness and corruption with which the Victorian Establishment was prepared to pursue a course of self-preservation was carried even further in dealing with the one man who threatened to reveal everything. This man was Ernest Parke, twenty-nine-year-old editor of the *North London Press*, who pinpointed in his newspaper the deliberate mishandling on the brothel investigation and trial. He attacked the police not only for allowing Hammond to escape to the Continent, but also for giving him so much time in which to do so that he managed to take his furniture with him. He attacked the court for passing a sentence of four months on Veck, who had been one of the worst offenders in an unsavoury case. Parke courageously pointed out, 'A clergyman facing a similar charge only last year, was sentenced for what were less serious offences to no less than life imprisonment'.

Parke's leading articles commented on men of title as well as Hammond being allowed to leave the country and defeat the ends of justice, because 'their prosecution would inculpate *more highly placed and distinguished personages*'.

This was a direct reference to Eddy, and Ernest Parke was getting too close to the truth. He had to be silenced. He had made one statement which laid him open to attack. He had named Lord Euston as a frequenter of the brothel. At first Parke's position looked unassailable. He had no less than six witnesses who claimed to have seen Euston entering or leaving

the house on different occasions, one of whom said he had
taken part in homosexual practices with him. The D.P.P.
documents confirm that Parke was correct in his allegations
about Euston. John Saul, a male prostitute, made a statement
which is in the file, in which he said:

> The young Duke of Grafton—I mean the brother to the
> present Duke was a constant visitor at Hammond's. He is a
> tall fine looking man with a fair moustache [This clearly
> means Euston] . . . I saw him myself last night. I know him
> well. He went to Hammond's with me on one occasion. He
> is not an actual sodomite. He likes to play with you and then
> "spend" on your belly.

Saul had no axe to grind, and everything to lose, by claiming
to have seen Euston at 19 Cleveland Street. And his words do
not have the ring of those of a man wanting to blacken Euston's
name maliciously. If that were true he would have denounced
him as 'a proper sodomite', or in his favourite words, 'a regular
Mary Ann'. It is important that Saul made this statement on
10th August and Parke did not become aware of the scandal
until September—so suggestions that Saul was perjuring
himself on Parke's behalf are unfounded. Saul had spoken the
truth, and the Government knew it. This is shown by several
hitherto secret documents in the D.P.P. file—letters from high-
ranking members of the Government who were involved in the
cover-up, including the Attorney-General and the Lord
Chancellor. It was agreed that Saul should not be charged
with perjury, as he most certainly would have been had they
believed for one moment that he had lied. Despite this, Euston,
at the instigation of a solicitor named Edward Henslow
Bedford, brought Parke to trial on trumped-up libel charges.
And Saul was dismissed by the judge as unreliable because he
was a homosexual! The 'contracted judge, counsels, witnesses
and plaintiff' described by Harrison fulfilled their function and
Parke was found guilty of criminal libel. He was sentenced to a
year's imprisonment. Silenced.

King Edward VII, Eddy's father, stipulated in his will that
after his death all his private papers were to be destroyed. His
instructions were carried out and the papers were burned by
Lord Knollys and Lord Esher. The reason for Bertie wanting
his archive destroyed was that he had lived such a profligate
life he had no wish for his darker secrets to become public know-

ledge. This was understandable. But Queen Alexandra made a similar request and all *her* papers were incinerated when she died. This has never been explained. Alix, as numerous biographers have said, was the nonpareil of virtue. It is inconceivable that she could have had anything to hide, unless Sickert's story was true. The destruction of her papers only begins to make sense in the light of Sickert's story about Cleveland Street, Jack the Ripper and the cover-up.

A myth has now to be exploded.

The Scotland Yard file contains hundreds of names, but none of them was considered a serious suspect, as is indicated by the fact that as soon as men arrested showed proof of identity they were released. The only three plausible suspects were named by Macnaghten, who did not put pen to paper until six years after the murders. Then he mentioned a Pole, a Russian (both unknown) and Montague John Druitt, none of whom had been mentioned in the case before. The foreigners have been untraceable, and only Druitt can be shown to have existed at all. But where, in 1894, did Macnaghten suddenly come across his name, for Druitt died at the end of 1888? Nowhere else in the file is Druitt mentioned, so he was not a suspect at the time of the murders. Conveniently he was dead and could not answer the charge that he was the Whitechapel Murderer. Walter Sickert described Montague Druitt as a scapegoat and accused Sir Melville Macnaghten, an instrument of the Freemasons, of concocting a case against him. He did not explain how Druitt came to be enmeshed in the web; he did not know. The complicated network that involved Druit in the case and enabled him to be set up as the scapegoat, ready to be denounced as the Ripper the moment any serious investigation took place, is fully described later in this chapter.

As early as 1889 the police were spreading the rumour that Jack the Ripper had died by drowning at the end of 1888. Mr Albert Backert, a leading member of the Whitechapel Vigilance Committee, was allegedly told this in March 1889 when he questioned the police about their inquiries. Senior officials of the police and Government helped to give the rumour wide acceptance when they mentioned it in their memoirs. Sir Melville Macnaghten claimed in *Days of My Years* that the Ripper committed suicide in the Thames. Sir John Moylan, Assistant Under-Secretary at the Home Office, wrote,

'It is almost certain that he escaped by committing suicide at the end of 1888'.

Sir Basil Thomson, an Assistant Commissioner of the C.I.D., thought the Ripper was 'an insane Russian doctor'. He wrote, '. . . the man escaped arrest by committing suicide in the Thames at the end of 1888'.

Two authors who have recently made detailed examinations of the case against Druitt are Tom Cullen in *Autumn of Terror* and Daniel Farson in *Jack the Ripper*. Both books are based upon private notes apparently written by Sir Melville Macnaghten, *copied* by his daughter, the Dowager Lady Aberconway, and *recopied* by the authors. Unfortunately in the various versions the original intention of Macnaghten seem to have been lost, for the notes used by Farson and Cullen vary in major points from Macnaghten's official notes, which are in the Scotland Yard file. Neither Farson nor Cullen was able to gain access to the Yard file, so only now is it possible to show that the whole basis of their case against Druitt is mistaken. Before examining the fatal errors in their theory, it is important to know the full content of Macnaghten's *official* notes. They are marked *Confidential* and are written in Sir Melville's own handwriting on white paper bearing only the small oval seal of the Metropolitan Police:

The case referred to in the sensational story told in 'The Sun' in its issue of 13th inst, & following dates, is that of Thomas Cutbush who was arraigned at the London County Sessions in April 1891, on a charge of maliciously wounding Florence Grace Johnson, and attempting to wound Isabelle Frazer Anderson in Kennington. He was found to be insane and sentenced to be detained during Her Majesty's pleasure.

This Cutbush, who lived with his mother and aunt at 14 Albert St. Kennington, escaped from the Lambeth Infirmary, (after he had been detained there only a few hours, as a lunatic) at noon on 5th March 1891. He was rearrested on 9th idem. A few weeks before this, several cases of stabbing, or jabbing from behind had occurred in the vicinity, and a man named Colicutt was arrested, but subsequently discharged owing to faulty identification. The cuts in the girls dresses made by Colicutt were quite different to the cut made by Cutbush (when he wounded Miss Johnson) who was no doubt influenced by a wild desire of morbid imitation. Cutbush's antecedents were enquired into by Ch. Inspr. (now Supt.) [unreadable], by Inspr. Race, and by P.S. McCarthy

C.I.D. (The last named officer had been specially employed in Whitechapel at the time of the murders there) and it was ascertained that he was born, and had lived in Kennington all his life. His father died when he was quite young, and he was always a 'spoilt' child. He had been employed as a clerk and traveller in the Tea trade at the Minories, & subsequently canvassed for a Directory in the East End, during which time he bore a good character. He apparently contracted syphilis about 1888, and,—since that time,—led an idle and useless life. His brain seems to have become affected, and he believed that people were trying to poison him. He wrote to Lord Grimthorpe, and others, and also to the Treasury, complaining of Dr Brooks, of Westminster Bridge Rd, whom he threatened to shoot for having supplied him with bad medicines. He is said to have studied medical books by day, and to have rambled about at night, returning frequently with his clothes covered with blood, but little reliance could be placed on the statements made by his mother or his aunt, who both appear to have been of a very excitable disposition. It was found impossible to ascertain his movements on the nights of the Whitechapel murders. The knife found on him was bought in Houndsditch about a week before he was detained in the Infirmary. Cutbush was a nephew of the late Supt. Executive.

Now the Whitechapel Murderer had 5 victims and 5 victims only,—his murders were
(i) 31st Aug '88. Mary Ann Nichols—at Buck's [sic] Row—who was found with her throat cut—& with (slight) stomach mutilation.
(ii) 8th Sept '88 Annie Chapman—Hanbury Street: throat cut—stomach & private parts badly mutilated & some of the entrails placed round the neck.
(iii) 30th Sept '88. Elizabeth Stride—Berner's [sic] Street: throat cut, but nothing in shape of mutilation attempted, & on same date Catherine Eddowes—Mitre Square, throat cut, & very bad mutilation, both of face & stomach.
(iv) 9th November. Mary Jane Kelly—Miller's Court, throat cut, and the whole of the body mutilated in the most ghastly manner.

The last murder is the only one that took place in a room, and the murderer must have been at least 2 hours engaged. A photo was taken of the woman, as she was found lying on the bed, without seeing which it is impossible to imagine the awful mutilation.

With regard to the double murder which took place on 30th Sept. there is no doubt but that the man was disturbed by some Jews who drove up to a Club (close to which the body of

Elizabeth Stride was found) and that he then, 'mordum satiatus', went in search of a further victim whom he found at Mitre Square.

It will be noticed that the fury of the mutilations <u>increased</u> in each case, and, seemingly, the appetite only became sharpened by indulgence. It seems, then, highly improbable that the murderer would have suddenly stopped in November '88, and been content to recommence operations by merely prodding a girl behind some 2 years and 4 months afterwards. A much more rational theory is that the murderer's brain gave way altogether after his awful glut in Millers [sic] Court, and that he immediately committed suicide, or, as a possible alternative, was found to be so hopelessly mad by his relations, that he was by them confined in some asylum.

No one ever saw the Whitechapel Murderer, many homicidal maniacs were suspected, but no shadow of proof could be thrown on any one. I may mention the cases of 3 men, any one of whom would have been more likely than Cutbush to have committed this series of murders:—

(1) A Mr M. J. Druitt, said to be a doctor and of good family, who disappeared at the time of the Millers Court murder, and whose body (which was said to have been upwards of a month in the water) was found in the Thames on 31st Dec.— or about 7 weeks after that murder. He was sexually insane and from private info I have little doubt but that his own family believed him to have been the murderer.

(2) Kosminski a Polish Jew and resident in Whitechapel. This man became insane owing to many years indulgence in solitary vices. He had a great hatred of women, especially of the prostitute class, and had strong homicidal tendencies: he was removed to a lunatic asylum about March 1889. There were many crimes connected with this man which made him a strong 'suspect'.

(3) Michael Ostrog, a Russian doctor, and a convict, who was frequently detained in a lunatic asylum as a homicidal maniac. This man's antecedents were of the worst possible type, and his whereabouts at the time of the murders could never be ascertained.

And now with regard to a few of the inaccuracies and misleading statements made by the 'Sun'. In its issue of 14th Feb., it is stated that the writer has in his possession a facsimile of the knife with which the murders were committed. This knife (which for some unexplained reason has, for the last 3 years, been kept by Insp. Race, instead of being sent to Prisoners' Property Store) was traced and it was found to have been purchased in Houndsditch in Feb. '91 or 2 years and 3 months <u>after</u> the Whitechapel murders ceased!

some asylum.

No one ever saw the Whitechapel murderer; many homicidal maniacs were suspected, but no shadow of proof could be thrown on any one. I may mention the cases of 3 men, any one of whom would have been more likely than Cutbush to have committed this series of murders:—

(1) A Mr. M. J. Druitt, said to be a doctor & of good family- who disappeared at the time of the Miller's Court murder, & whose body (which was said to have been upwards of a month in the water) was found in the Thames on 31st Decr.- or about 7 weeks after that murder. He was sexually insane and from private info. I have little doubt but that his own family believed him to have been the murderer.

(2) Kosminski - a Polish Jew - & resident in Whitechapel. This man became insane owing to many years indulgence in solitary vices. He had a great hatred of women, specially of the prostitute class, & had strong homicidal tendencies; he was removed to a lunatic asylum about March 1889. There were many circs connected with this man which made him a strong "suspect".

(3) Michael Ostrog, a Russian doctor, and a convict, who was subsequently detained in a lunatic asylum as a homicidal maniac. This man's antecedents were of the worst possible type, and his whereabouts at the time of the murders could never be ascertained.

And now with regard to the case of the

The vital page of Macnaghten's notes

The statement, too, that Cutbush 'spent a portion of the day in making rough drawings of the bodies of women, and of their mutilations' is based solely on the fact that 2 <u>scribble</u> drawings of women in indecent postures were found torn up in Cutbush's room. The head and body of one of these had been cut from some fashion plate, and legs were added to show a woman's naked thighs and pink stockings.

In the issue of 15th Inst. it is said that a <u>light</u> overcoat was among the things found in Cutbush's house, and that a man in a <u>light</u> overcoat was seen talking to a woman in Backchurch Lane whose body with arms attached was found in Pinchin St. This is hopelessly incorrect! On 10th Sept. '89 the naked body, with arms, of a woman was found in some sacking under a railway arch in Pinchin St: the head and legs were never found nor was the woman ever identified. She had been killed at least 24 hours before the remains (which had seemingly been brought from a distance) were discovered. The stomach was split up by a cut, and the head and legs had been severed in a manner identical with that of the woman whose remains were discovered in the Thames, in Battersea Park, and on the Chelsea Embankment on 4th June of the same year; and these murders had no connection whatever with the Whitechapel horrors. The Rainham mystery in 1887, and the Whitehall mystery (when portions of a woman's body were found under what is now Scotland Yard) in 1888 were of a similar type to the Thames and Pinchin St. crimes.

It is perfectly untrue to say that Cutbush stabbed <u>6</u> girls behind—this is confounding his case with that of Colicutt.

The theory that the Whitechapel murderer was left-handed, or, at any rate, 'ambidextrous', had its origin in the remark made by a doctor who examined the corpse of one of the earliest victims; <u>other doctors did not agree with him.</u>

With regard to the <u>4</u> additional murders ascribed by the writer in the Sun to the Whitechapel fiend:—

(1) The body of Martha Tabram, a prostitute was found on a common stair case in George Yard buildings on 7th August 1888; the body had been repeatedly <u>pierced</u>, probably with a <u>bayonet.</u> This woman had, with a fellow prostitute, been in company of 2 soldiers in the early part of the evening. These men were arrested, but the second prostitute failed, or refused, to identify, and the soldiers were accordingly discharged.

(2) Alice McKenzie was found with her throat cut (or rather <u>stabbed</u>) in Castle Alley on 17th July 1889; no evidence was forthcoming and no arrests were made in connection with this

case. The <u>stab</u> in the throat was of the same nature as in the case of number 3.

(3) Frances Coles in Swallow Gardens, on 13th February 1891—for which Thomas Sadler, a fireman, was arrested, and, after several remands, discharged. It was ascertained at the time that Sadler had sailed for the Baltic on 19th July '89 and was in Whitechapel on the night of 17th idem. He was a man of ungovernable temper and entirely addicted to drink and the company of the lowest prostitutes.

(4) The case of the unidentified woman whose trunk was found in Pinchin St on 10th Sept. 1889—which has already been dealt with.

M. L. Macnaghten
23rd Feb. 1894

Investigating Farson's submission that Druitt was the murderer, it is illuminating to examine several statements he claims were made by Macnaghten:

No one ever saw the Whitechapel murderer (unless possibly it was the City P.C. who was on a beat near Mitre Square) and no proof could in any way ever be brought against anyone, although very many homicidal maniacs were at one time or another suspected. I enumerate the cases of three men against whom the police held very reasonable suspicion. *Personally, and after much careful and deliberate consideration, I am inclined to exonerate two of them.*

The sentence which I have put in italics is vital to Farson's theory that the third suspect, Druitt, was in Macnaghten's mind the real killer. But in his official notes at the Yard, which must be considered more reliable than Farson's copy of a copy, Macnaghten wrote:

No one ever saw the Whitechapel murderer, many homicidal maniacs were suspected, but no shadow of proof could be thrown on any one. I may mention the cases of 3 men, *any one of whom* would have been *more likely* than Cutbush to have committed this series of murders. [My italics.]

Here we see no inclination to exonerate two of them, just the names of three men, *any one of whom* might have been Jack the Ripper.

Farson and Cullen claim that an even more impressive in-

dictment of Druitt appeared in Lady Aberconway's copy of her
father's notes. Once again, nothing like it appears in the real
notes. According to the two authors, Macnaghten wrote:

> . . . I have always held strong opinions regarding No. 1
> [Druitt] and the more I think the matter over, the stronger do
> these opinions become. The truth, however, will never be
> known, and did, indeed at one time lie at the bottom of the
> Thames, if my conjectures be correct.

These words do not appear in the original notes. In the real
notes Macnaghten made no claim to have any strong suspicions
regarding Druitt. He was merely one of three *possibles*. There
was no mention, either, of the truth having lain at the bottom
of the Thames.

Now look at the actual reference to No. 1, in which both
authors differ seriously from the real notes. Cullen and Farson's
version is reproduced on the left and the real Macnaghten's
notes on the right:

No. 1 Mr M. J. Druitt, a doctor of about forty-one years of age and of fairly good family, who disappeared at the time of the Miller's Court murder, and whose body was found floating in the Thames on 3rd December, i.e. seven weeks after the said murder. The body was said to have been in the water for a month, or more—on it was found a season ticket between Blackheath and London. From private information I have little doubt but that his own family suspected this man of being the Whitechapel murderer; it was alleged that he was sexually insane.	(1) A Mr M. J. Druitt, said to be a doctor and of good family, who disappeared at the time of the Millers Court murder, and whose body (which was said to have been upwards of a month in the water) was found in the Thames on 31st Dec.—or about 7 weeks after that murder. He was sexually insane and from private info I have little doubt but that his own family believed him to have been the murderer.

The discrepancies are at once apparent: In the genuine notes
there is no mention of Druitt's age; they say Druitt was found
in the Thames on 31st December (which is correct). Cullen and
Farson's version says 3rd December, which by no stretch of the

imagination was seven weeks after Kelly's murder on 9th November—it was a mere three weeks and three days. A further mistake is made in the revised edition of Farson's book, when the date of the finding of Druitt's body is changed yet again—to 13th December! The real notes make no mention of a season ticket, and the wording of the two pieces is quite different. Thus the notes used by Messrs Farson and Cullen as the basis of their indictment of Druitt appear to be *rough and inaccurate copies*. Whether the mistakes occurred in Lady Aberconway's first transcription, or in the subsequent copies, it is impossible to say. Over so many years and in so many versions it is hardly surprising that statements have emerged which have little bearing on the originals.

Armed with the idea that Macnaghten suspected Druitt and exonerated the other two suspects named, Farson and Cullen set out to find evidence.

The evidence produced by Farson is seriously flawed. Patiently, and with the help of two full-time researchers, he traced a Dr Lionel Druitt who was listed in the *Medical Directory* until 1887, after which date his address was given as Australia. Lionel turned out to be Montague's cousin. Farson also found the death certificate of his suspect at Somerset House and discovered that Druitt was a barrister, not a doctor as Macnaghten had stated.

He found that Druitt was born at Wimborne in Dorset in August 1857. In January 1870 he went to Winchester College, where he proved a successful all rounder. He made rapid progress academically, was an active member of the Debating Society and excelled at cricket. In 1876 he was awarded a scholarship to New College, Oxford, where he did moderately well. He left in 1880, having achieved a B.A. Druitt turned to law, and in May 1882 was admitted to the Inner Temple. He was called to the Bar, before the benchers of the Inns of Court, in 1885. He took chambers at No. 9 King's Bench Walk, which he maintained until his death, but he appears to have had little success as a barrister, and eventually became a full-time master at a school in Blackheath, where he had been teaching at least since 1883.

Farson's next piece of 'evidence' seems insubstantial, but it appears to be the foundation of his argument. He states that he received a letter from a Mr Knowles who said he had once seen a document in Australia called *The East End Murderer—I knew him*. It was apparently written by a Lionel Drewett, Druitt or

Drewery. Unfortunately, Farson cannot produce the letter because, he says, it disappeared along with other papers relevant to Jack the Ripper in a dossier someone borrowed but never returned. Farson does not remember Knowles's address, so the latter cannot be traced and questioned about the document he may or may not have seen. What is more frustrating is that Farson did not immediately contact Knowles to ask vital questions, like: 'When and where did you see the document?'; 'Do you have a copy?'; and most important of all, 'Did it name the murderer?' In fact, no questions at all were asked of the man who, Farson himself says, provided him with *crucial* evidence.

'The value of this [Knowles's] letter in identifying Jack the Ripper can hardly be exaggerated', he writes, although he does not have even the address of the man who wrote it. The letter was placed in a file which was later stolen. Farson had noted from the purloined letter, however, that *The East End Murderer —I knew him* had been published privately by a Mr Fell of Dandenong, a mountain settlement some twenty miles east of Melbourne, in 1890. He goes on to say that if it could be proved the document was written by M. J. Druitt's cousin Lionel, then it would be beyond coincidence—and Druitt must have been the Ripper. This seems a prodigious leap from mere possibility to accepted fact. Farson no longer regards the existence of the document as merely possible, but suddenly, without any corroboration, that possibility has been transformed in his mind to fact, and he is already talking about, 'If it can be proved it was written by Montague's cousin . . .'

Another important piece of investigation glossed over is that Knowles is supposed to have claimed *The East End Murderer—I knew him* could have been written by someone called Drewett or Drewery. No investigation into this possibility appears to have been conducted; it is tacitly assumed that the document did exist, that it was written by Lionel Druitt, and that all Farson has to show is that Lionel the author was also Lionel the doctor, Montague's cousin. Farson then reminds us that the *Medical Directory* showed Dr Lionel Druitt moved to Australia in 1887.

In Farson's revised edition he quotes a correspondent who states that in column seven of the death certificate of Druitt's mother, who spent her last years in a lunatic asylum, there is written: 'Emily Knowles, present at death, Manor House, Chiswick'.

With no stronger evidence than this coincidence of common surnames, Emily Knowles is coupled with the present-day Mr

Knowles who wrote the missing letter, a mountainous piece of conjecture with no hint of supporting evidence; Farson knows nothing more about either Knowles than the name. The suggestion is that Emily Knowles was a woman looking after Mrs Druitt at the asylum, and that she held vital information after Montague's last visit to his mother: 'This was conveyed by a member of her family to Lionel, enabling him to write the document'. (!)

By this stage Farson seems convinced that Druitt was the killer. But:

(1) He has not proven that the document to which he refers even existed.

(2) He has not shown, if it did, that Lionel Druitt wrote it.

(3) He has not examined the argument that if Montague were the murderer, his cousin would hardly have wanted to publicize the fact. And in the unlikely event that Lionel was seeking notoriety through a connection with the Ripper, firstly he would not have had to arrange for the piece to be published privately—newspapers and publishers would have snapped it up immediately; and secondly, if he was seeking notoriety he would hardly have had his work published in a place so small and remote as Dandenong, where so few would have read it. Dandenong has little more than six thousand inhabitants now. In the 1890s it was a cluster of huts, and certainly no printer would have found a livelihood there.

(4) He has not discussed the likelihood that whoever wrote the piece, it may have named someone completely different from Montague Druitt. Farson does not even mention this as a possibility.

(5) He does not mention that literally thousands of statements have been made by people claiming to know the identity of the Ripper, and that *The East End Murderer—I knew him,* even if it existed, may have had no significance at all.

Despite what several Druittists have claimed, Farson produces no concrete evidence that the document existed. What he does produce appears to be fourth-hand hearsay which would not be admissible in any court of law, claiming that an amateur criminologist called Maurice Gould claimed he had been in Australia from 1925 to 1932, and that there he met two people who claimed they knew the identity of the Ripper. Their information, it is said, came from papers belonging to a Mr W. G. Fell.

Farson continues:

> Today, Gould admits that details are blurred at such a
> distance, but he remembers that one of the two men was a
> freelance journalist called Edward MacNamara who 'knew
> this Mr Fell of Dandenong who died in 1935' and said that
> Fell housed a man called Druitt who left him papers proving
> the Ripper's identity: 'These he would not part with unless
> he received a considerable sum, £500 I think, which I had
> not got in those days and so *what I wrote was from memory from
> the scant examination I had of them*'. [my italics]

Not only is the information Farson proffers as corroboration
fourth-hand, but it is apparently based on something written
from *memory* after a *scant* examination. It is not explained how
the two men Gould met in Australia had knowledge as early as
1932 of Mr Fell's death in 1935. Nor is it explained that the
Australian registries of births and deaths have no record of the
death of a W. G. Fell any time between 1933 and 1937, which
rules out Mr Gould's testimony.

However, armed with what he calls a 'double confirmation
of names', from the blurred memory of Gould and from the
untraceable Knowles, Farson flew to Australia. He drove to the
Dandenong Ranges, and at a place called Lang-Lang he
heard of a shopkeeper called Fell. Unfortunately, he was no
relation to the elusive printer.

If Farson produced no evidence the document existed, the
BBC with all their efforts and resources, concluded it did not,
and in so doing seem to have destroyed Farson's whole case
against Druitt. In a Telex message to Humphrey Fisher, Head
of Documentaries at the Australian Broadcasting Commission
in Sydney, Paul Bonner asked for information on the alleged
document. On 9th April 1973 he received this reply from
researcher Leone Buchanan:

> Humphrey Fisher passed on your request to me concern-
> ing Dr Lionel Druitt and the publication of *The East End
> Murderer—I knew him*. So far no luck. Have checked Sydney
> libraries and spent three days in Melbourne checking every
> available source including libraries, historical societies,
> criminologists, archivists, private collectors, publishers and
> newspapers. Druitt's publication is not listed in Australian
> bibliographies and a search of directories around 1890 reveals
> no such person as W. G. Fell. Traced daughter and grand-

daughter of Druitt who have no knowledge of Dr Druitt being in Dandenong or of his writing the article. Apparently he was in Tasmania during that time.

This seems to destroy Farson's theory once and for all. If Dr Lionel Druitt was in Tasmania when Farson claimed he was at Dandenong then he could not have written the document—which seems not to have existed anyway, because if it had some trace of it would surely have been uncovered by Buchanan's exhaustive research. And finally it would seem that W. G. Fell did not exist either!

Lionel Druitt's only published work in Australia was in fact a four-page article dealing with urine infection, which appeared in a medical magazine.

As if he has established not only that the document existed, but also that Lionel Druitt was its author, Farson goes on to ask:

What personal knowledge could Lionel have had which made him accuse his cousin? Here I am able to produce another piece of crucial evidence. I discovered from the *Medical Directory* that Dr Lionel Druitt had a surgery at the Minories in 1879. This is the first link between Druitt and the East End of London, the absence of which has been so baffling until now. Montague was about to leave Oxford at that date, but again I find the association beyond coincidence.

However, Dr Lionel Druitt did not have a surgery in the Minories in 1879, and there is no mention of him in the *Medical Directory* for that year. The reference which is confusing Farson appears in fact in the *Medical Register*, a different publication entirely. This reference does indeed list Druitt at Minories, E. in 1879. But at the most this means he was assisting the doctor who regularly practised at that address, and he was not there for more than a few months. This is shown by the fact that the *Medical Directory* and the *Medical Register* for the years either side of 1879 give Druitt's address as 8 Strathmore Gardens, which was clearly his permanent address. Unfortunately, this misunderstanding about Lionel Druitt's connection with the Minories has become the basis of the next major part of Farson's theory. He suggests that Lionel, four years older than Montague, 'might well have felt it his duty to look after the boy when they were both in London'. But he gives no evidence to show Montague was ever in the East End of London, or even that he knew his cousin Lionel.

'It is reasonable to assume', says Farson, 'that Montague might have visited Lionel there. . . . It is conceivable that he even lived there himself after Lionel had left, and that at some time Lionel had grounds for suspicion.'

So, instead of producing *evidence* to link Montague with the East End, Farson tries to convince us of his suspect's guilt by stating 'it is reasonable to assume' he stayed at the Minories for nine years after Lionel left, even though all this time Montague had rooms at No. 9 King's Bench Walk. A quick check of both the *Medical Register* and the *Medical Directory* for every year between 1879 and 1889 shows that at no time could Montague have stayed at No. 140. It was occupied permanently by doctors. Firstly Doctors J. O. Taylor and Thomas Thyne practised at the address, to be succeeded by Dr John Sell Edmund Cotman. Despite Farson's assertion, it is *un*reasonable to assume any connection between Druitt and the Minories, unless there is supporting evidence.

Farson then returns to his amateur criminologist Maurice Gould, who claims to have spoken to a former librarian from Poplar on the Isle of Dogs, which borders on Ripper territory. Gould is quoted as saying, 'From some recess in the library he [the librarian] produced an old, either Voters' List or a Directory, which listed an M. J. Druitt as living in the Minories'.

Farson says he later tried to trace the reference but without success, and 'further enquiries indicate that the ex-librarian is dead'.

Once again Farson's evidence can be traced back via hearsay to a dead man. The first half of his case is based on a letter he cannot produce from a man who cannot be traced. The second half is based on the unsubstantiated testimony of a dead man. Old librarians die, but Voters' Lists and Directories live on. I have examined every directory covering the Minories in the seventies, eighties and nineties, and in none of them is the name M. J. Druitt mentioned.

The case to show a connection between Druitt and the Minories has the strength of gossamer, yet Farson proceeds to detail what he sees as the importance of that thoroughfare. It is not simply their position in the East End, he says:

They have a particular significance in the story of the Ripper. On September 29th, 1888, the Ripper wrote from Liverpool: 'Beware, I shall be at work on the 1st and 2nd inst., in

Minories at twelve midnight, and I give the authorities a good chance, but there is never a policeman near when I am at work'.

Then he quotes part of a further letter from Liverpool received after the double murder of 30th September:

What fools the police are. I even give them the name of the street where I am living.

As far as Farson is concerned these letters can have been written by only one person, Montague the Ripper. But yet again one single idea turns out to be fraught with fatal weaknesses. There is no evidence whatsoever to show the real murderer wrote the two letters from Liverpool. There is nothing to indicate Druitt ever went to Liverpool or had any connections with the city. If Farson had seen the Scotland Yard file he would know it contains hundreds of letters from cranks all over the world. They are written in many languages; many an East End street and numerous nights between September 1888 and the end of the year are mentioned. With that wealth of material one could prove anything—providing of course one accepts the Ripper wrote every letter received by the police and Press, and that in between murders he travelled as far off as Barcelona and Philadelphia to post his crazy messages.

But the most misleading point about the two Liverpool letters is Farson's juxtaposition of the last two sentences of one with the reference to the Minories in the other. 'What fools the police are. I even give them the name of the street where I am living', is used to create the impression that the writer of the letter lived in the Minories. What Farson does not mention is that 'the street where I am living' plainly refers to the address at the top of the letter—Prince William Street, Liverpool!

This analysis of Farson's book reveals no evidence at all to incriminate Druitt. He has not shown Druitt was anywhere near the scenes of the murders nor that he ever went to the East End. And he has no evidence to show Druitt had a motive for killing whores.

Montague John Druitt was not Jack the Ripper. The truth of this is to be found in the barrister's cricketing career. The first murder, that of Nichols, took place at Whitechapel in the early hours of Friday, 31st August. *The very next day* Druitt was in

the West Country playing cricket. The second murder, Annie
Chapman's, took place about 4.20 on the morning of Saturday,
8th September. Six hours later Druitt was playing cricket at the
Rectory Field at Blackheath for the Blackheath Cricket Club.

'Of course this does not disprove the case against Druitt in
any way', Farson writes, and then suggests feebly, 'It might
confirm that his nerve was strong'. He continues:

> Certainly it was practical, for the journey to Blackheath
> from Spitalfields was a short and easy one. There is no reason
> why a man should not commit murder and go on to play a
> good game of cricket a few hours later. Despite the excessive
> slowness of the game he might even regard it as a release.

By the time he gets to discussing the killer's state of mind,
Farson has obviously forgotten the picture he painted of the
strong-nerved Druitt elaborately mutilating Chapman, then
going on to play cricket. He first quotes Dr Magnus Hirschfeld,
author of *Sexual Anomalies and Perversions*, who makes the point
that:

> The sexual murderer does not know the sinister, bestial
> desire to kill that lies dormant within him, to come to life at
> the first unfortunate opportunity.

Farson goes on to say that Hirschfeld suggests the sexual
murderer is hardly aware of what he is doing, and that he
murders in a state of sexual intoxication. He then quotes
Colin Wilson, who says that after the murder he thinks the
killer would suffer:

> intense depression, the 'morning after' feeling, revulsion
> from the bloodstained clothes, the feeling 'Did I do that?' . . .
> I suspect that Jack the Ripper was a slave to this craving for
> killing, like a drug addict, but still ashamed of it.

Farson comments:

> I am sure that Wilson is right. Apart from the question of
> self-acknowledged responsibility, this does not conflict with
> the conclusions of Hirschfeld but carries them still further.

But it is hardly consistent with Farson's earlier comment about
Druitt playing cricket only hours after committing a savage
murder.

In his concluding chapters, Farson elaborates on Sir Melville Macnaghten's words: 'From private information I have little doubt but that his family believed him to have been the murderer'. Farson discusses this in regard to William Druitt, Montague's brother, a solicitor from Bournemouth who testified at Montague's inquest. Farson writes:

> We may suppose that William, who represented the family, believed that his brother committed the murders. But . . . why? The suicide in the Thames is no evidence in itself. Yet at the very point where the evidence might seem weakest, I can see its strength. William must have had proof of Montague's guilt. Furthermore, this proof must have been conclusive; William was not searching for notoriety, on the contrary, and he would hardly have drawn attention to his suspicions without good reason. Equally the police would not have accepted his statement without proof.

We must remember that Sir Melville Macnaghten's notes did not express the opinion of the police as a whole. For police, Farson should substitute 'Macnaghten'. Secondly, as Macnaghten's *official* notes show, he did not *accept* the statement that the family believed Druitt was the Ripper. He merely reported their suspicion, which in itself was meaningless. Many families had suspicions about certain of their members, as the Yard *Suspects* file proves. That did not make them all Jack the Ripper. And thirdly, if the police had had proof, as Farson alleges, Macnaghten certainly would have included it in his notes.

Farson quotes the letter found in Druitt's pocket after he was dragged from the Thames, and which was read out at the inquest:

> Since Friday I felt I was going to be like mother and the best thing for me was to die.

But this does not support the case against Druitt, it weakens it. Would a man who had committed five brutal murders accompanied by horrific mutilations over a period of ten weeks sit down and write, several weeks after the final murder, that he had been feeling apprehensive about his state of mind *since Friday*? The idea that he had not become just a little worried about his behaviour between 31st August and 9th November is almost comic.

In the revised edition of his book Farson admits the possibility that Druitt did not commit suicide but was murdered by his family. His reasoning, in part, is sound. Druitt's pockets were filled with stones. A swimmer is not likely to choose death by drowning, and a person who cannot swim would have no need to weight his body. But Farson harps back to the fictitious connection with the Minories and quotes a correspondent as saying:

> I would say that they [Druitt's family] overpowered him—drugs? injection?—they had medical knowledge and so presumably access to 'knock out drops'—and then carried his unconscious body to the Thames and then heaved his stone-laden body into it. (Minories to Thames—200 yards?) Justice was done if not legally.

Yet as we have seen, Druitt was in no way connected with the Minories. And if he had been, No. 140 where Farson says Druitt lived is considerably more than two hundred yards from the river; it is nearer nine hundred. Though the reasoning that Druitt was murdered is sound, it is hardly credible that his own family could have been responsible. Even if the Druitts had certain knowledge that Montague was a desperate maniac, and had been responsible for the Jack the Ripper murders, surely the last thing they are likely to have done is murder him. If they had taken any action it would have been to place him in an asylum like his mother. So, if his family did not murder Druitt, who did?

Sickert said from the beginning that Druitt had been a scapegoat, but he did not know how he had been selected. If this was true, those involved in the cover-up would have been questing for a likely candidate on whom to place the blame for the murders. And Druitt, alone in London, nervous and unhappy, would have been an ideal choice. Of course, it would have been hopeless bringing him to trial—conviction would have been impossible, and the accompanying publicity highly dangerous. But if he committed suicide, and a note was found on his body expressing fear for his sanity, then the case would be well and truly sewn up.

The Honourable Society of the Inner Temple have records to show that Druitt kept up his chambers at No. 9 King's Bench Walk until his death. This is confirmed by the *Post*

Office Directory of London. It is almost certain that if he was murdered, he was taken from *this* address to the Thames. King's Bench Walk runs right down to the Victoria Embankment. But without solid facts all this is speculation, with little more validity than Farson's writing about Druitt. If Druitt was a scapegoat, he must have been set up. Someone somewhere along the line must have chosen him. If Sickert was right in his suggestion, there had to be a link between Druitt and the other sides of the case. But where?

There is a series of links that taken singly could be dismissed as coincidence. Combined, they form a pattern which is undeniable:

(1) Michael Harrison has found that Prince Eddy's tutor, and later governor, Canon John Neale Dalton, was educated at the same school at Blackheath where Druitt became a master. Whether Dalton continued his association with the school, and indeed exerted any influence there, it is impossible to say. Once again, it is only possible to speculate that if he did he could have been responsible for one of the most baffling aspects about Druitt's tragic life, his mysterious dismissal from the school. Druitt taught there for at least five years, and was dismissed shortly before his death. No one has been able to find out why.

(2) Thomas Toughill, who has developed his own theory about the identity of the Ripper, has established another connection, albeit an indirect one, between Druitt and Eddy. Druitt's brother was in the same regiment as the artist Frank Miles—and Miles' brother was Eddy's equerry.

(3) Having established Miles as a second link between Druitt and Eddy, we find that Miles lived in Tite Street, Chelsea—and that across the road, at No. 9, lived Sir Melville Macnaghten, the man responsible for connecting Druitt's name with the Ripper case.

(4) Next door to Miles at No. 28 Tite Street lived the artist Whistler, Walter Sickert's erstwhile mentor whom Sickert visited regularly.

(5) At No. 16 Tite Street lived the homosexual Miles's former lover, Oscar Wilde—and Wilde was another close friend of Sickert whom Sickert used often to visit.

(6) Hesketh Pearson pointed out in his biography of Wilde that another distinguished visitor used to call on Wilde at Tite Street—Eddy's father, the Prince of Wales. Parties were held

at Wilde's house at which Sickert, Eddy's father and Miles were among the regular guests.

(7) Macnaghten was a likely guest at these same parties, though this is not definite. As well as his link with Sickert at Tite Street, Macnaghten and Sickert were fellow-members of the Garrick Club.

(8) Yet another fact connects Druitt with the Royal Family. After the notorious Mordaunt divorce scandal in which the Prince of Wales was implicated in 1869, Lady Mordaunt was conveniently certified insane and placed in an asylum where she spent the rest of her life. Whether she was really insane is open to some doubt, but the fact remained that her incarceration was fortunate for the Prince of Wales. The records of the Lunacy Commission show that only about twelve lunatics in the whole country were of sufficient importance or interest to warrant regular reports. Tracing the records through the years, one fact cannot be missed: two names appear regularly together in that small list of inmates—Lady Mordaunt and Mrs Ann Druitt, Montague's mother.

(9) Another interesting connection between Druitt and Eddy is via Eddy's best friend James Kenneth Stephen, whom Harrison named as the Ripper. Stephen's brothers were both barristers like Druitt. Harry Lushington Stephen was at No. 3 King's Bench Walk (Druitt was a few yards along at No. 9) and Herbert Stephen was immediately opposite Druitt's chambers, at No. 4 Paper Buildings.

(10) The Stephens were all patients of Sir William Gull, the man Sickert names as the prime mover in the Ripper case.

(11) Druitt was surrounded by people who had close links with the account of the Ripper murders told by Sickert. The eleventh link takes us beyond the civilized purlieus of King's Bench Walk and Paper Buildings into No. 9 King's Bench Walk itself. Several solicitors and barristers shared No. 9 King's Bench Walk with Druitt—one of whom was Reginald Brodie Dyke Acland, the brother of Sir William Gull's son-in-law.

(12) Dyke Acland's father, Sir Henry Wentworth Acland, was Honorary Physician to Eddy's father and a close friend of Gull.

(13) Acland was also a friend of Holman Hunt, the Pre-Raphaelite painter—whose studios had been at Cleveland Street.

(14) The final link is the vital one. The solicitor who instigated the second part of the Cleveland Street cover-up, Edward Henslow Bedford, lived at No. 9 King's Bench Walk, the same

address as Druitt. Law Society records show that Bedford practised at the address between 1867 and 1898, and subsequently at 52 Arbour Square, Whitechapel, close to the police station. During his time at King's Bench Walk he was twice in partnership, but between 1879 and 1898, the period during which Druitt shared the address, he practised alone. The building is not vast; it is a three-storey, flat-fronted house; Bedford and Druitt would undoubtedly have known each other well.

It seems beyond coincidence that the man who played a major role in the second part of the cover-up should live at the self-same address as the person used as a scapegoat in the third part. Bedford was in the best possible position to evaluate Druitt, bring him to the notice of those in charge of the cover-up, and also set up his murder.

To sum up: an amazing set of facts, all of which can be verified by documents open to the public, not only confirm Druitt was a scapegoat by linking him with every aspect of the case. They also provide definite links between every part of Sickert's narrative, parts which until now have appeared unconnected. Druitt, Eddy, the Prince of Wales, J. K. Stephen, Sir Melville Macnaghten, Sir William Gull and all the goings-on at Cleveland Street are linked together, just as Sickert claimed. And as final establishment of his credentials, Sickert himself has links with all of them.

CHAPTER NINE

All Roads lead to Dorset Street

Apart from the curious fact that Inspector Abberline was in charge of both the Ripper case and the Cleveland Street brothel case, other incidents link Cleveland Street—and indeed the Royal Family—with the East End murders.

The importance of one connection between the Royal Family and Jack the Ripper has so far been missed: Queen Victoria was passionately concerned about the Ripper murders. This was not, however, a concern stimulated by a monarch's conscientious desire for law and order. Victoria had a special interest. In a year when murder was commonplace throughout England, she took an active interest in the *first* Ripper murder and ordered the Prime Minister to take steps that would prevent a sequel. Only a person with some inside knowledge can recognize in a single killing the beginning of a series—especially if the second murder has not yet occurred. In a telegram to Salisbury, sent after Kelly's murder on 9th November, Victoria reminded him: 'You promised me when the first murder took place to consult your colleagues about it'.

As this indignant memorandum indicates, unless the Queen instructed her Prime Minister to take personal action over every murder that occurred in England—which she did not—then Victoria knew Nichols's killing was the first of a series the moment it happened. Had she urged action after *Chapman's* death her concern would have been understandable, for by then it was obvious that a pattern of murder was developing. But murder was so common in Whitechapel in 1888 that her specific concern with Nichols indicates a deeper knowledge.

Murder was so much a part of life in the East End that when a woman called Emma Smith was attacked by three men and stabbed to death on Easter Monday, 1888, the newspapers did not bother to report it. Two witnesses who testified at Kelly's inquest said they had heard the cry, 'Murder!' but it was such a common cry in the neighbourhood they both ignored it. There were about five hundred inquests into unexplained deaths in the Whitechapel district alone in 1887, the year before the Ripper murders. Cullen wrote:

> In scanning the press for this period one is astounded by the number of reports of women who had been beaten or kicked to death, jumped on until they were crushed, chopped, stabbed, seamed with vitriol, eviscerated, or deliberately set afire. In the preceding year thirty-five murders were recorded in the Home Counties alone (seventy-six murders if one includes infanticides), and of this number only eight convictions were secured, the majority of these crimes remaining unsolved forever.

Crime comes in waves, and 1888 was the crest of the wave for crimes of violence, especially in the East End where they happened every day. Unless Sickert's story is correct it is hard to explain Queen Victoria's preoccupation with Nichols's murder. At the time the Queen started demanding action it was an apparently unremarkable murder with nothing to distinguish it from a dozen others in Whitechapel that year. Only later did it turn out to be the first by Jack the Ripper.

A further provable connection between the murders and Cleveland Street was mentioned by Sickert himself. Fifty yards from the hovel where Marie Kelly was murdered stood Providence Row Women's Refuge, run by nuns. This was the East End convent from which Sickert said Kelly had first been brought to Cleveland Street. One of the founders and a leading committee member of Providence Row was a solicitor called Edmund Bellord. He was a partner in a firm of estate agents called Perkins and Bellord, whose offices were at none other place than Cleveland Street. They owned much of the property in the area—including, incidentally, Lord Salisbury's house in nearby Fitzroy Square.

Perhaps the most important connection between the West End and the East End was that mentioned by Marie Kelly herself. At her inquest the man she had been living with, Joe

Barnett, said 'When she left Cardiff she said she came to London. In London she was first in a gay house in the West End of the town. A gentleman there asked her to go to France. She went to France but she told me as she did not like the part she did not stay there long. She lived there about a fortnight.'

Though many authors have dismissed this as fantasy on the part of Marie Kelly, it is nevertheless remarkably consistent with the story told by Sickert. Not only does it seem inescapable that the gay house in the West End was Sickert's studio in Cleveland Street, Sickert also said he had taken Kelly to Dieppe, which would account for her trips to France with 'a gentleman'.

Sickert maintained that his personal involvement in the case ended at Cleveland Street, but that he knew who the killers were, the motive for the killings and how they were carried out. He believed four of the Ripper victims knew each other, though he did not produce any evidence in support of this claim. Eddowes, he said, was murdered only because she was mistaken for Kelly. He did not know why. He said the four companions, Kelly, Chapman, Stride and Nichols, were blackmailing someone connected with the events in Cleveland Street, though once again he left a gap in the story by not explaining who. The blackmail drew attention to the whores and brought about their murder.

No theorist has suggested *any* of the victims knew each other, let alone hinting at an association between four of them. Their bodies were found over a wide area encompassing Whitechapel, Spitalfields and Aldgate. There certainly appears at first glance to be nothing to connect them, except that they were all prostitutes. But if any of the victims did know each other, it would shed completely new light on the case. . . .

The first observation—and even this seems to have eluded previous writers—is that although the victims' bodies were found over a large area in three different districts, they all lived in one tiny part of Spitalfields. This degraded neighbourhood included Dorset Street, which was known as the most evil road in London, along which policemen would walk only in pairs, White's Row, Fashion Street, Flower and Dean Street and Thrawl Street. They were all short roads; the longest (Fashion Street) was only a hundred and eighty yards long, and Dorset Street was little more than a hundred yards long. This is the picture:

DORSET STREET. Annie Chapman lived in a common

lodging house at No. 35. Marie Kelly lived thirty yards away on the same side of the street in Miller's Court, which was part of No. 26. It was disclosed at Kelly's inquest that before moving to Miller's Court she had lived at another common lodging house in Dorset Street. Exactly where is not known. As well as living so close to each other, Chapman and Kelly both frequented the same pub, the Britannia on the corner of Dorset Street and Crispin Street. This new evidence has not previously come to light because at Chapman's inquest the pub was referred to as the Ringer's, and at Kelly's it was described by its correct name, the Britannia. As Caroline Maxwell's previously unpublished statement, given in full in Chapter 4, shows, the Britannia was owned by a Mrs Ringer and known to the locals as the Ringer's.

FASHION STREET. Catherine Eddowes often lodged at No. 6. Stride sometimes stayed at a lodging house in the same street, but which number is not known. Fashion Street was fifty yards from Dorset Street.

FLOWER AND DEAN STREET. Mary Nichols lodged for a time at a house called the White House. This was only yards away from No. 32 where Stride often dossed. A short way along from No. 32 was Eddowes's main address, No. 55. Flower and Dean Street was less than a hundred yards from Dorset Street.

THRAWL STREET. Nichols's chief address was at No. 18. This was near No. 6, the address of Eddowes's sister, whom Eddowes often used to visit. Thrawl Street was a hundred and eighty yards from Dorset Street.

Considering that there were 233 common lodging houses in Whitechapel, Spitalfields and Stepney from which Jack the Ripper could have selected his victims, it must surely be significant that he killed women from addresses so close to each other. Even without further evidence, it seemed a strong possibility that the victims knew each other. But there was still more evidence to come.

Timothy Donovan, deputy of the common lodging house at 35 Dorset Street, told the Chapman inquest that Annie Chapman had lived there for the four months prior to her murder, except for the last week, during which time he had not seen her until the Friday evening. He had known her about sixteen months.

The address of victim number three, Elizabeth Stride, has always been reported as Flower and Dean Street, and it was disclosed at her inquest that she had also lodged in Fashion

Street. She had in fact dossed in both these streets, but that was
only part of the story. The house reported to have been Stride's
regular address was No. 32 Flower and Dean Street, but
Elizabeth Tanner, deputy of the common lodging house at that
address, told Stride's inquest:

'I have seen the body of the dead woman at St George's
Mortuary and I recognize it as that of a woman who had
lodged in our house *on and off* for the last six years.' (My italics.)

From this statement it is plain that Stride spent little of her
time at this address. The view is strengthened by the dialogue
which followed between Coroner Wynne Baxter and Mrs
Tanner:

CORONER   Who is she [the deceased]?
TANNER   She was known by the nickname Long Liz.
CORONER   Do you know her right name?
TANNER   No.

Most of the Spitalfields lodging houses were appallingly over-
crowded, but if Stride had been a regular lodger at No. 32
Mrs Tanner would surely have known her name. If Stride was
not in fact living where until now it has been assumed she was,
what was her address? The answer is to be found in another part
of Widow Tanner's evidence:

CORONER   Do you know any of her male acquaintances?
TANNER   Only of one.
CORONER   Who is he?
TANNER   *She was living with him.* She left him on Thursday
          to come and stay at our house, so she told me.
          [My italics].

The man Stride had been living with was a waterside labourer
called Michael Kidney. That she had spent most of her time
with Kidney, and not at either Flower and Dean Street or
Fashion Street, was borne out by Kidney's testimony:

I have seen the body. It is Long Liz. *I've known her for about
three years and she has been living with me nearly all that time.* I
left her in Commercial Street as I was going to work. I
expected her to be at home but when I got home I found she
had been in and gone out. She was subject to going away
whenever she thought she would. During the three years
I've known her she has been away from me altogether about

five months. I've cautioned her the same as I would a wife. It
was drink that made her go. But she always came back again.
I don't believe she left me on Tuesday to take up with any
other man. I think she liked me better than any other man. I
didn't see her again until I identified the body in the mortuary.

Kidney's testimony shows us how Stride's address has gone
down on historical record as 32 Flower and Dean Street.
When the Ripper struck her down she just happened to be in
the midst of one of her bouts of drunkenness which took her off
to that address. And the temporary doss house she drifted into
was put down as her permanent abode. These were the days
before the precise methods advocated by Conan Doyle in his
Sherlock Holmes stories had been adopted by the real police;
when names, ages and addresses were regarded, with a certain
contempt, as mere formalities. But names, ages and addresses
can and do catch murderers.

Long Liz Stride was apart from Kidney for only five months
in three years, and that five months consisted of odd jaunts
into a drunken independence. Most of the time between 1885
and her death she was living with Kidney. But where did they
live? Several writers have coupled the information about
Stride's connection with Flower and Dean Street with the fact
that she cohabited with Kidney, and concluded that they lived
together in Flower and Dean Street. This is incorrect. One vital
fact that was revealed at Stride's inquest has not so far been
noted. The *Daily News* of 6th October gave Michael Kidney's
address as 35 Dorset Street, *the self-same lodging house where
Annie Chapman had lived for four months prior to her death.* This was
the house where Elizabeth Stride had lived with Kidney. This
was the house from which she had decamped a few days
before her murder, just like Chapman. *Both victims had lived at
the same house, and both had kept away from it in the days leading up to
their deaths.*

A report in the secret Home Office file, recording Coroner
Baxter's summing-up at the Stride inquest, confirms this
conclusion: 'For the last two years the deceased had been living
at a common lodging house in Dorset Street, Spitalfields, with
Michael Kidney, a waterside labourer'.

Suddenly we find that three of the four Ripper victims whom
Sickert claimed knew each other all came from Dorset Street.
Two of them were living at the same house. Two frequented the
same pub. The evidence that they knew each other seems over-

All roads lead to Dorset Street

whelming. The fourth victim whom Sickert said was part of the same circle, though she was murdered nearly a mile away in Bucks Row, lived less than a hundred yards from the others, and doubtless frequented the same pub. Sickert's version of the East End murders was beginning to have real meaning. In a metropolis the size and character of the East End it is inconceivable that a random killer could have cut down, in places up to nearly a mile apart, four women who just happened to know each other. It is clear that whatever Jack the Ripper's motive, he (or they) knew the identity of the victims. It is not surprising so few writers have made this point: most theories are based upon the idea of a maniac perpetrating random murders.

Another factor vital to Sickert's story is that the Ripper's intended final victim was Marie Kelly. In 1867 there were an estimated 80 000 prostitutes in London. If anything this figure had increased by the eighties. Out of 80 000, Jack the Ripper killed five. Can it have been an accident that two of his five victims, the last two, were called Mary Ann Kelly? The odds against this happening by accident are astronomical, even though Kelly was a fairly common name. In addition, the real Kelly and the victim who merely used the name were the only Ripper victims to receive facial mutilations. Despite her fondness for the French version of her name, a fantasy perpetuated on her death certificate, the real Kelly was not known by many people in Dorset Street as Marie Jeanette. As the evidence of her inquest shows, she was known by some as Mary Jane, by others as Mary Ann. Can it be coincidence that Catherine Eddowes, who lived only fifty yards from the real Kelly, used the name Mary Ann Kelly? Eddowes often called herself Kelly because she lived with a man called John Kelly.

This must surely be the explanation lacking in Sickert's story, the reason why Eddowes was mistaken for Kelly and died in her place.

When Eddowes was dead the Ripper did not strike again for six weeks. She had called herself Mary Ann Kelly, and the killers thought they had the real Kelly. The details of her murder, like the mysterious facial mutilations, support this idea, as will be shown in Chapter 10. When the mistaken identity was realized Kelly was done to death and the Ripper murders were brought to their final, horrid crescendo exactly thirty-nine days after the death of Eddowes. This, too, will be seen to have significance.

All Ripper roads lead to Dorset Street. Dorset Street leads inexorably back to Cleveland Street. An elderly nun at the Roman Catholic convent in Harewood Place, W.1, only a few minutes' walk from Cleveland Street, had an interesting story to tell when the BBC interviewed her in 1973. In 1915 she had been a novice at Providence Row, directly opposite the pub where Kelly and Chapman had rubbed shoulders daily. She clearly remembered an old nun who had been there at the time of the Ripper murders telling her that 'if it had not been for the Kelly woman, none of the murders would have happened'.

CHAPTER TEN

The Masonic Killers

The suggestion that Freemasons were behind the Jack the Ripper murders was first laid before the public in *Butchery*, the third episode of the BBC series on the Whitechapel Murders. Scriptwriters Elwyn Jones and John Lloyd attributed the idea to their fictional policeman Detective Chief Superintendent John Watt. In so doing they unfortunately distorted the truth for the purpose of dramatic impact. Barlow and Watt's dialogue on the Freemasonry idea was separated by three episodes (or three weeks) from Sickert's story, which was told by his son in Episode Six. There was every indication that the Sickert account and the accusation of the Freemasons were unconnected. In fact the indictment of the Masons was an integral part of Sickert's story. It was purely as a result of a comment by Joseph Sickert that researcher Ian Sharp went to the London Library in St James's Square one afternoon in January 1973 to see if there was any traceable connection between the world's most mysterious society and its most mysterious series of murders. The evidence he uncovered should have appeared as corroboration of Sickert's six-minute narrative, or at least allied to it. Jones and Lloyd chose instead to include it in their script as a separate line of inquiry, and the true import of Walter Sickert's story was lost. Barlow and Watt's examination of the Masons was of necessity restricted to a few minutes. This brevity, and the fact that the idea was presented as just another theory bobbing on a sea of speculation, showed the idea badly. It came over as unlikely as Donald McCormick's complicated theory that a member of a Russian sect called the Chlysty might

have felt impelled to kill and mutilate whores, and as in-
substantial as Robin Odell's suggestion that the Ripper was a
Jewish ritual slaughterman inspired by the rigid doctrines of the
Talmud to rid the world of the taint of harlotry.

Had the Freemasons theory been anchored in a serious
attempt to explain who the killer or killers were, and why the
murders should have been perpetrated by Masons, it would
have been meaningful. But as jetsam the idea floated across our
television screens and for most of us sank into the Sargasso of
forgotten ideas, the crowded oblivion where all but the most
memorable of television's welter of communication is consigned.

Sickert's story also suffered because of the format of the
series. Viewers had never before seen such a hybrid programme,
where facts mingled inextricably with fiction. They knew Barlow and Watt were figments of a writer's imagination; many
people wondered if their investigation was enriched with
imaginary pieces of evidence. For all these reasons, and the
fact that the series was broadcast in midsummer when both
stations, faced with a much depleted audience, have made a
practice of churning out their dross, *Jack the Ripper* went with a
whimper rather than a bang. Jones and Lloyd turned their six
scripts into book form, and *The Ripper File* was published in
March 1975. But still the Freemasons idea was separate from
the Sickert narrative, and it was no more deeply investigated
than it had been on television.

Walter Sickert's assertion that the murders were masterminded by a group of extremist Freemasons and perpetrated
according to Masonic ritual is in fact a sensational idea. If true,
it would knock eighty-five years of theories out of joint. Like the
rest of the Sickert story, however, it took the form of a bald
statement, and the painter produced no shred of evidence in its
support. If Sickert had been lying this one statement would have
been his undoing. But, unsubstantiated as the idea was, it
became the strongest proof in the investigation so far that he
had spoken the truth. The evidence produced by Ian Sharp and
myself shows that the murders were indeed Masonic. Once
again, a single truth seems to wreck all other theories about the
murders, for no previous suspect except Prince Eddy himself
was a Mason. And the case against Eddy, as has been explained,
was quite without foundation.

Researching the mysteries of Freemasonry is an exacting and
difficult task, but it is possible. There have been enough
reliable exposures of the secret brotherhood to enable a

conscientious researcher to build up a clear picture of its activities. Before examining the undeniable connections between Masonry and Jack the Ripper, it is helpful to know something of the background and nature of Freemasonry.

It is a secret society which originated in England in the Middle Ages. It developed alongside several other guilds or incorporated crafts. The dearth of highly skilled craftsmen in the building industry imposed upon stonemasons in particular a need to move about the country in order to earn a living. Masons had to go where the work was. They travelled from place to place to assist in building the magnificent cathedrals and abbeys whose advent closed the door on the Dark Ages. Their craft was jealously guarded against interlopers. Apprenticeships were hard to obtain, and rigorous where achieved. Masons rapidly came to realize that the itinerant nature of their livelihood made them particularly vulnerable, and to protect themselves from exploitation they formed themselves into a sort of primitive trade union. It was a time when a number of professions were setting up guilds, and like the real trade-unions five hundred years later, none of them was national. Each guild was limited to a city or borough, and the stonemasons organized themselves at a local level into 'Lodges'. An idiosyncrasy of the masons which had an important effect on their evolution was that employers as well as employees were granted membership of the Lodges. Because the masons were migratory a greater degree of national unity was achieved within their guild than in those of other professions. This ensured greater uniformity in working conditions between one district and another, and as the strength of the masons grew in comparison to other professions, so did their determination to remain dominant. Because a mason could not work all his life in one place, and because each Lodge was constantly welcoming masons from other areas, the esoteric aspect of the craft was developed. Lodges all over the country agreed to adopt secret signs, passwords and handshakes so that a mason coming to a strange place could be recognized by his brothers as a genuine craftsman.

As the centuries passed the free and accepted masons, or freestone masons, evolved from a guild into a social organization. Lodges were set up abroad, notably in France. Eventually representatives of other skilled professions, and later still senior members of any middle and upper class professions, were permitted into the fraternity. By the eighteenth century Freemasons were, in practice, linked to their skilled predecessors only in name and in the form of their ritual. They had become a quasi-religious secret society, membership of which was extremely difficult to achieve, and highly desired by those who could not gain admittance. Brothers helped each other in business and on the social ladder. In many professions it became common for a Freemason to be given promotion purely because he was a Mason. The practice survives today.

Imagination and myth had by this time insinuated themselves deeply into the society's everyday working, and its actual origins became obscured by a fabulous tale of a heroic birth thousands of years before. Freemasonry's beginnings are now variously attributed by initiates to the days of the Roman Empire, to the Pharaohs, the Temple of Solomon, the Tower of Babel and even to the building of Noah's Ark. Of all the myths woven into the background of Freemasonry, the building of Solomon's Temple is the most sacred. On that great event much of Masonry's secret ritual is based.

In its own words Freemasonry is 'a peculiar system of morality, veiled in allegory and illustrated by symbols'. It proclaims itself as an organization founded on the practice of social and moral virtue.

Even though an initiate is bound by an oath of secrecy that imposes death on the betrayer, in its lower degrees Freemasonry is arguably quite respectable. It must be admitted that Masons as a body are among the most generous donors to charity. Several writers have claimed that one cannot be both a Freemason and a Christian, and until 1975 a Roman Catholic suffered excommunication for joining the fraternity because the Vatican proscribed Freemasonry and regarded it as 'subversive and anti-clerical'. Now, under certain circumstances, it is possible for a Catholic to obtain permission from his bishop to become a Mason, although Catholics in general still eye the brotherhood with deep suspicion. Despite this, it is not until a Mason is initiated into the higher degrees that he becomes truly pagan.

As Masons progress into higher degrees, their god undergoes a basic alteration. No one can become a Freemason unless he professes to believe in one Supreme Being. Freemasons call him the Great Architect, who created the universe with one sweep of his compasses. Combined as he is in the early degrees with an oath to honour the precepts of the Bible, this god is the benevolent counterpart of Jahweh and Allah; under any name he is the god of love, the Almighty Father. Degree by degree the per-

The 'Bloody Sunday' riot, Trafalgar Square, November 1887
Photo Radio Times Hulton Picture Library

Walter Sickert in
1884

Joseph Sickert in
1973
Photo Harry Jackson

Walter Sickert and his third wife Thérèse Lessore in 1939, three years before he died

Photo Cecil Beaton

Prince Eddy about 1890
Photo Radio Times Hulton Picture Library

Is the facial resemblance
between Princess Alexandra
(*right*) and Alice Margaret
Crook (*far right*) inherited?
See p. 41
*Photo Radio Times Hulton
Picture Library*

Annie Elizabeth Crook about
1886

Sickert family photograph

Sickert family photograph

Lazarus breaks his fast.

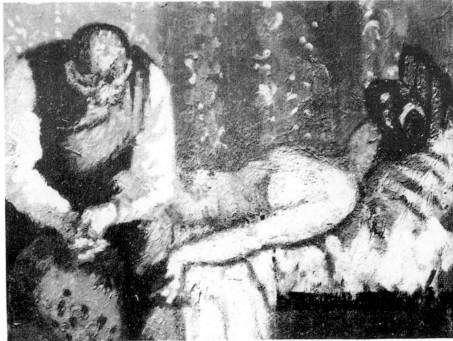

The Painter In His Studio (self-portrait)
  Reproduced by kind permission of Henry Lessor

Ennui
  Reproduced by kind permission of the Tate Gallery, London

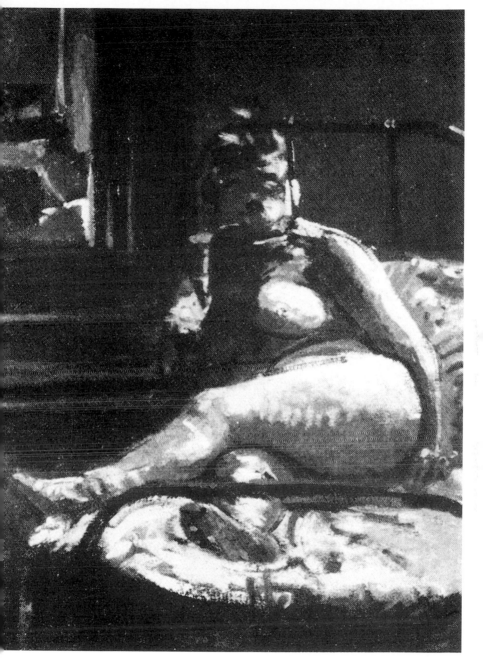

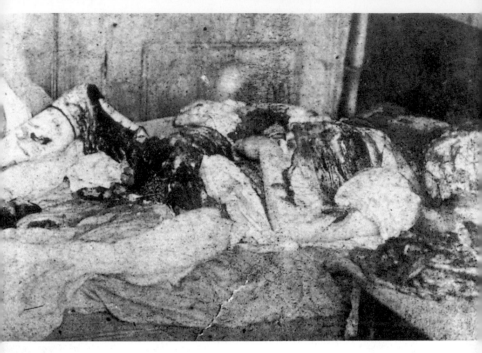

The Scotland Yard photograph of the mutilated remains of Marie Kelly, referred to in the Macnaghten papers

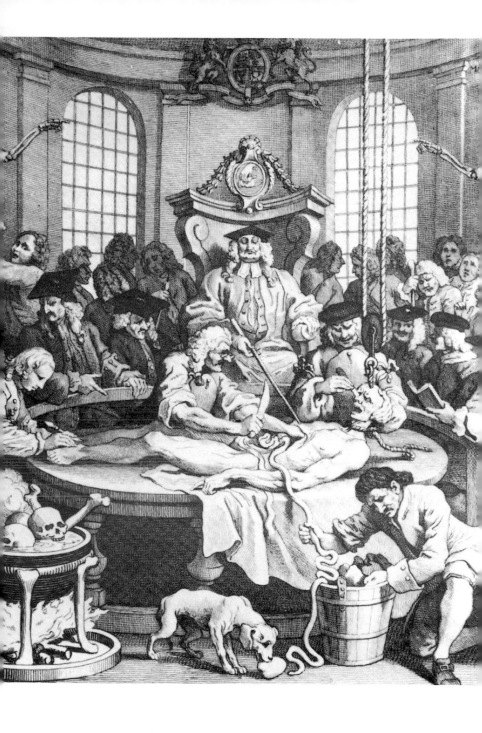

Lord Salisbury

Sir William Gull

Photo Radio Times Hulton Picture Library

Gull's grave at Thorpe-le-Soken

Sir Charles Warren

Robert James Lees at th
age of eighty-one
Photo Psychic N

Sir Robert Anderson

Nos. 108 to 119 Wentworth Dwellings, Goulston Street—scene of the writing on the wall. The writing was found just inside the doorway on the right-hand wall. Until 1975 Ripper experts had assumed this building had been demolished, as the writing had been wrongly reported to have been found at 'Peabody Buildings'. Richard Whittington-Egan discovered the true location during the research for his *A Casebook on Jack the Ripper*. No photograph of the building has previously been published
Photo Leonard Knight

Joseph Sickert pays a sad visit to the tobacconist's shop in Cleveland Street where the whole Ripper episode had its origins. The shop has since been taken over by the Middlesex Hospital
Photo Harry Jackson

An affectionate portrait of Walter Sickert painted by his son in 1975

Photo Leonard Knight

sonality of this godhead changes imperceptibly, until in the highest degrees the strange god of the Freemasons is revealed as Jah-Bul-On. This weird entity is a composite personality comprising Jahweh, the god of the Christians and Jews; Osiris, the mummy-like god of the dead in Ancient Egypt; and Baal, the pagan god whom the Israelites identified with the devil. Hence, while Masons will profess they worship only one god, they have attributed three personalities to that god, one of which is diabolical. While it is inaccurate to call advanced Freemasons devil-worshippers in a strict sense, they nevertheless accord this devil great importance in the governing of the universe, they treat him as an equal of the Christian God and they do pay him homage. This religious ambivalence was used against the Masons in the second part of the nineteenth century when Leo Taxil, a Frenchman since denounced as a liar, claimed to have definite proof of Masonic devil-worship. Whether or not Taxil's 'proof' was genuine, his claims were based on fact. Albert Pike, the great Masonic authority of the nineteenth century and Grand Commander of the Southern Jurisdiction of the Supreme Council at Charleston, USA, wrote in 1873 when he gained sufficient seniority to learn of Jah-Bul-On that he was disquieted and disgusted by it:

> No man or body of men can make me accept as a sacred word, as a symbol of the infinite and eternal Godhead, a mongrel word, in part composed of the name of an accursed and beastly heathen god, whose name has been for more than two thousand years an appelation of the Devil.

Yet this is exactly what advanced Freemasons are made to accept, and this is the deity they worship.

At the lowest degree, that of the Entered Apprentice, an initiate swears on pain of death and ghastly mutilation to obey not only the precepts of Freemasonry but also those of the Bible and the laws of the land in which his Lodge operates. The further he progresses through the hierarchy, the more the laws of the Bible and society are discarded and the more sacred become the laws of Masonry. Having passed what is known as the Royal Arch, a Mason owes allegiance only to his brother Masons.

An illustration of this progression from being a member of society to one independent of society's laws appears in the following. It is an extract from the oaths taken at two degrees, that of the Master Mason, the highest of the lower degrees, and that of the Royal Arch Mason, the first step in the long climb up to the ultimate degree, the thirty-third.

In a Master Mason's initiation ceremony he swears that the secrets of another Master Mason, 'given to me in charge as such, and I knowing them to be such, shall remain as secure and inviolable in my breast as in his own, when communicated to me, murder and treason excepted; and they left to my own election. . . . '

Thus, up to and including the degree of Master Mason, an initiate has the right to act as a normal responsible member of society and report to the authorities any Mason who may be engaged in murder or treason. But beyond the Royal Arch this is no longer true. In the initiation ceremony of a Royal Arch Mason he promises 'that a companion Royal Arch Mason's secrets, given me in charge as such, and I knowing them to be such, shall remain as secure and inviolable in my breast as in his own, *murder and treason not excepted*. . . . '

This fundamental change between the degrees alters a Mason's entire standing in society. Now he is accorded more immunity than a king or president. William Morgan, an American Mason who wrote a book called *Freemasonry Exposed*, published in 1826, declared:

> The oath taken by Royal Arch Masons does not except murder and treason; therefore, under it, all crimes can be perpetrated.

The full truth is more disturbing than this, for in the same oath the Royal Arch Mason swears

> that I will aid and assist a companion Royal Arch Mason, when engaged in any difficulty, and espouse his cause, so far as to extricate him from same, if in my power, *whether he be right or wrong* . . .

Thus, when a Freemason passes the Royal Arch he is not only prohibited on pain of death from exposing a fellow-Mason involved in treason or murder, *he is also compelled to assist him in covering up his crimes*.

Sir Charles Warren, Commissioner of the Metropolitan Police at the time of the Ripper murders, was one of the country's leading Freemasons. In 1861 he passed the Royal Arch, and from that moment on was under compulsion to assist any senior Mason in escaping punishment for the worst crimes he might have decided to commit. In the twenty-seven years between his passing the Royal Arch and the Whitechapel Murders, Warren became not only one of England's highest-ranking Masons, but one of the most powerful in the world. A Lodge in South Africa was named after him; in England he was a founder of the Quatuor Coronati Lodge of Masonic Research and Past Grand Sojourner in the Supreme Grand Chapter; and in 1891 he became District Grand Master of the Eastern Archipelago.

Only his supremacy in Freemasonry seems able to explain his appointment as Commissioner of the Metropolitan Police in 1886, and also the mysterious fact that his dismal failure in that office, recognized by the Government, Press and public, was awarded not with disgrace but a knighthood. 'Thus', wrote Warren's grandson, Watkin Williams,

> in receiving the decorations of G.C.M.G. and K.C.B. while still only a Regimental Lieutenant-Colonel, Warren established a record which was never before attained and can seldom since have been equalled, even during the days of the Great War.

All that for being the worst police commissioner in the history of Scotland Yard!

But did Warren fail in his duty? Although from every normal viewpoint he did, there is just one way in which his apparent incompetence could have been a dramatic triumph worthy of a knighthood. If the Whitechapel Murders were committed according to Masonic ritual—and it will presently be shown that they were—then Warren served the Freemasons to perfection in concealing facts. In the light of the evidence contained in this chapter, it is even conceivable he was appointed Commissioner purely to assist in the cover-up of the murders. Several of his actions while in office support this suggestion. The first was that he forced non-Mason James Monro, head of the C.I.D., to resign *just before the Whitechapel Murders began.* The second was that he appointed high-ranking Mason Sir Robert Anderson as Monro's successor *on the eve of Mary Nichols's murder.* Anderson's strange behaviour on taking office, described fully in the final chapter, also supports this suggestion. The final act on Warren's part which suggests he may have been appointed purely to protect the Masons during the reign of Jack the Ripper was that he himself resigned and quickly disappeared from the scene *only hours before the murder of Marie Kelly*. It was almost as if he *knew* the final murder was imminent. His rapid departure from office certainly ensured that any clues that may have been left were cold before they could be followed up. For Warren did not pass on the message that he was resigning—and so his order that no one should enter the scene of any murder without his permission was not countermanded until the afternoon of the day Kelly died, or about three hours after the police arrived. From 10.45 in the morning until 1.30 in the afternoon the investigating officers kicked their heels outside Kelly's room, waiting for orders from Warren. The Commissioner's conduct during the murders, examined in detail later in this chapter, certainly supports the suggestion that his sole function was to operate a cover-up. After resigning as Commissioner, Warren threw himself full time into his Masonic activities.

The Whitechapel Murders are not the first killings to have been attributed to Freemasons. There is evidence to suggest that Mozart was poisoned, and several scholars believe Masons were responsible. Mozart was a Freemason, as were most of the Austrian courtiers in the latter part of the eighteenth century. It is known that Vienna's highest Masons were angry at Mozart leaving the brotherhood in his last years. And they were outraged over what they regarded as a betrayal of their secrets in *The Magic Flute*. There was certainly something suspicious about the composer's death. Although a post-mortem examination is supposed to have revealed no traces of poison, it was reported that the body swelled up after death, which gave rise to speculation about foul play. To this day no one knows where Mozart's body was buried. He was to have been interred in the cemetery of St Marx, outside the walls of Vienna. Unaccountably, the small group of friends who had attended the funeral service turned back at the city gates and did not accompany the body to the graveyard. They all said later that their reason for turning back was that there had been rain and snow. But records at the Vienna Observatory show the day was dry, calm and chilly. And there is no trace of Mozart's grave in the cemetery.

Probably the most notorious murder laid at the door of the Masons was the mysterious slaying of William Morgan, author of *Freemasonry Exposed*. After desperate attempts by Masons to prevent Morgan publishing his work—attempts which included imprisoning him on trumped-up charges (shades of Ernest Parke), his rooms being ransacked and papers stolen, and threats to his life by so-called pillars of society—*Freemasonry Exposed* was finally published. Morgan was soon after kidnapped and done to death, allegedly by Masons. The murder is shrouded in mystery and evidence was frantically covered up (!), but the nationwide outcry against Masons in America, and the rapid rise of a powerful Anti-Masonic Movement seems justified by the evidence of people involved with Morgan.

It is unlikely ever to be known for certain if these two murders were committed by Masons. All that is certain is that both men died untimely deaths, and both had earned the antipathy of the brotherhood. If they were Masonic murders Freemasons in general were not responsible. On each occasion (from what can be gathered so long after) it would have been the work of an extreme Lodge, or extreme members of several Lodges. Though neither crime would have been plotted with the consent of all Masons, every advanced initiate must share the blame. For every Mason who has passed the Royal Arch has willingly helped to create the perfect matrix for crimes of violence. His promise not only to condone but to assist in the concealment of murder, treason and any other crime has brought about the situation where murder can be committed and the murderers go for ever undetected.

The fog of secrecy which envelops Freemasonry makes it virtually impossible to divine any more than the day-to-day workings and the rituals of the society. But a translation of some original documents, allegedly stolen from one of the most influential and highly initiated leaders of Freemasonry in France at the turn of the century, gives an indication of the plans and ambitions of at least some of its leaders. The documents were gathered together and first published in England by Eyre and Spottiswoode in 1920. The so-called *Protocols* are explicit: absolute power is the ambition, at least of the Freemasons in the highest degrees, and nothing, not even human life, must stand in its way. It would be ludicrous to suggest that these documents show Freemasonry as a whole to be evil, or that Masons are all aiming to take over the world. It has been shown that in the lowest degrees Masons are, on the whole, ordinary law-abiding citizens who have no knowledge of the total allegiance and appalling demands made on initiates to higher degrees. But with such fanatical writings set down as 'protocols' by high Masons, it needs only an extreme or lunatic fringe to take them absolutely literally. Of all the hundreds of thousands of Freemasons in England in the 1880s, there were bound to be these lunatic fringes. And a peculiar sort of lunacy did inspire the Ripper killings. Here, then, are some of the *Protocols*:

(1) Our motto must be "All means of force and hypocrisy".
(2) Only sheer force is victorious in politics, especially if it is concealed in the talent indispensible for statesmen. *Violence must be the principle*, cunning and hypocrisy must be the rule of those governments which do not wish to lay down their crown at the feet of the agents of some new power.

The second protocol describes almost exactly the dilemma facing Salisbury with the misconduct of Eddy and the blackmail from Marie Kelly and her cronies. He was surrounded by 'the agents of some new power'—socialists, anarchists, republicans—and he dealt with the problem, said Sickert, in just the way prescribed in the protocol. Violence, indeed, became the principle, and cunning and hypocrisy coalesced in a near-perfect cover-up.

(3) In order to obtain our ends we must have recourse to much slyness and artfulness.

Once again, so much slyness and artfulness has been brought into play on the murderous field of the Ripper that no one has been able to get near the truth working, as all previous investigators have, from the outside. It has taken Walter Sickert, reconnoitring from within the tangled web, to point the way and show that the spider at the centre is in reality a horde of tarantulas.

(4) The main success in politics consists in the degree of secrecy employed in pursuing it. The action of a diplomat must not correspond with his words. To help our world-wide plan, which is nearing its desired end, we must influence the governments of the Gentiles [the Masonic term borrowed from Hebrew and used to mean non-Masonic] by so called public opinions, in reality pre-arranged by us by means of that greatest of all powers—the press, which, with a few insignificant exceptions not

worth taking into account, is entirely in our hands. Briefly, in order to demonstrate our enslavement of the Gentile governments in Europe, we will show our power to one of them by means of *crimes of violence*, that is to say by a *reign of terror*.

The documents containing the *Protocols* were stolen thirteen years after the Whitechapel Murders, but they were not new even in 1901. Had the reign of terror described in the fourth protocol already happened by the time the documents were stolen? *Had it happened in Whitechapel in 1888?* The effect Jack the Ripper had on the people of the East End, and indeed on the whole country, has been described with complete accuracy as a *reign of terror*. And it was brought about by *crimes of violence*. Was the murder of the five whores perpetrated not only for the motive of self-protection already described, but also to demonstrate the far-reaching power of Freemasonry to initiates the world over?

(5) We must secure all instruments which our enemies might turn against us. We shall have recourse to the most intricate and complicated expressions of the dictionary of law in order to acquit ourselves in case we are forced to give decisions, which may seem overbold and unjust. For it will be important to express such decisions in so forcible a manner, that they should seem to the populace to be of the highest moral, equitable and just nature. Our government must be surrounded by all the powers of civilization among which it will have to act.

Freemasons are here seen to condone manipulation of the law in order to conceal their own unjust methods. Precisely this attitude on the part of Salisbury and his colleagues made it possible for the blatantly illegal inquest on Marie Kelly to be accepted, and for the perversion of justice concerning the Cleveland Street brothel case to be carried out.

(6) In politics, governments and nations are satisfied by the showy side of everything; yes, and how should they have time to examine the inner side of things when their representatives only think of amusements? The nation holds the power of a political genius in special respect and endures all its high-handed actions, and thus regards them: "What a dirty trick, but how skilfully executed!" "What a swindle, but how well and with what courage it has been done!"

Here the Freemasonic code applauds the fraudulent and the illegal, providing they are accompanied by guile or audacity, as were the Ripper crimes.

(7) It is necessary for us to acquire the services of bold and daring agents, who will be able to overcome all obstacles in the way of our progress.

Once more the accent is on the bold and daring, qualities which summarize the Ripper's style and astounded all who heard about the crimes.

(8) The services of the police are of extreme importance to us, as they are able to *throw a screen over our enterprises, invent reasonable explanations* for discontent among the masses, as well as punish those who refuse to submit.

Tom Cullen, the BBC researchers and I all arrived at the conclusion that the police had hidden the truth. Sir Charles Warren, described in his biography as a zealous Mason, unquestionably *threw a screen* over the Masons by erasing the writing on the wall found after the murder of Eddowes, and he *invented a reasonable explanation* for his *un*reasonable behaviour.

(9) The grandness of our might will require that suitable punishments should be awarded, that is to say, that they should be harsh even in the case of the smallest attempt to violate the prestige of our authority for the sake of personal gain.

This instruction might have been an exact description of the events in Sickert's story. Kelly and the other whores were operating some sort of blackmail (an 'attempt to violate the prestige of our authority for the sake of personal gain'), and they were indeed harshly punished. Freemasonry also dictates that in certain circumstances a Mason will be buried twice, and that he will die by his own greatest achievement. As will be shown in the next two chapters, this is what happened to two of the men named by Sickert as the Rippers.

The translator of the *Protocols* claimed they were in the form of minutes which were removed from a large book of notes for lectures. They were signed, he said, by Freemasons of the highest rank, the thirty-third degree.

It must be stated that the *Protocols* have been the subject of debate since they first appeared in print. Hitler twisted their meaning and alleged that they proved the existence of a worldwide conspiracy by the Jews, and used them in a hopeless attempt to justify his extermination programme. Chiefly because of the Nazi atrocities many writers have attacked the *Protocols* as forgeries. The argument continues to rage, and there are strong points both for and against.

An important point to bear in mind is that they had been in existence a long time before they were finally published. And they bear such uncanny resemblance to the events surrounding the Ripper case, it seems inescapable that they exerted an influence. Forgeries or not, the product of fanatical minds or not, the fact is they have been taken in deadly seriousness by thousands of people. It will be shown that Sir William Gull, fanatically inclined and almost certainly insane towards the end of his life, was just the sort of high Mason to take the *Protocols* literally, as he did the whole of Freemasonry's allegory and ritual. And it is Sir William Gull's alleged conduct *as a result* of the *Protocols* and other Masonic lore, not the genuineness of that lore itself, which is under discussion.

Of course, even accepting for a moment that there were no question of the documents' authenticity it would still be ludicrous to believe that they form the code by which all Freemasons live. Most Masons do not progress beyond the third degree[1], so the vast majority of Freemasons before the *Protocols* were published would never have heard of them.

But what they would have conveyed to those high initiates who not only read them but took them seriously, is fascinating and disturbing.

They say that Freemasons applaud violence, terror and crime providing it is carried out in a *crafty* manner. One section of the notes says humour is all-important and the most appalling crimes may be committed under its cloak. The one Ripper letter likely to have been genuine suggests that Jack the Ripper was

---

[1] Initiates to the third degree are called Master Masons. The name conveys an idea of great seniority. Few Master Masons or Freemasons below the third degree realize that the degree they regard as so advanced is in reality close to the bottom of the Masonic ladder, which stretches up to rarefied heights once a Mason passes the Royal Arch. The humble station of the Master can be judged by the exalted titles bestowed on initiates thirty degrees above him. The highest Masons, who arrogantly called themselves 'the grandest organization in the world', assume such pagan titles as Grand Inspector Inquisitor Commander, Sublime Prince of the Royal Secret and the patently blasphemous Prince of Jerusalem.

going about his crimes in just this way, committing ghoulish murders with a Puckish sense of fun. If Masonic supremacy appears in jeopardy, it is re-established by a show of strength, by crimes of violence, perpetrated to demonstrate the continuing power of Freemasons for the benefit of brothers abroad. If the strength of Masons high in the Government was being threatened by the self-interest of Marie Kelly, it is consistent with the *Protocols* that crimes of violence would have been committed to re-establish Masonic authority in the eyes of Masons everywhere. And Kelly and her confederates would have received the penalty meted out to those who betray the brotherhood. This is exactly what happened.

It is here that the three main aspects of Sickert's story—the knife-edged political situation, the behaviour of members of the Royal Family and the consequent fear of the Masons for their own survival—come together historically. Eddy's father, the Prince of Wales, was installed as Most Worshipful Grand Master of England on 28th April 1875. As the years passed and the political situation in England grew more dangerous to the established order, there is evidence to show that the Prince's Masonic brothers were becoming deeply concerned about his profligate life, which appeared to be growing worse rather than better.

In 1881 the Prince received a letter signed 'A Freemason', but which appears rather to be the work of a representative body of Masons of the Grand Lodge. The letter contains a thinly disguised attack on his behaviour and a warning of the dangers he could bring upon the throne and his colleagues in the secret brotherhood. The letter—on the surface warm, friendly and full of admiration—is revealed as a bitterly sarcastic indictment when viewed in the light of the Prince's character. The Prince of Wales's notorious conduct was known all over Europe and America, yet the letter from the Masons refers to his 'pure career' and 'sober and virtuous life'. It says in part:

> In writing, dear brother, I do not address you as a Prince of Wales, for some of our Princes of Wales have been drunken, riotous spendthrifts, covered in debt, and deep in dishonour [a perfect description of Bertie]; but you, dear brother, instead of being such a one, figure more reputably as the erudite member of a Royal Geographical Society, or as a steady fellow of the Worshipful Company of Fishmongers . . .

If Junius[1] were alive today, his pen would not dare to repeat its fierce attack on another Prince of Wales. Junius charged George, Prince of Wales, with quitting the arms of his wife for the endearments of a wanton, with toying away the night in debauchery, and with mocking the sorrows of the people with an ostentatious prodigality. But your pure career, your sober and virtuous life, would win laudations even from Junius's ghost. You are an English gentleman, as well as Prince of Wales; a good and kind husband in spite of being Prince of Wales; with you woman's honour is safe from attack, and sure of protection. The draggled and vice-stained plumes of your predecessors' escutcheons have been well cleaned and straightened by modern journalism, and the Prince of Wales' feathers are no longer (like the Bourbon fleur de lis) the heraldic ornament of a race of princes *sans foi, sans moeurs*.

The irony is poisonous. If there was one quality of Bertie's which was beyond doubt it was that *no* woman's honour was safe from his attack. If he had only one unfailing habit, it was quitting the arms of his wife for the endearments of a wanton. Every intelligent person in the land knew of his debauchery. As the sarcasm continued undiluted, the letter took on a warning tone and went on to underline the fact that Freemasonry was more powerful than princes:

Fit were you as profane to make the journeys to the Altar, for fame writes you as sober and chaste, as high-minded and generous, as kind-hearted and truthful. These are the qualities, oh Albert Edward, which hid your disability as Prince, when you knelt bare-kneed in our audience chamber. The brethren who opened your eyes to the light [a reference to the blindfold with which an initiate is 'hoodwinked'], overlooked your title as Prince of Wales in favour of your already famous manhood. Your career is a pleasant contrast to that of George Prince of Wales. Yet because you are as different from the princes whose bodies are dust, while their memories still remain to the historian as visible monuments of shame, I write to you, not as an English Prince, but as brother Master Mason . . .

I do not indeed regard your title of Duke at all in writing to you, for when we find a Duke of Newcastle's property in the hands of Sheriff's Officers, his title a jest for bankruptcy

---

[1] Junius was the writer of a series of anonymous letters published in Woodfall's *Public Advertiser* in London between January 1769 and January 1772. He is generally thought to have been Sir Philip Francis (1740–1818).

messengers, and the Duke of Hamilton's name an European byword, it is pleasant to be able to think that the Duke of Cornwall and Rothesay [one of Bertie's many titles] is not as these Dukes are; *that this Duke is not a runner after painted donzels, that he has not written cuckold on the forehead of a dozen husbands,* that he is not deep in debt, has not, like these Dukes, scattered gold in filthy gutters, while deaf to the honest claims of justice.

My italics in this passage indicate the most bitter pieces of sarcasm, for the words used ostensibly to praise Bertie best describe his debaucheries. Then comes the unmistakable warning to change his ways, or else:

We know, brother, that you would never have voluntarily enrolled yourself in the world's grandest organization, if you had been as these. It would have been perjury if you had done so—perjury which, though imperially honoured at the Tuileries, would be scouted with contempt by a Lancashire workman.

The Prince knew that the greatest threat to the established order, and hence the Masons, was the ordinary working man, whom he was constantly alienating by his anti-social behaviour, and whose consequent resentment was being whipped into hatred by the republicans.

I write to you as a fellow Master Mason, as to one on an equality with myself, so long as you are true to your Masonic pledge, less than myself whenever you forget it. I address this epistle to you as a fellow-member of a body which teaches that man is higher than king; that humanity is beyond church and creed; that true thought is nobler than blind faith, and that virile, earnest effort is better far than dead or submissive serfdom.
. . . *You have joined yourself to the Freemasons at the right moment, for true Freemasonry is about to be more powerful than Royalty. . . . In England, even at this hour, we are—if the organs of blood and culture speak truly—very near forgetting the use of a Queen. . . .*

The anonymous writers went on to draw the future king's attention to the Royal Families of Europe so recently overthrown, and to warn him against a similar fate. Throughout the letter, cloaked in the transparent guise of gushing *bonhomie,* one feeling comes through clearly: the Prince of Wales must cease his dissipated life or the throne will topple, *and that poses a threat to the Masons which cannot be countenanced.*

Now to the specific connections between Jack the Ripper and Freemasonry. Masonry is based on a peculiar system of ritual and allegory, and at each degree, in addition to bloody, pagan oaths, an initiate is made to perform certain mimes which represent the penalty he is to pay should his oath be betrayed.

In the lowest degree, that of the Entered Apprentice, part of the penalty for revealing Masonic secrets is to have the throat cut from left to right. The 'penal sign' of the Entered Apprentice has thus become a left-to-right movement of the hand across the throat. It has been general knowledge for years that four of the five Ripper victims had their throats cut in just this way. Unfortunately, since 1939 when William Stewart's *Jack the Ripper: A New Theory* appeared, the facts about Elizabeth Stride have been somewhat confused. Stewart believed there were only four Ripper murders, and somehow he made the mistake that Stride's throat was cut in the opposite direction to the wounds inflicted on Nichols, Chapman, Eddowes and Kelly. He wrote:

> In each of the Ripper murders the victim was killed by the throat being cut from left to right. This characteristic alone marked the murder of Elizabeth Stride as not being the work of Jack the Ripper.

It is hard to explain how Stewart reached this conclusion, but he was wrong. Two statements in the Scotland Yard file show conclusively that Stride's throat was cut from left to right, just like the other victims, and in the precise manner of the Entered Apprentice Freemason.

The first statement is by Dr Bagster Phillips, who examined Stride's corpse. He said:

> I affirm that she was seized by the shoulders, placed on the ground, and that the perpetrator of the deed was on her right side when he inflicted the cut. I am of opinion that *the cut was made from the left to the right of the deceased*.

The second and more exhaustive of the two reports is in fact only a copy of a four-page medical report in the Home Office file. The document was written by Dr Thomas Bond, consulting surgeon to the Metropolitan Police's 'A' Division, who performed a post-mortem examination on Kelly's body. It was one of the many pieces of evidence suppressed at Kelly's inquest. In the report, Bond referred to the previous murders.

He was including Stride when he stated that

> In the first four [murders] the throats appear to have been cut from left to right.

Thus the first Masonic parallel is noted: all Jack the Ripper's victims were dispatched according to an age-old Masonic ritual.

Another important statement in the Yard file, the contents of which have never been released, is the assertion by Dr Ralph Llewellyn, who examined the body of Nichols, that her throat had been cut *after* the mutilations to the abdomen. This would be fairly easy for a doctor to determine. Llewellyn's statement raises one vital question. If the severing of the carotid artery was not performed to kill the victim, what possible reason could there have been for inflicting the wound? It is surely inescapable that Nichols's throat wound was inflicted purely for a symbolic purpose. In *The Complete Jack the Ripper*, Donald Rumbelow put a convincing case for the Ripper victims having been strangled and then mutilated after death. Rumbelow's evidence strengthens the view that the cutting of the throats was for no practical purpose. It is surely significant that the act is such a sacred part of Freemasonic ritual.

In addition, the subsequent mutilations to the victims' bodies were carried out according to Masonic tradition. It is not disputed that these injuries were also caused after death. We have exact details of only three of the five women's mutilations, Chapman, Eddowes and Kelly. The first victim, Nichols, was given no more than a cursory glance by Dr Llewellyn when she was first found, so there is no reliable description of the precise form her mutilations took. By the time Llewellyn examined her fully her body had been stripped and washed by mortuary assistants. Stride's corpse escaped with a slit throat before any mutilations were begun. But the injuries of all three women given the full treatment by the Ripper, and whose bodies were fully examined, bear striking similarities to each other—and extraordinary parallels with the ritual killings of Freemasonry. A contemporary report of Chapman's corpse said:

> The intestines, severed from their mesenteric attachments, had been lifted out of the body *and placed on the shoulder of the corpse*.

And Dr Frederick Brown said at the inquest on Eddowes:

> The abdomen was all exposed. The intestines were drawn

out to a large extent *and placed over the right shoulder*. A piece of the intestine was quite detached from the body and placed between the left arm and the body.

Under questioning Dr Brown was quite definite on the point that the intestines had been placed on the shoulder 'by design'. This was definitely Masonic. By far the greater part of Masonic ritual and allegory is based upon the mythical murder by three apprentice Masons, Jubela, Jubelo and Jubelum, of the Grand Master Hiram Abiff, in charge of building Solomon's Temple. Having murdered Hiram the apprentices fled, but they were discovered near the coast at Joppa and they were themselves murdered,

> *by the breast being torn open and the heart and vitals taken out and thrown over the left shoulder.*

This has become the chief instruction for dealing with traitorous Master Masons. The description of Chapman's injuries was the section of his evidence which Dr Bagster Phillips tried desperately to suppress at the inquest (see pp. 108–10).

The incredible part about the Nichols murder was that it was not realized that she had been disembowelled until her body reached the mortuary. It appears that she was not so badly mutilated as the subsequent victims, but, if her vitals had not been thrown over her shoulder, she had certainly been 'torn open' in true Masonic style. And it is interesting that according to Dr Llewellyn, when she was found in Bucks Row her legs were both extended, as if she had been formally laid out.

The one inconsistency is that Masonic ritual specifies 'the left shoulders' and Eddowes's intestines were placed on her *right* shoulder. The discrepancy might be explained by the fact that Mitre Square, where Eddowes was found, was the most vulnerable of all the murder sites. She was butchered more elaborately than any of the other victims except Kelly, and in less time. The timing of the murder would have meant that not a second could be lost in depositing the body where it was found. In the hurry to arrange the body in a Masonic way it is possible that the point about *which* shoulder was overlooked. This is especially likely because, according to Sickert, Gull remained in the carriage and the actual arrangement of the corpse on the ground was undertaken according to Gull's instructions by Netley.

Dr Brown told the Eddowes inquest of another deliberate piece of mutilation: 'A triangular flap of skin had been reflected

from each cheek . . . ' These two triangles have a precise
Masonic relevance. The sacred sign of Masonry is *two triangles*,
which represent the altar top of the Holy Royal Arch.

The similarities between the killing of Marie Kelly and a
Masonic ritual murder are striking, as an engraving by William
Hogarth shows. *The Reward of Cruelty*, the final stage of Hogarth's *Four Stages of Cruelty* series—ostensibly a caricature of the
medical profession—in fact shows a Masonic ritual killing in
progress, and bears an uncanny resemblance to the mutilation
of Kelly. Hogarth was a Mason, and one of the first to expose
the fraternity. There are Masonic symbols in many of his
engravings, but this particular work was his most frank.
Hogarth drew the Masonic parallel in this particular work by
depicting the victim *formally laid out* on a dissecting table with a
screw in his head supported by ropes and a pulley. This screw
or drill is called a Lewis, and corresponds to the Lewis which
supports two of the most important pieces of Masonic impedi-
menta, the rough ashlar and the perfect ashlar. Now compare
Kelly's injuries, as described in *The Times*, with the fate of
Hogarth's victim:

The poor woman lay on her back entirely naked. . .

Hogarth's victim lies on his back entirely naked.

*Her throat had been cut from ear to ear, right back to the spinal
column. . . .*

Hogarth's victim has a Masonic 'cable tow' around his neck,
which is clearly defined in Masonic ritual as representing the
cutting of the throat.

*Her ears and nose had been cut off, and the face otherwise slashed
until its features were completely obliterated. . . .*

Hogarth's victim is in the process of being facially mutilated.
One of the *three* Masonic killers in the picture is cutting at the
eye with a surgeon's knife, which also corresponds to the
Eddowes murder where the eyelids were slit.

The stomach and abdomen had been ripped open. . . .

This is happening in Hogarth's picture.

*The lower portion of the body, including the uterus, had been cut
out. . . .*

The detail of the engraving is inadequate to tell whether any internal organs are missing (and, of course, a man has no uterus), but the lower portion of the body has definitely been cut out.

Kelly's heart was also cut out, and Hogarth's victim has suffered the same treatment. Finally, in one version of the engraving, the left hand of the victim lies across the left breast, in the same position as Kelly's. This is confirmed by a photograph of Kelly's body in the Yard file. The left arm of Annie Chapman, the only other murder where the killer had time to arrange the corpse as he chose, lay in the same position. Elizabeth Stride's *right* arm lay across her breast. One final parallel between the Masonic murder depicted by Hogarth and the butchery of Kelly is that the final Ripper victim had her legs and feet skinned. One of the killers in the engraving is skinning the foot with a sharp scalpel.

Sickert said the murders were carried out by three people. Hogarth depicts *three* Masonic killers. Freemasons do in fact regard three as the perfect number, and Masonic mimed killings are traditionally carried out by three Masons, in memory of the sacred myth of Jubelo, Jubela and Jubelum. *Three* years after Kelly's death, in 1891, the Clarence and Avondale Lodge, named after Prince Eddy, was set up at the Masonic Hall at Leytonstone, close to where Kelly was buried.

Most writers have mentioned one curious detail of the murder of Annie Chapman, but it has never been properly explained. Some writers, like Farson who is confused by it, have made no attempt to explain it. Others do not even mention it, and others still, like Stewart, claim implausibly that it had no significance. Farson's feeling about the detail was close to the truth. He wrote:

> Even more bewildering was a curious detail that seems inexplicable, though I cannot help feeling that it has significance: two brass rings, two new farthings, and a few coins were laid out neatly around the feet of the corpse.

Farson was correct in attaching significance to the act, but beyond this brief mention he said no more. The act of placing brass rings and the other items by the body was Masonic, an act of twisted symbolism. Brass is the sacred metal of the Masons because Hiram Abiff was a worker in brass. He supervised the moulding of the two great hollow brass pillars which stood at the entrance to Solomon's Temple, and which have become the symbol of Freemasonry. Two brass rings side by side look exactly like two hollow brass pillars in cross-section. The other more obvious Masonic aspect of the episode is that before a Mason is initiated to any degree he is divested of all metals such as coins and rings.

Here, once more, the cover-up rears its head. The rings were removed shortly after Chapman's body was found, and Coroner Wynne Baxter was told they had been stolen by the killer. This is another point which seems to have escaped previous writers on the Ripper. On page 61 of his book, Rumbelow wrote:

> As if he was taking part in some elaborate ritual the killer had laid the two rings he had torn from her fingers, some pennies and two new farthings at the woman's feet.

Yet eleven pages later, in summarizing the words of Coroner Baxter at Chapman's inquest, he wrote:

> Two things were missing from the body, he said. Chapman's rings, *which had not been found*, and the uterus, which had been taken from the abdomen.

These two statements are at variance, yet no writer has so far mentioned the inconsistency, let alone explained it. The first question is, were the rings in reality arranged with the coins at Chapman's feet or was the first statement mistaken? There was no mistake, as statements in the Press at the time of the murder confirm. The rings and coins were seen and noted by several journalists. The strongest support of this is that they were observed by the first journalist at the scene of the murder, Oswald Allen. In a report that appeared in the *Pall Mall Gazette* only hours after the murder was discovered, Allen wrote:

> A curious feature of this crime is the murderer had pulled off some brass rings which the victim had been wearing and these, together with some trumpery articles which had been taken from her pockets, *were placed carefully at the victim's feet*.

How can the subsequent disappearance of these items be explained? The first person on the scene after the police and journalists was Dr Phillips, already shown in Chapter 8 to have been involved in the cover-up. He was eager at the Chapman inquest to conceal the Masonic nature of her injuries. He is the most likely person to have been responsible for eliminating the clue of the brass rings.

Hours after the Chapman murder the Leather Apron rumour first swept London. It is now impossible to trace the actual source of this rumour, as it appears to have been generated spontaneously in several different places around the East End. Intriguingly enough, the most important Masonic vestment is the *leather apron*. This garment is actually made of lambskin, but Masons always refer to it as their 'leather apron'.

This striking connection between the Whitechapel Murders and the Masons brings us back to the slaughter of Catherine Eddowes in Mitre Square. For in this murder the *apron* once again appears to have significance. A portion of Eddowes's apron was cut off by the murderer. It was not torn off in frenzy but removed with a clean cut, calmly and deliberately. Why? If the sole purpose of taking the piece of apron was to wipe blood from the Ripper's hands or knife, what possible reason could he have had for taking up much valuable time cutting off a section of the garment? Other parts of her copious clothing would have presented a far easier and quicker way of cleaning himself, her voluminous petticoats for example. Once again, the practical explanation does not make sense. There was no practical reason for the act. Therefore we are left with the alternative, that the apron was cut off for a *symbolic* purpose, just like the cutting of the throats after death, the posthumous mutilations and the careful arrangement of items at Chapman's feet.

There was even significance in the thirty-nine days that were allowed to elapse between the murder of Eddowes and that of Kelly. Thirty-nine is a meaningful number to Freemasons, arrived at by multiplying the 'perfect' number, three, by the 'favourite', thirteen. In other words it is the ideal, the perfect number of favourites.

It was the audacious murder of Eddowes above all the others that gave the Ripper a reputation for having supernatural powers. How could a man waylay Stride shortly before one o'clock, murder her, walk half a mile and find Eddowes, take her to Mitre Square, butcher her, arrange her body in the most meticulous manner and escape undetected, all in forty-five minutes? Sickert's contention that Eddowes was picked up by the three killers in their carriage, murdered inside it and then placed in the square later, alone seems to answer the problem.

A counter to the carriage argument is that the vehicle would have been heard. This is true, but hearing does not necessarily mean either noticing or remembering. In the early days of

Ripper literature the suggestion was made that the murderer was an 'invisible man'. This meant the sort of person whose presence in the streets would have been so commonplace he would not have been noticed. A policeman, for instance, would have been blotted from a person's subconscious in this way. The same is true of the sound of a vehicle. Admittedly no one reported hearing a carriage pass the scene of any of the murders. This is because the sound of vehicles passing through the streets late at night was so common in the East End at that time, and so much a part of the general background of living, that no one would have noticed it. As the testimony of witnesses at several of the inquests showed, the streets at all hours of the day and night were bustling with cabs, delivery vehicles and the wagons of market workers and slaughterhouse employees. Bucks Row, where witnesses specifically mentioned they had heard nothing all night, was not only traversed throughout the night by noisy slaughterhouse wagons, it was also next to a railway line. None of these sounds registered in the minds of witnesses, and the noise from the wheels of Netley's coach would have been indistinguishable from the sound of a passing wagon.

Sickert's carriage notion provides a plausible explanation for another baffling aspect of the case, the seemingly inexplicable fact that the killer or killers commanded sufficient confidence in their victims for the women to go willingly with them. After the death of Chapman no tart, however down on her luck, would have gone into a dark square with a strange man. But when the nationwide hue and cry was after solitary Jack, the bestial lurker in the shadows, the last people to fall under suspicion would have been two gentlemen and their driver travelling through the East End in their carriage. The dialogue which would have snared little Eddowes and banished her fears can be imagined:

'Good night to you, madam. This is hardly the time or the place to be alone in these dark days. May we offer you a lift to your destination?'

The cockney tarts who haunted the twilight world of Whitechapel were rarely treated as human beings, let alone as ladies. The problem of tempting the victims inside the coach would have been easily overcome by appealing to their vanity and reminding them of the faceless terror that was stalking the night outside. It would have been a simple irony to convince the women that in entering the carriage they were finding safety from Jack the Ripper. The murders taking place in a vehicle alone explains why so little blood was found at the 'site' of each killing.

Mitre Square was in the wrong direction for Eddowes when she was released from Bishopsgate Police Station after sobering up. Her only reasonable destination at that time of night would have been her doss-house in Spitalfields. That she was planning to go to Spitalfields is confirmed by her own words as she left the police station. At the inquest jailer George Hutt told City Police solicitor Mr Crawford that as Eddowes left him she said, 'I shall get a damned fine hiding when I get home'.

CRAWFORD   I gather from that you thought she was going home?
HUTT   Yes.

That she eventually finished up in the opposite direction from the way she would have taken to Spitalfields is a good indication that she was taken to Mitre Square. But why? On the face of it, it was the last place a killer would choose. Rumbelow described the 'enormous risks' taken by the Ripper in performing his operation there:

Mitre Square had three entrances—one from Mitre Street and passages from Duke Street and St James's Place. On two sides of the square there were warehouses, belonging to Kearley and Tonge, with a watchman on night duty. On the third side, opposite where the body was found, there were two old houses, one of which was unoccupied and the other lived in by a policeman. On the fourth side were three empty houses. Every fifteen minutes during the night the square was patrolled by a police constable: at 1.30 a.m. the square had been empty when he strolled through, at 1.45 a.m. he had found a body.

The Times thought that:

The assassin, if not suffering from insanity, appears to be free from any fear of interruption while on his dreadful work.

Even though the murder did not take place in the square but inside the carriage, Mitre Square still presented an enormous risk during the few brief minutes Netley took to deposit the body. Why was it so essential a spot to lay Eddowes that all these risks were taken?

It will be remembered that according to Sickert the killers thought that in Eddowes they had found Marie Kelly. This was to have been the last murder, and consequently the most overtly Masonic. Mitre Square has strong Masonic significance. In fact it is fair to say it was the most Masonic of all places in London, except for the great hall of the Grand Lodge itself. The square was literally riddled with Masonic connections. Its name, for a start, was entirely Masonic. *Mitre* and *Square* are the basic tools of the Freemason, and they play a large part in Masonic ritual and allegory. They were implements used by the original stonemasons, and in his initiation ceremony an Entered Apprentice is presented with the tools of a stonemason and told by the Master: 'These tools we apply to our morals'. In *The Builders, A Story and Study of Masonry*, Joseph Fort Newton described the Square as 'a symbol of truth'. The name Mitre Square first appeared in an Ordnance Survey map of 1840. It had been named after the Mitre Tavern, an important meeting-place for Masons in the eighteenth and nineteenth centuries.

Two other important connections exist between Mitre Square and Freemasonry. It had been the scene of a murder in 1530 that in some respects paralleled the mythical murder of Hiram Abiff, the bedrock of so much of Masonry's allegory. Like the murder of Hiram, it took place in a hallowed place, for in the sixteenth century Mitre Square was the site of the Priory of the Holy Trinity. A woman was in the Priory praying at the high altar, just like Hiram in Solomon's Temple before his murder, when she was set upon by a mad monk. He did her to death and later killed himself, by plunging the knife into his own heart. The scene of the murder, the victim at prayer and the subsequent violent death of the killer all correspond to the mythical incident which is the hallowed core of Freemasonic tradition.

This peculiar holiness was consolidated two and a half centuries later when Mitre Square became the meeting-place of Masons belonging to Hiram's Lodge. So strong were its links with Masonry that it continued as the centre of a flourishing Masonic activity well into the nineteenth century. The Mitre Tavern, at the entrance to the square, became the meeting-place of two other Lodges, the Union Lodge and the Lodge of Joppa. The latter is once again closely related to the murder of Hiram, for it was near the coast at Joppa that the three apprentice Masons were found hiding. Evidence that Mitre Square was particularly sacred to Masons is found in the names of the Lodges which met there. *Hiram's* Lodge and the Lodge of *Joppa* are more closely bound up with the central theme of Masonry than any of the other Lodges around London in the

1800s. These lesser lodges included such names as the Ark Lodge and the Lodge of Prosperity. Only the most important Lodges met at Mitre Square. Apart from the brethren of Hiram's Lodge and the Lodge of Joppa, however, Mitre Square was still a hive of Masonic activity. A few yards away, the Tailor's Arms in Mitre Street was the rendezvous of the Lodge of Judah.

One of the country's chief Lodges, and almost certainly the one to which Sir William Gull belonged, was the Royal Alpha. It met almost entirely in the West End, and most notably at the King's Arms in Brook Street, Mayfair, close to Gull's residence at No. 74. The lodge had only two meeting-places outside the West End—Leadenhall Street and the *Mitre Tavern*, providing a direct link between Gull and Mitre Square.

The savage murder of 1530 might almost be considered a link between the killing of Hiram and the murder of Catherine Eddowes. For though the Masonic parallels in the first Mitre Square murder are strong, its details also resemble the fourth Ripper killing. In both cases it was a woman who fell victim to an apparently insane killer, and in both cases the victims were butchered with a knife. So, there are points of contact not only between the murder of Eddowes and the murder of the unknown woman in 1530, but between both these and the mythical murder of Hiram Abiff. It seems likely that Mitre Square became so sacred a place for Masons because of the 1530 outrage. It was no accident that the killers sheltering under the single identity of Jack the Ripper chose Mitre Square as the venue for their intended final victim's discovery.

Hanbury Street, where Chapman was found, was another important Masonic meeting-place. The Humber Lodge and the Lodge of Stability had met regularly at the Black Swan and the Weaver's Arms, both in Hanbury Street and one on either side of No. 29, where Chapman's body was found.

Finally, the most conclusive proof of all that the murders were Masonic is to be found in following the trail of that missing piece of Eddowes's apron. The cloth, soaked with blood, was found by P.C. Alfred Long, lying in the passage of Wentworth Dwellings, model dwellings in Goulston Street. These dwellings have been wrongly identified by previous authors as 'Peabody Buildings'. Above the cloth, on the wall of the passage, was a chalked message. Until now, the exact content of the message has not been known. The wording has been reported differently in almost every book on the Ripper. But the Private Letter Book of the Metropolitan Police, a collection of confidential letters now at the Public Record Office, contains the original copy of the message. A note from Sir Charles Warren to the Permanent Under-Secretary to the Home Office, Godfrey Lushington, says:

> I send you a copy of the writing on the wall at Goulston Street.

Attached to the letter is a document, photographic copies of which are contained in the Home Office file. It shows the exact wording and layout of the message, and there has been an obvious attempt to copy the handwriting style of the original:

> The Juwes are
> The men That
> Will not
> be Blamed
> for nothing

Until the discovery of the writing on the wall, Sir Charles Warren had not ventured into the East End. The news of the message brought him scurrying from Whitehall as fast as a carriage could convey him. Major Smith of the City Police, never on the best of terms with Warren, had already decided to allow courtesy to go by the board. Hearing the news of the chalked message, he authorized Inspector McWilliam to send three officers to Goulston Street to photograph it. At last the Ripper had left a clue.

The murder had taken place just inside City Police territory, but the writing on the wall was within Warren's domain. When the City policemen appeared with their bulky photographic equipment Warren had already arrived. He forbade them to take any pictures, and proceeded with a course of action that has not been properly explained or justified. This was the only real clue ever left by Jack the Ripper. *Yet Warren washed it away.* He later gave the excuse that he had feared anti-Jewish riots would be sparked off by the reference to 'Juwes'. Even if this were true it does not explain why he would not allow the City men to photograph the message. The pictures could have provided vital evidence, and the writing could have been erased after being photographed. It does not explain why he did not accept the advice of several senior policemen at the scene and have just the word 'Juwes' erased. It does not explain why he did not merely have the message covered with a cloth. It was, after all, in the hallway of a building that could easily have been cordoned off.

What, then, was Warren trying to hide? What possible reason could he have had for so blatantly destroying evidence? The whole episode remains incongruous until we realize there is only one reason why a senior police officer would go to great lengths to defeat the ends of justice. That is when the officer owes allegiance to a master higher even than justice. It has been shown that Warren was one of the world's most advanced and powerful Freemasons. He had long since sworn to assist a fellow-Mason in murder or treason by concealing evidence. This is clearly what Warren was doing in Goulston Street. But what was it in that scrawled message that pointed the finger at a Freemason? The evidence lies in the word 'Juwes'. This was not, as Warren tried to convince critics, and many authors have subsequently averred, a misspelling of the word Jews. *For the Juwes were the three apprentice Masons who killed Hiram Abiff and who are the basis of Masonic ritual.*

It is impossible to find out if some of the lesser-known people in Sickert's story were Masons. The chief characters certainly were. Warren, Gull, Anderson and Salisbury were all well advanced on the Masonic ladder. Salisbury, whose father had been Vice Grand Master of All England, was so advanced that in 1873 a new Lodge was consecrated in his name. The Salisbury Lodge met at the premier Masonic venue in England, the Freemasons' Hall in Great Queen Street, London.

Can there be any doubt that the Ripper murders, the subsequent cover-up, and also the cover-up surrounding the Cleveland Street brothel case were carried out by a band of extremist Freemasons? Even Lord Euston, the prime mover in the last, brutal part of the Cleveland Street cover-up, was a prominent Mason. And despite the fact that he was known to be a frequenter of the homosexual brothel, his Masonic career flourished in the wake of the scandal. The moral virtue which Freemasons profess to hold sacred was clearly of little importance when Lord Euston was made Grand Master of the Mark Masons. But then his promotion was not in recognition of his morals. It was Masonic blood-money for the service he had rendered in silencing Ernest Parke.

CHAPTER ELEVEN

Sir William Gull

The reaction of most Ripper experts to Walter Sickert's account of the murders is unqualified disbelief. The general feeling was summed up by Colin Wilson, author of *A Casebook of Murder*, when he wrote after Joseph Sickert's television appearance, 'In my own view, it is the most unlikely story so far'.

Farson and Rumbelow have since made passing references to the broadcast in their books, and have dismissed it on the strength of one fundamental objection. Their main argument against the whole Sickert saga appears to be: Sir William Gull could not have been an active member of the Ripper party because in 1887 he suffered a stroke.

There is a great deal of evidence that vindicates Sickert's accusation of Gull. Before the positive side of the case is explained, however, the sole objection to Gull's participation in the murders can be proved groundless.

The statement which has given rise to the mistaken idea that Gull was little more than a cripple after 1887 is contained in the *Dictionary of National Biography*. The entry on Gull says in part:

> In the autumn of 1887 he was attacked with paralysis, which compelled him to retire from practice; a third attack caused his death on 29 Jan. 1890.

From this statement it appears impossible for Gull to have been one of the Ripper party, least of all the protagonist. But this reference to Gull's illness is an over-simplification, and other sources provide a more accurate account.

The truth is to be found in the words of Dr Thomas Stowell, who had his information from Gull's own daughter. He wrote that Gull had 'a slight stroke in 1887'. Just how slight that stroke was is shown in the following passage, taken from *In Memoriam—Sir William Gull*, an affectionate tribute to Gull that appeared shortly after his death :

He was then [October 1887] at his home in Scotland, intending almost immediately to return to work after his autumn holiday, and while walking alone in the grounds was seized with paralysis. *He did not lose consciousness, but fell on one knee and was able to walk to the house with assistance.* [My italics]

This was hardly a serious attack, as the *Dictionary of National Biography* suggests. So mild was the so-called 'stroke' that Gull *walked* back to his house. Even though he ceased to attend patients in 1887, he still led an active life. His son-in-law, Theodore Dyke Acland, explained in *William Withey Gull, A Biographical Sketch*, that :

Sir William took an important part in the public work of his day. From 1856 *to 1889* he served on the Senate of the University of London. [My italics]

Gull religiously filled in the forms every year for his professional details to be recorded in the *Medical Register*. He last appeared in the *Register* in 1889, so at least until the end of 1888, when the 1889 edition was compiled, he regarded himself as an active medical man. Why then, if he was well enough right through to 1889 still to be serving on the Senate of the University of London, did he relinquish his practice in 1887? Events following Gull's illness are outlined in the 1892 edition of Wilks and Bettany's *Biographical History of Guy's Hospital :*

Sir W. Gull had had two or three short illnesses before the one which was the commencement of his fatal malady, but at this time he was well and enjoying himself in Scotland, near Killiecrankie, when he was seized with *slight* paralysis on the right side and aphasia. This was in October 1887. He recovered in great measure and returned to London, where he remained for some months comparatively well. Friends who then saw him did not discern much difference in his looks and manner, but he *said* he felt another man, and gave up his practice. He subsequently had three epileptiform attacks, *from which he rapidly recovered*, but on January 29th, 1890, he was suddenly seized with an apoplectic attack, fell into a state of coma, and gradually passed away. [My italics]

This passage emphasizes the slightness of Gull's 1887 attack. The observation by Wilks and Bettany that Gull's friends hardly noticed any difference in him after the 1887 'stroke' is another indication of its mildness. Could their statement that Gull 'said' he felt another man suggest he may have been misleading people into believing he was too ill to continue his practice?

The truth about Gull's 1887 illness was that he suffered slight paralysis, not even a stroke in the usual sense of the word. But even assuming his 1887 attack was a stroke as he insisted, it was of such a minor nature that it need hardly have affected his life at all. A stroke is a sudden loss of consciousness, the senses and voluntary motion, caused generally by the rupture of a blood-vessel in the brain. None of these symptoms were apparent in Gull. There are two types of stroke, major and minor. Dr Alan Barham Carter, an expert on this sort of illness and the author of *All About Strokes*, defines a minor stroke as occurring 'when the damage is small, limited in extent and often reversible so that death of the [brain] cells does not occur'.

Dr Barham Carter explained that a normally strong man can make a complete recovery even from a major stroke, in which brain cells are permanently destroyed. Gull was a more than normally strong man. He has been described by one writer as of medium height, but 'of great strength and vigour', and the *Dictionary of National Biography* pays tribute to his 'great powers of endurance'. It is surely not hard to accept that an attack as mild as that suffered by Gull would prove a negligible impediment in the life of a man of his *exceptional* strength. It is important to note that his constitution was not impaired by serious illness. All his life he was remarkably healthy, except for a single attack of enteric fever.

Had Farson and Rumbelow heard the full story they would never have raised Gull's illness as an objection to his taking part in the murders. Neither writer interviewed Joseph Sickert before publishing the criticisms which stemmed from Sickert's six-minute television narrative. With this in mind, they cannot be blamed for drawing the conclusions they did. Not only was a story that defied précis impossibly condensed so that vital details were lost, several aspects of the original account were actually distorted in the miniaturization process. Thus viewers heard:

> She [Marie Kelly] was killed as the last of five women in a way that made it look like the random work of a madman.

Walter Sickert never made this statement. He insisted that all the victims except Eddowes knew each other, that Nichols, Chapman, Stride and Kelly were participating in a sordid blackmail attempt, and that Eddowes was murdered in mistake for Kelly. But the greatest flaw in the broadcast was that it lacked all detail. It was not explained, for instance, that Sickert said the murders, excepting those of Kelly and Stride, were committed in a moving carriage, and hence Gull would have needed to expend relatively little physical effort in his part of the murders. Sickert said Gull first induced unconsciousness in the victims by feeding them black grapes impregnated with poison. Then, as they lay motionless in the carriage, he would perform the Masonic mutilations with the help of Anderson. This means the physical strain on Gull would have been small. John Netley would later undertake the strenuous task of placing the corpses in the street. On more than one occasion he was helped by Anderson, but Gull never left the carriage.

The notion that Farson and Rumbelow have discredited—that of a solitary Gull skulking through the alleys of the East End and alone butchering his victims, then eluding the hue and cry on foot—was clearly farcical. But Sickert never suggested anything like that.

If any doubts remain as to Gull's physical ability to sit in a carriage and perform his Masonic surgery upon four women over a period of ten weeks, it will be valuable to bear in mind the much greater physical and mental effort exerted—not spasmodically as in the case of the Ripper murders, but constantly and under great pressure—by sufferers of one or more *major* strokes. To repeat: at worst Gull suffered the mildest stroke it is possible to suffer without it passing unnoticed. Dr Barham Carter again:

> Many famous people have had a stroke, but the ones I shall mention here are some of those who have made great contributions to the world after a *major* stroke, thus showing

that the catastrophe need not be the end of a man or woman's career.

He recalled the major stroke suffered by Louis Pasteur:

> On 29 December Pasteur was able to walk without any support, and after this rather slow recovery came the remarkable future. His energies and enthusiasm seemed to be in no way diminished and he formulated all his famous theories of immunity and vaccination in the years following his stroke.

Pasteur underwent *years* of intense strain and gruelling work in the course of his revolutionary research, after a *major* stroke.

Dr Barham Carter described Churchill:

> He made a good recovery from the [major] stroke of 1949 and won the election of 1951, becoming Prime Minister. In spite of *a succession* of minor strokes in 1950 and 1952 and a bigger one in 1953, he undertook the full duties of his office successfully, and there is nothing to show that at this time he had lost any of his former fire and judgement. In fact at that time he also took the burden of the Foreign Office on his shoulders and was very successful in his decisions concerning our relationship with other countries.

In 1953 Churchill was seventy-nine, eight years older than Gull at the time of the Whitechapel Murders. It is certain that the combined job of Prime Minister and Foreign Secretary takes more physical fitness and strength than performing Gull's alleged part in the Jack the Ripper killings, which were spread over a period of two and a half months. If we accept the fact that a man nearly eighty can be Prime Minister and Foreign Secretary after two major strokes and a succession of minor ones, we must accept that a man many years younger is capable of being a carriage-bound Jack the Ripper a year after an attack so slight he didn't even collapse.

Finally, having been told Sickert's description of the murders, Dr Barham Carter said,

> There is no doubt that a man aged seventy-two, physically strong and active, who has had a minor stroke, could have lived a perfectly normal life and could have committed the Whitechapel Murders in the manner described by Sickert.

Many writers have asserted that Jack the Ripper was a doctor. Of a hundred and three published theories which I have examined, more than a quarter state the Ripper was a doctor or a medical student. Most theorists who believe a medical man was responsible for the murders base their reasoning on the comments of Dr Ralph Llewellyn and Dr Bagster Phillips, who stated at the inquests of Nichols and Chapman that the murderer must have possessed some anatomical knowledge. The opinion was widely accepted, and the suspicion which fell on medical men generally was skilfully evoked by Dennis Halsted in his book *Doctor In the Nineties*. Halsted was a doctor at the London Hospital at Whitechapel at the time of the murders, and he too described the 'great surgical skill' employed by the Ripper. That medical men were the chief suspects at the time of the killings is confirmed by a file at the Home Office devoted to accusations against doctors and policemen, and by the large number of medical men listed in the *Suspects* file at Scotland Yard.

Two doctors who examined the body of Eddowes, divisional police surgeon Dr George Sequeira and the medical officer of health for the City of London, Dr William Saunders, were of the opinion that no anatomical knowledge had been displayed. But the view that the murderer *did* possess some knowledge of surgery is vindicated by the more precise evidence of other doctors.

At the Nichols inquest, Dr Llewellyn said, 'The murderer must also have had some rough anatomical knowledge'.

Dr Phillips said at the Chapman inquest, 'There were indications of anatomical knowledge. The whole of the body was not present, the absent portions are from the abdomen. The way in which those portions were extracted showed anatomical knowledge.'

The Lancet, the journal of the medical profession, made the comment that the murders were 'obviously the work of an expert—of one, at least, who had such knowledge of anatomical or pathological examinations as to be enabled to secure the pelvic organs with one sweep of the knife'.

Dr Frederick Brown, the City Police surgeon who performed the post-mortem examination on Eddowes, was quite definite: 'Anyone carrying out this deed would need a good deal of knowledge as to the position of the organs in the abdominal cavity'.

Brown would not be deflected from his stand by the conflicting opinion of Sequeira and Saunders. Under questioning he continued, 'It would take a great deal of skill and of knowledge as to the position of the kidney to remove it. The kidney could easily be overlooked, for it is covered by a membrane.'

The last comment confirms finally that, whoever was responsible for the Ripper murders, he or they possessed *some* anatomical knowledge, and probably a great deal.

With this fact in mind several theorists have built up their cases around the understandable notion that a surgeon was responsible. Sickert, however, in asserting that Gull was the chief Ripper, went against the mainstream of opinion, for Gull was a physician. On the surface a physician seems far less likely than a surgeon to have been the perpetrator of the Ripper's lethal surgery, and if Sickert had been spinning a yarn he would have been much more likely to have cast a surgeon as the killer.

As always, Sickert's unlikeliest statements prove true when examined in depth.

Colin Wilson points out in *A Casebook of Murder* that the French murderer Eusebius Pieydagnelle did not start murdering until his family insisted he give up being a butcher (to which he had been attracted by his fascination for blood) and become a lawyer; while carving up animals his sadistic craving had been entirely satisfied. This wrecks the theories about berserk surgeons. The blood-lust of a mad surgeon would have been satiated in the course of his everyday work.

In reality a physician is a far more plausible candidate for the Ripper, for he would rarely perform any extensive surgery. Even though the killer had surgical skill, it seems clear, even taking into account the unfavourable conditions in which the mutilations were performed, that he had neither the experience nor the training of a surgeon. The member of society whose surgical ability must always rank second only to that of the surgeon is undeniably the physician.

William Withey Gull was born in the parish of St Leonard, Colchester, on 31st December 1816. His father was John Gull, a humble barge-owner on the river Lea. William was the youngest of eight children, two of whom died in infancy. The family moved to Thorpe-le-Soken in Essex in about 1820. Shortly afterwards William's eldest brother was offered a scholarship to Christ's Hospital, but proud John Gull refused to allow it, declaring that none of his children would ever depend on charity.

John died of cholera in London in 1827. Thereafter William's mother Elizabeth brought up the children to the best of her ability and limited means, teaching the three boys and three girls that 'whatsoever is worth doing, is worth doing well'. Young William was educated at a small village school, but insisted all his life that he had received his real education from his mother, a woman of great intellectual power and keen insight.

One of his favourite quotations in early life was:

> If I was a tailor
> I'd make it my pride
> The best of all tailors to be;
> If I was a tinker
> No tinker beside
> Should mend an old kettle like me.

The children were given a strict Christian upbringing, Mrs Gull observing all the saints' days, wearing black during Lent and feeding the family fish and rice pudding on Fridays.

In 1832 Mrs Gull moved with her family to Thorpe, an estate near to Thorpe-le-Soken owned by the authorities of Guy's Hospital in London. Adjacent to the estate was the parish of Beaumont whose rector, Mr Harrison, was a nephew of Benjamin Harrison, the Treasurer of Guy's. It seems the rector was deeply fond of Mrs Gull, and one of the many affectionate acts in his selfless and gentlemanly wooing was to welcome William to the Rectory every other day for private tuition. During this secure, happy period in his childhood, William developed a fascination for collecting fauna and flora. The influence of Rector Harrison gradually eroded the boy's adolescent desire to go to sea, and instilled in him a firm ambition to become a doctor.

His motto of later years had not yet found expression in words, but its sentiment was already a living part of his character:

> If thou do'st purpose aught within thy
>   power
> Be sure thou do it, though it be but
>   small.

Once he had made up his mind to enter medicine, nothing could discourage him. For a short time he was an usher at a small country school at Lewes, in Sussex. But in 1837, just before his twenty-first birthday, he finally met Benjamin Harrison and was accepted as a pupil at Guy's Hospital. He was given two rooms at Guy's, was paid £50 a year and given every opportunity to study. Determined to succeed and so display his gratitude to Harrison, he applied himself diligently to his studies, and in his first year won every prize available. He graduated as a B.A. in Medicine at the University of London in 1841, obtaining honours in Physiology and Comparative Anatomy, in Surgery and in Medicine.

The following year Gull was appointed to teach Materia Medica at Guy's and was given a small house in King Street, E.C., and a salary of £100 a year. His zeal for medicine brought rapid promotion, as did his decision at this time to become a Freemason. In 1843 he was appointed Lecturer on Natural Philosophy at Guy's. The same year he became Resident Superintendent of a small asylum for twenty insane women, which formed part of the hospital.

Three years later he gained a gold medal in his M.D. degree at the University of London, the highest honour in medicine the University could bestow. For the next ten years at Guy's he was Lecturer on Physiology and Comparative Anatomy. Meanwhile he was elected Fullerian Professor of Physiology at the Royal Institution of Great Britain, he became a Fellow of the Royal College of Physicians and Resident Physician of Guy's Hospital.

In 1848 Gull married Susan Ann, daughter of Colonel Lacy of Carlisle, and they had a son, Cameron, and a daughter, Caroline.

Gull's name became a household word after 1871, when the Prince of Wales contracted typhoid while staying at Sandringham. Queen Victoria was adamant that her favourite man of medicine, Sir William Jenner, the Royal Physician, should treat her son, but in the event the unknown Gull was introduced to Princess Alexandra—and Jenner stood by merely as second opinion. The prince recovered under Gull's ministrations, and in 1872 he was created a baronet and appointed the Prince of Wales's regular physician. He later became Physician Extraordinary, then subsequently Physician in Ordinary, to Queen Victoria.

It was said of Gull that 'few men have practised a lucrative profession with less eagerness to grasp at its pecuniary rewards'. That may or may not be true, but Gull left behind him

£344 000 plus lands, an estate unprecedented in the history of medicine and a material achievement than can rarely have been equalled by any doctor since. Sir Edward Muir, Serjeant Surgeon to the Queen and President of the Royal College of Surgeons, who died in October 1973, left only £87 000— which is a minute fraction of Gull's fortune, considering the way inflation has eaten away the value of the pound since 1890. The Marquess of Salisbury, a more eminent man than Gull, who was not only Tory Prime Minister but also the latest in the long line of wealthy Cecils who as senior Ministers had played an important part in ruling England since the days of Elizabeth I, left only £300 100 when he died in 1903. By today's standards Gull the barge-owner's son would have been a multi-millionaire.

Gull had definite contact with leading Conservative politicians, being a friend of Disraeli and the most important doctor in England by the time Salisbury was Prime Minister. It is certain he knew Salisbury. Gull's son-in-law, Theodore Dyke Acland, was an intimate friend of the Cecil family and attended both Gull and Salisbury, signing both their death certificates. In his role as Royal Physician, Gull is quite likely to have known of Prince Eddy's illegitimate child.

Surprisingly, there are more people than Sickert who point an accusing finger at Gull when it comes to the East End murders. For instance, in the Chicago *Sunday Times-Herald* of 28th April 1895 there appeared a story under the heading *Capture of Jack the Ripper*. It recounted a story told by a well-known London physician, Dr Howard. Howard, his tongue loosened by drink, claimed he was one of twelve London physicians who had sat as a court of medical inquiry and as a commission in lunacy upon a brother physician, who had been responsible for the Jack the Ripper murders. It said:

> Jack the Ripper was no less a person than a physician in high standing and in fact was a man enjoying the patronage of the best society in the West End of London.
>
> When it was absolutely proved beyond peradventure that the physician in question was the murderer, and his insanity fully established by a commission *de lunatico inquirendo*, all parties were sworn to secrecy. Up to the time of Dr Howard's disclosure this oath has been rigidly adhered to.
>
> He was a physician in good standing, with an extensive

practice. He had been ever since he was a student at Guy's Hospital, an ardent and enthusiastic vivisectionalist.

The report goes on to say that after the inquiry, the unnamed physician was at once removed to a private asylum at Islington,

> and he is now the most intractable and dangerous madman confined in that establishment. In order to account for the disappearance of the doctor from society a sham death and burial were gone through.

In true American journalese, the report finishes with:

> None of the keepers know that the desperate maniac, who flings himself from side to side in his padded cell and makes the long watches of the night hideous with his piercing cries is the famous Jack the Ripper. To them, and to the visiting inspectors he is simply known as Thomas Mason, alias number 124.

Allowing for the sensational treatment which any such story was bound to have received in America at that time, there is still a hard core of provable fact. There was, for instance, an asylum at Islington—called St Mary's—but its records have been destroyed. And in 1896 an Islington "pauper" called Thomas Mason died—at exactly the age Gull would have been had he lived.

It is important to note that Walter Sickert never mentioned this newspaper report. He is unlikely even to have known about it. Therefore, *if* it was referring to Gull, it is completely independent corroboration of his story.

The Dr Howard quoted in the report can only be Dr Benjamin Howard who was listed in the *Medical Register* in the eighties and nineties. Howard was an eminent American physician residing in London. He qualified as a doctor in New York in 1858, and the *Medical Directory* shows he often travelled abroad—to Paris, Vienna and Berlin, and especially to the United States, which is consistent with the report that he was in America in 1895. Investigating Howard's background produced a single gleaming fact in the murk of the Ripper case, a fact which yet again stretches the imagination too far to allow it to be dismissed as coincidence. And if it is not coincidence it means Walter Sickert must have spoken the truth. For Dr Howard's London address was the St George's Club in Hanover Square—and the St George's Club ran a hospital at 367

Fulham Road, where Annie Elizabeth Crook died. This new evidence indicates how the Freemasons in charge of the cover-up could have handled the incarceration of Annie Elizabeth. If the physician Howard denounced as the Ripper was indeed Gull, Howard becomes a direct link between Gull and Annie Elizabeth. Howard, almost certainly a Freemason like so many of his fellow doctors, could well have been one of several Masonic members of the St George's Club who connived in Annie Elizabeth's elimination after she and Prince Eddy were parted. As such, Howard would have been an ideal choice to serve as one of the twelve doctors needed to conduct the secret lunacy hearing on Gull—*if* Gull was the physician he was talking about, and so far it is not established that he was.

As Howard did not name the man he claimed was the Ripper, it is necessary to identify the suspect by taking his statement point by point:

> He was no less a person than a physician in high standing and in fact enjoying the patronage of the best society in the West End of London.

No statement could be more true of Gull. He was Physician in Ordinary to the Queen, and his patients were drawn from the Royal Family and the nobility. Gull himself used to boast that his practice, at 74 Brook Street, Mayfair (the heart of the West End), was probably larger than that of any other physician at any period.

> Ever since he was a student at Guy's Hospital . . .

As has been shown, Gull entered Guy's as a student in 1837. This clue narrows the field enormously, for only a limited number of West End physicians of high standing had studied at Guy's.

> . . . he had been an ardent and enthusiastic vivisectionalist.

Gull was exceptionally outspoken in his defence of vivisection, as his evidence before the Royal Commission on Vivisection in 1875 showed. He was the best-known supporter of the cause in this country, and in 1882 wrote a sixteen-page article in *The Nineteenth Century* expressing his ardent support of the practice of experimenting on animals. Arguing that 'the good we may obtain to ourselves by physiological experiment should outweigh the immorality of the process', and that 'our moral susceptibilities ought to be bribed and silenced by our selfish gains', he energetically defended the infliction of pain on animals if it resulted in advances in medicine. In answer to a charge that vivisectionist Claude Bernard had invented a stove to enable him to watch the process of 'baking dogs alive', Gull wrote:

> "Baking dogs alive! How horrible and disgusting!" would be a natural exclamation. What purpose could there be in anything so cruel? This we shall see directly.

And he proceeded to justify in the strongest possible terms this and other experiments in the cause of 'human life and the relief of human misery'.

Dr Howard's story mentions that the physician who was Jack the Ripper had a wife who survived him, and there is reference to their one son. Both these facts are true of Gull, who also had a daughter.

Another important point is that the Ripper was described by Howard as a West End physician. Of course, in 1888 there were many West End physicians. But of them all, only one disappeared—ostensibly through his death—shortly after the year of the Ripper. This was Sir William Gull. This fact comes to light in the writing of a man who was, ironically, trying to prove a diametrically opposite viewpoint. William Stewart, in his book *Jack the Ripper: A New Theory*, wanted to establish that the murderer could not have been a West End doctor. He wrote:

> I have made a complete list from the *Medical Register* of the practitioners residing in the West End prior to August, 1888, and defined the West End by a square.
> At the top left-hand corner of this square I placed Harlesden, at the top right-hand corner Camden Town, at the bottom right-hand corner Charing Cross, at the bottom left-hand corner Hammersmith. In the list of practitioners in this area I included all those who were employed in hospitals. By comparing this list with the obituary of practitioners for the year subsequent to November, 1888, I discovered that no West End doctor's name was missing. In other words *all* the medical men in the West End who were practising before the murders were alive and practising for at least a year or two afterwards.

Stewart's last statement is wrong, however. As has been explained, Sir William Gull is supposed to have died in January 1890, only fourteen months after the last murder, so he was not alive and practising for a year or two after the murders. There are two possible reasons for Stewart's mistake. The first is that he was careless, the second that for a specific reason he did not include Gull on his first list. The second alternative is more likely, because a repetition of Stewart's exhaustive survey shows that except for the error over Gull, he was entirely correct in his statement. No other eminent West End doctor did die in the two years following the Whitechapel Murders. So Stewart builds up the evidence against Gull even more strongly.

He excluded Gull from his original list because, though he was seeking to prove that no West End *doctor* was Jack the Ripper, he did not in fact check every doctor, merely every *practitioner*. As Gull had retired in 1887 he could not be described as a practitioner, and for this reason Stewart did not include him on his first list. Consequently, when he came across Gull's obituary notice he would not have considered it relevant. But even though Gull had retired, he remained a resident of Brook Street, and could still be accurately described as a West End doctor, the description used by Howard.

Thus Stewart carefully exonerated all West End practitioners by his patient research, leaving as suspects a mere handful of retired doctors, including Gull. A more thorough check of obituaries than Stewart undertook, and also a full check of entries in the *Medical Register* and *Medical Directory*, shows that of this handful of suspects, only Gull died in the period immediately after the murders. These findings show two things. Combined with the fact that all the details of Howard's story fit him, they show that Gull was certainly the doctor described in the Chicago article as Jack the Ripper. Perhaps more importantly, they show that if the Ripper was a doctor Gull is the only possibility.

Others have accused Gull of being the Ripper. He is the doctor referred to in another accusation—the now famous story of the spiritualist medium Robert James Lees who is supposed to have identified the Ripper by his clairvoyant powers and, after the murder of Kelly, led the police to the home of a West End physician, who was later secretly removed to an asylum.

It is not necessary to believe in clairvoyance to see the value of

the Lees story. Whether he came by his knowledge through
supernatural or natural means is a matter for debate, and
doubtless most people would incline toward the latter view. But
the fact that he did know something—probably through his
close contacts with the court—seems inescapable. And the real
value of the Lees story will become apparent later when his
testimony is seen to correspond minutely with a story told by
Gull's own daughter.

The chief objection to the Lees story is that several commenta-
tors have claimed it did not appear in print until 1931. If it had
had any foundation in truth, the argument runs, some reference
to it would have come to light before then. This objection wilts
under the statement that the Lees story first appeared in print
thirty-six years earlier than 'Ripperologists' have until now
believed. It appeared in the final section of the article in the
Chicago *Sunday Times-Herald* in April 1895. Before Ian Sharp
discovered it for the BBC, this article had never been quoted. It
does not even appear in the Association of Assistant Librarians'
comprehensive catalogue of Ripper literature, *Jack the Ripper or
The Mysteries of the East End*. The Chicago article was omitted
from this admirable bibliography only because until 1973 it had
lain forgotten since the year it appeared.

Even 1895, seven years after the murders, was not the
beginning of the Lees story; it was merely the first time it had
been committed to print. The story had wide circulation, in
London at least, as early as July 1889—only nine months after
the murders. This is confirmed by a note in the *Letters* file at
Scotland Yard. Admittedly this is from a crank who signed
himself 'Jack the Ripper', but the writer's state of mind is
immaterial. Only his knowledge counts. The contents of the
letter show that the story of Lees having helped the police run
Jack the Ripper to earth was known forty-three years earlier
than critics of the story have stated. The letter, received at the
Yard on 25th July 1889, says:

Dear Boss
        You have not caught me yet you see, with all your
cunning, with all your "Lees" with all your blue bottles.
                                        Jack the Ripper

For the story to have gained this sort of acceptance as early as
July 1889 means it must initially have been told (or leaked out)

a few weeks after the murder of Kelly, which fits in with Lees taking part in the hunt for the Ripper in November 1888, as the story claims.

Despite the fact that the story has since been grossly exaggerated, to the extent that some apocryphal versions refer to more than twenty murders, it is possible to get back to the bare bones. I have studied every available version of the story, removed the inconsistencies and inventions of later writers, and retained only those points which are common throughout. I then compared what was left with the original story told by Lees himself, a very different tale from the one which has come down to us via sensational reporters. The original story comes from Lees's great-niece, Mrs Emily Porter of Wembley, who knew 'Uncle James' extremely well until she was about twenty, when he died. The story he told her tallied almost exacty with the story which remained after the embellishments of sensational writers had been trimmed away.

Lees was a highly respected medium whose clairvoyant powers were so highly developed that at the age of nineteen, it was said, he was called before Queen Victoria to make contact with the dead Prince Albert. Lees later became the leader of the Christian Spiritualists in England. He was a close friend of Disraeli, and accompanied him on his last walk before his death. He ran a spiritualist centre at Peckham, was a leading socialist, and a friend of Keir Hardie, later a leader of the Labour Party.

The original and unembellished story told by Lees was that at the time of the Ripper murders he was at the height of his powers. One day he was writing in his study when he became convinced that the Ripper was about to commit another murder. He went to Scotland Yard but was given little attention because there had been a spate of cranks and theorists assailing the police each day (see Chapter 14). But that night there was indeed a Ripper murder. Lees was so shocked by the accuracy of his vision that on the advice of his doctor he took a holiday abroad. One day, on his return, he was riding with his wife in a London omnibus. Suddenly he began to experience a renewal of the strange sensations which had preceded his former clairvoyant condition. The omnibus ascended Notting Hill. When it stopped at the top a man got on.

Leaning over to his wife Lees remarked earnestly, 'That is Jack the Ripper'.

His wife laughed at this and told him not to be foolish.

'I am not mistaken', he replied, 'I feel it.'

The omnibus travelled the entire length of Edgware Road, turning into Oxford Street at Marble Arch. At this point the man got out, and Lees determined to follow him. About half way down Oxford Street, Lees told a constable of his 'supernatural' knowledge, but again he was met with derision. The policeman even threatened laughingly to 'run him in'. On reaching Apsley House the Ripper, in a nervous state, jumped into a cab and was driven rapidly down Piccadilly. Eventually Lees found a police inspector willing to take him seriously. After the final murder on 9th November Lees concentrated his powers on the vision of the man he had seen. He led the inspector to a West End mansion, the home of one of the most celebrated physicians in London. Once inside, the inspector spoke to the physician's wife. In the course of a searching interrogation she confessed that she did not believe her husband was of sound mind. She had been horrified to note that whenever a Whitechapel Murder occurred he was absent from home. When accused, the doctor admitted that his mind had been unbalanced for some years, and that of late there had been intervals of time during which he had no recollection of what he had been doing. The physician could sometimes be calculatingly cruel, at other times extremely kind. He said that he had on one or two occasions found himself sitting in his rooms as if suddenly aroused from a long stupor, and in one instance he had found blood on his shirt-front, which he had attributed to nosebleed. On another occasion his face had been badly scratched.

Here the Lees story dovetails with the testimony of Dr Howard, for according to Lees the physician was committed under a false name by twelve doctors to a private asylum. To conceal the truth it was announced that the doctor had died. A coffin was filled with stones, and his funeral caused a great stir.

Though Lees did not name the doctor to whom he claimed to have led the police, there are clues in the story that again point directly to Gull. These clues, combined with the fact that Lees was plainly describing the same physician as Howard, who *was* accusing Gull, make it certain that he too was saying, 'Sir William Gull was Jack the Ripper'.

The clues in Lees's story that point to Gull are:

(1) The route taken by the Ripper in avoiding Lees—

beginning at Marble Arch, going half-way along Oxford Street and back down Piccadilly—traces a wide U-turn with Gull's house at 74 Brook Street almost at its centre. Few doctors who were among 'the most celebrated physicians in London' lived in that relatively small area, which excludes Harley Street.

(2) Another clue is to be found in the timing of the doctor's discovery by Lees. It was shortly after the last murder on 9th November 1888. It is a curious fact that Sir William Gull wrote his will only eighteen days after this date, on 27th November 1888. What prompted Gull to prepare his will at this time is not known. It was more than a year since his stroke in October 1887, and he had suffered no attacks since. In fact, according to his death certificate, he had only two attacks all told, the second proving fatal. Shortly after his recovery from the first seizure would have been an understandable time for his thoughts to turn in the direction of his will, but they did not. Throughout the rest of 1887 and the whole of 1888 he was a perfectly fit man —yet only a few days after the time Lees claimed he had led the police to the Ripper, Gull unaccountably chose to make arrangements for the division of his estate after his death.

(3) A third clue concerns the sham death and burial of the physician in Lees's and Howard's stories. This bogus funeral is supposed to have caused 'a great stir'. Gull's funeral caused so much of a stir that a special train had to be laid on, and mourners included some of the most influential men in London —Lord Justice Lindley, Sir Joseph Lister, Sir Henry Acland and Gull's best friend in later life, Sir James Paget, Serjeant Surgeon to Queen Victoria. Gull was interred near his father and mother at the village churchyard at Thorpe-le-Soken. Country folk from villages as far as twenty miles away tramped to the graveyard on the day of the funeral and lined the route of the coffin from the railway station to the church.

(4) The physician run to ground by Lees was described by him as being sometimes a surprisingly kind man, at other times cold and calculatingly cruel. This sums up Gull's character perfectly. He would alternate between moods of warmth and benevolence in which no kindness was too much, and temperamental sloughs during which he appeared about as human as a pillar of stone. In her book *How Charles Bravo Died*, Yseult Bridges showed just how callous Gull could be:

> Dr Johnson, a man of middle age who had attained some eminence in his profession, was strictly orthodox in his out-

look and methods, and therefore the antithesis of Sir William Gull. The former, for instance, had refrained from telling his patient, "You are poisoned", because he lacked actual proof of it; or, "You are dying", because that was contrary to the ethics of his profession.

But the latter had no hesitation in telling him bluntly both these truths. "On my own responsibility and without previous consultation," he informed the court [Bravo's inquest] "I told Mr Bravo he was a dying man."

Charles . . . was struggling to sit up. "Am I dying?" he asked Sir William desperately.

"You are very ill and in all probability you have not very many hours to live, but of course as long as there is life there is hope."

"Is there really no hope for me?" he asked again, as though unable to accept his fate. Sir William felt his pulse and heart. "There is very little life left in you. In fact you are heart-dead[1] now."

Yet Gull was praised for his kindness to patients and on 31st January 1890 a letter signed 'R.A.' appeared in *The Times* and described how Sir William had treated a gentleman 'with failing health and fortune'. Gull administered first medicine, which failed to work, and then the sum of thirty guineas. He was renowned for this sort of kindness, but he was widely criticized, too, for the other side of his nature. On one occasion he displayed his inhuman streak in a manner even more overt than that in the Bravo episode. Ironically, the story is recounted in one of the affectionate memoirs of Gull which appeared after his death—*In Memoriam, Sir William Gull*. He had been attending a poor patient with heart disease and after the man's death he was extremely anxious to perform a post-mortem examination. Permission was obtained with great difficulty, but with the proviso that nothing was to be 'taken away'. A devoted sister of the dead man was present during the examination to ensure fair play. Rather than deal with an intensely delicate situation with as much sensitivity as possible, Gull deliberately cut out the dead man's heart before her eyes, put it in his pocket and said, 'I trust to your honour not to betray me'.

So saying, he left with the heart of the speechless woman's brother still reposing in his pocket, and the mutilated corpse lying before her on the dissecting table.

[1] This has often been reported as the even more callous: 'In fact you are half dead now'.

Without becoming unduly influenced by Robert Louis Stevenson's *Dr Jekyll and Mr Hyde*, published two years before the murders, it is true to say that the 'split personality' has been recognized by psychiatrists as the not uncommon state now defined as schizophrenia. The malady is prevalent among those who suffer great mental and emotional pressure, though it rarely reaches the proportions described in grim detail by Stevenson. Once in a while, however, such a case does arise, illustrating the fact that the character of the doctor described by Lees is not so unbelievable as many may think. In October 1974 a young husband was jailed by an Old Bailey judge for raping a nurse. The court heard that the defendant was twenty-four, outwardly a normal, happily married man, but that he could 'turn into' a brutal sex attacker. His defence counsel told the court that apart from the indecent assaults he had committed on five women, he was in no way vicious or unpleasant. 'Except when his trouble is upon him, he is a perfectly normal young man. These things are almost outside his control'. Other Jekyll and Hyde cases worth studying are that of Edward Paisnel, the notorious 'Beast of Jersey' and, more recently, that of Peter Cook, the Cambridge Rapist. Paisnel was sentenced to thirty years' imprisonment in 1971 for thirteen sex offences against young children: wearing a grotesque mask and spiked suit he had terrorized the island for eleven years and been obsessed with witchcraft and the atrocities of Gilles de Rais, the original Bluebeard. Despite the evil side of his nature, Paisnel was nevertheless a kind and generous man who loved small children.

As his conduct in the post mortem episode and the Bravo case suggest, Gull was not a conventional man. He regarded himself as a law unto himself. He frequently showed he had little thought for the feelings of others, and did not hesitate to hurt freely. He suited his word to his actions, for one of his sayings was: 'Morals and religion have no true and firm basis'.

It was written of him: 'Of all evils, he looked upon ignorance as the worst'.

This gives some idea how he might have regarded an ignorant servant, Marie Kelly, who dared put his Masonic colleagues and himself in danger with her loose tongue. An arrogant man, he bowed to no higher authority once he had made up his mind. Therefore, once set on disposing of Kelly in whatever way he thought appropriate, he would have let nothing stand in his way. Many thought his strong physical

resemblance to Napoleon went beyond outward appearance.
It was said of him:

> Having once formed an opinion and determined upon a
> line of action, he carried it out unhesitatingly, uninfluenced
> by any thought of consequences. He was unswerving in his
> ideas of right and wrong, uninfluenced by other people's
> views and opinions. His insight into truths which lesser
> minds were blind to see and powerless to grasp, and a life-
> long experience that his vast capacities generally placed him
> in the truest relation to things, developed in him an absolute
> confidence in the infallibility of his own judgement in certain
> points.

Gull's three 'epileptiform attacks', mentioned by Wilks and
Bettany, are possibly significant here. Epileptiform attacks are
caused by abnormal brain activity following brain injury.
Epileptic fits range from mild 'absences' to generalised convul-
sions in which the person falls down unconscious. In certain
types of epilepsy, notably temporal lobe, there might be a long
period of 'automatism' in which the sufferer might wander away
and in rare instances be violent, a state that sums up the
symptoms of the doctor in Lee's story.

Yet the argument may still be raised that if Lees had really
led the police to Sir William Gull's house there would be a
record of the events in the secret files. It has already been
shown, however, that a cover-up has taken place. Any papers
relating to Lees and Gull would therefore have been a vital
part of the evidence to be suppressed. This is precisely what
seems to have happened. Of all the papers contained in the
secret files of the Home Office and Scotland Yard, only one file
is incomplete. This is Home Office File A49301, in which it is
noted that thirty-three out of fifty-one items were destroyed or
missing when the file was put together in 1893. Can it be
coincidence that this is the file containing accusations against
doctors and policemen?

Two points make the circumstances surrounding Gull's
death suspect, points which become understandable when applied to a man who was secretly committed to an asylum when
the world believed he was dead. They go beyond showing that
the doctor in the Lees and Howard stories was Gull and confirm
that everything described in those stories actually happened.

(1) In his last years Gull was attended by three doctors—Dr
Hermann Weber, Dr Charles Hood and his own son-in-law

Theodore Dyke Acland. While there is no specific law for-
bidding a doctor from certifying the death of a relative, it is
generally considered preferable he should not do so. This is
especially true where a patient is being treated by several
doctors, only one of whom is related to him, as was the case
with Gull. Proper practice dictates that the death certificate
shall be signed by a doctor not related to the deceased. This is
because it could subsequently be suggested that the patient did
not die from the cause stated by the doctor. Relatives are
considered more likely to have a motive for falsifying a death
certificate than non-relatives. In the case of Sir William Gull,
his death-certificate was signed, contrary to good practice, by
his son-in-law. The allegations that Gull did not die in 1890
but was placed in an asylum would explain this odd departure
from convention.

(2) It was not until late 1888—shortly after the final Ripper
murder—that Gull really dropped out of the public eye. This
contradicts the myth that he was too ill to take part in public
life from October 1887 onward, and places his retirement from
society remarkably close to the date Lees led the police to the
Ripper. The reason given for his disappearance from society
generally during 1889 was that he suffered further strokes that
year. This was a lie. His death certificate proves conclusively
that he suffered no apoplectic attacks of any kind between the
first in 1887 and the second two days before his death. The
certificate states under cause of death:

> Cerebral
> Haemorrhage
> Hemiplegia
> 1st attack Oct 10 1887
> 2nd do Jan 27 1890
> Certified by
> Theodore Dyke Acland
> M.D.

The known facts do not fit in with Gull being a broken man
after 1887. For more than a year after this he was active. Then
for no apparent reason (certainly not a physical illness) he did
drop out of society, and his death was announced in January
1890. But the facts *are* consistent with his being under restraint
after the last Whitechapel Murder. It would obviously have
been too dangerous for Gull's death to have been announced

immediately after the end of the murders. The coincidence would have been blatant, and would have been spotted, for instance, by Stewart. A reasonable time lapse had to be allowed lest suspicion fall upon Gull and then, naturally, upon his Masonic colleagues. But his sudden withdrawal from society after Kelly's murder had to be explained. It was consequently announced that he had suffered further strokes, a statement which his death certificate shows beyond doubt was a complete fabrication.

The name under which the physician in Howard's story was certified—Thomas *Mason*—brings to mind the Freemasonic tradition that in certain circumstances a Mason will die by his own greatest achievement. Gull, said Sickert, was in his element removing the troublesome by certifying them insane. Now there is completely independent evidence that this was the ultimate fate of Gull himself. What more appropriate name for a certified Freemason than Mason, a pun horribly consistent with the humour described in the Masonic *Protocols* as so essential?

Slowly the evidence builds up. The physician Howard described was undoubtedly Gull. From clues contained in Lees's story it can be seen that the doctor he spoke of was also Gull. That both men independently described different but overlapping episodes in the same drama strengthens this argument. The fact that both stories fit in perfectly with established facts and with Sickert's narrative—again quite separate from the others—and that the details of Gull's last days reported in the past do *not* fit in with established facts, such as those on his death certificate, adds enormous weight to the case against him.

To secure a conviction in a British court the prosecution must prove its case beyond all reasonable doubt. The densely crowded dock in the trial of Jack the Ripper, however, more realistically requires proof beyond a shadow of doubt. In the case against Sir William Gull we can finally get close to that long-awaited certainty. There is quite independent proof that Lees's story implicating Gull was perfectly true.

This is contained in the writings of an eminent surgeon and Ripper expert, Dr Thomas Stowell, CBE, MD, FRCS, etc. Stowell said he had been told a story by Gull's own daughter, Caroline:

> She was the wife of Theodore Dyke Acland, M.D., F.R.C.P., one time my beloved Chief. I knew them both

intimately and often enjoyed the hospitality of their home in Bryanston Square over many years.

That Stowell was telling the truth in this is borne out by the fact that in his will Dyke Acland directed that Stowell be appointed one of his trustees and executors, and he left him a valuable Pre-Raphaelite painting. Plainly, Stowell was indeed a dear friend of Gull's daughter and her husband. He continued:

> Mrs Acland's story was that at the time of the Ripper murders, her mother, Lady Gull, was greatly annoyed one night by an unappointed visit from a police officer, accompanied by a man who called himself a medium and she was irritated by their impudence in asking her a number of questions which seemed to her impertinent. She answered their questions with non-committal replies such as 'I do not know,' 'I cannot tell you that,' 'I am afraid I cannot answer that question.'
>
> Later Sir William himself came down and in answer to the questions said he occasionally suffered from 'lapses of memory since he had a slight stroke in 1887'; he said that he once had discovered blood on his shirt.

The resemblance between this story and that told by Lees is uncanny. There can be no doubt that they describe the same incident. Admittedly there *appears* to be a discrepancy in the fact that Lady Gull reacted with non-committal replies and the physician's wife in Lees's story confessed she did not think her husband was of sound mind. But the initial reaction of the wife in the Lees account must have been exactly the same as that of Lady Gull in Caroline Acland's story; Lees described the 'searching interrogation' of the physician's wife, but no interrogation would have been necessary had she been willing to answer questions about her husband. It is also clear that Caroline Acland's account does not tell the whole story. Why did Lady Gull give *non-committal* replies? If the questions of the medium and the inspector had been so impertinent she would surely have simply thrown them out. If Lady Gull was being non-committal it means she did not wish to commit herself either way about her husband's alleged involvement in the murders. If he had been innocent, the last thing she would have been is non-committal.

Plainly, Caroline Acland knew no more than she told Stowell. She was unaware that her story was any more than an interesting tale about two foolish visitors received by her parents at the time of the Jack the Ripper murders. She loved her father deeply, and even named her son Theodore William Gull Acland, so the last thing she would have wished is to have suggested Gull was the Ripper.

The astonishing aspect of Stowell's article is that he was apparently trying to prove the Ripper was Eddy, Duke of Clarence. He quoted the Caroline Acland story in support of his theory that Gull came by the blood on his shirt by medically examining Eddy after one of the murders. Stowell studied the Ripper case for many years before publishing his findings in *The Criminologist* in 1970. Though he never named his suspect, except by the letter 'S', it is generally accepted that he wanted readers to think he was accusing the Prince without actually saying so. Interviewed on television, he remained adamant in his refusal to state positively that his suspect was Eddy. Why? Having scattered a plethora of clues pointing in Eddy's direction, there would have been no reason to refuse committing himself—unless in reality he did not suspect Eddy at all. Even more intriguing was the fact that on 9th November 1970, the 82nd anniversary of the murder of Marie Kelly, a letter from Stowell appeared in *The Times* in which he denied he had said or even thought Eddy to have been the Ripper. Writing this curious, unexplained letter must almost have been Stowell's last act, for in *The Times* of the following day a brief report announced the death *on November 9th* of Dr Thomas Stowell. According to his son, Dr Thomas Eldon Stowell, all the papers and notes the old man had built up during a lifetime of studying the Whitechapel Murders were destroyed unread as soon as he had died.

Old Stowell's final emphatic statement that he had not even *thought* Eddy was the Ripper takes on a new significance when considered in the light of another passage in his article, 'It was said that on more than one occasion Sir William Gull was seen in the neighbourhood of Whitechapel on the night of a murder'. This points the finger directly at Gull, yet Stowell camouflages it with the feeble suggestion that 'It would not surprise me to know that he was there for the purpose of certifying the murderer to be insane'. (!)

In the same article he revealed that rumours had been current at the time of the murders which said positively Gull was the Ripper. Read carefully, Stowell's whole article is clearly intended to create the *impression* that Eddy was his suspect. But the only evidence he produced pointed the finger at Gull!

Because old Stowell's papers were so unaccountably destroyed, we have no idea where he discovered the evidence which incriminates Sir William Gull. It is implausible to suggest that Stowell invented the evidence, because if he were romancing he would have been far more likely to invent evidence to support his case against 'S'.

There seems to be only one clue as to why Stowell behaved so oddly after discovering evidence against Gull. This is to be found in his will:

> I bequeath my Grand Lodge Masonic clothing to Cheselden Craft Lodge . . . my Grand Chapter Clothing and P.Z. jewel to Cheselden Chapter . . . and the remainder of my Masonic jewels and books to Cornubia Lodge No. 450.

P.Z. means Stowell was a Past Zerubbabel, the principal Freemason among a group of initiates who have all passed the Royal Arch. The important function of a Past Zerubbabel is to perform the final rite in the ceremony of closing a Royal Arch Chapter. The words Stowell would have chanted in so doing might well be applied to his act of trying to conceal the truth about Gull's complicity in the Whitechapel Murders:

> Companions, nothing now remains but, according to ancient custom, to lock up our secrets in a safe repository, uniting in the act of Fidelity, Fidelity, Fidelity, Fidelity.

What more safe repository was there for the Masonic secret Stowell had uncovered about Gull than to lock it up in a veiled accusation of Prince Eddy?

Exactly what motivated Stowell in writing his article it is now difficult to say. Though he appeared to want everyone to believe Eddy was the killer, it seems from the contents of his article and his feeble excuse for Gull's presence in Whitechapel that he could in reality have intended *Gull* to be implicated, without having the responsibility of pointing the finger himself. In his peculiar, unfathomable way Stowell planted other clues incriminating Gull. The earliest clue suggested Gull did not die when he is supposed to have done, which again supports the three independent claims that Gull was the doctor sent to an asylum under a false name. Stowell told Colin Wilson that he had found in Gull's private papers the information that 'S' had not died of pneumonia as he is reported to have done in 1892, but that he had died of syphilis. This would be truly remarkable, because Gull is supposed to have died two years earlier in 1890, in which case he could have known little about how 'S' died. Was this strange claim by Stowell yet another cryptic accusation of Gull, explaining in his own peculiar way that '*Sir William Gull did not die in 1890*'?

A deeper study of Stowell's strange behaviour opens up yet another possibility. His article could have been designed, not to *conceal* Gull's guilt, but to *proclaim* it in such a way that he could not be held responsible by his Masonic elders.

In an interview after the publication of his article Stowell explained that he would not name his suspect because he had no wish to embarrass the family of the suspect, to whom he owed so much. Stowell had no known contact with the Royal Family and certainly *owed* them nothing. But he owed the family of Sir William Gull, in the person of Caroline Acland and her husband, a great deal. Another point which supports the idea he was pointing a camouflaged finger at Gull is the following statement in his article:

> To support this fantasy [that the murderer was a medical man] it was not unnatural for the rumour mongers to pick on a most illustrious member of my profession of the time— perhaps of all time—Sir William Gull, Bt., M.D., F.R.C.P., F.R.S.

Harrison reacted to this enigmatic statement thus:

> On the contrary, one would have thought that to pick on one of the most illustrious medical men of his day would have been the most unnatural thing in the world.

This assessment is accurate, but it does not go far enough. An exhaustive study of the Ripper case reveals no such rumours as those alluded to by Stowell. Until August 1973, three years after Stowell's article, Gull had not been denounced as the Ripper in public. Only Sickert has done so since. What then did Stowell mean? Having seen the avalanche of discussion and speculation on the Ripper since 1970 it is now difficult to recreate the frame of mind of readers when Stowell published his dissertation accusing 'S'. In November 1970 no mention had ever been made of Prince Eddy or Gull in connection with the Ripper murders. Few ordinary people had heard of either of them. Stowell then made the statement, which is quite untrue, that 'it was not unnatural for the rumour mongers to pick on . . . Sir William Gull'.

The inescapable conclusion is that Stowell, in making a deliberately inaccurate statement about a man who had never been publicly mentioned in connection with the Ripper, was in fact accusing that man. The denunciation of Gull was veiled in Stowell's apparent preoccupation with Eddy only to confuse Stowell's Masonic elders. But anyone with a comprehensive knowledge of the Ripper case would have known that he was accusing Sir William Gull.

A summary of the evidence so far shows Sir William Gull was a Freemason of influence; that he suffered from mental attacks in which he would have behaved strangely and even violently; that many lies have been woven around his death to make it appear natural; that he himself was a weird, unpredictable man; that he was seen in Whitechapel on the nights of the murders; and that by his own admission he had woken up in his rooms to find blood upon himself.

He was indicated as being Jack the Ripper by Walter Sickert, Dr Benjamin Howard, William Stewart, Robert James Lees, Dr Thomas Stowell and even his own daughter Caroline.

Sir William Gull had a personal connection with the whores of the East End. The *Dictionary of National Biography* makes the passing comment in the entry on Gull that 'He was a close friend of James Hinton'. That innocuous statement hides facts which are crucial when considered in the light of Sickert's indictment of Gull as the whore-ripping East End killer. Gull was more than a close friend of Hinton. Until Hinton's death in 1875 they were lifelong best friends. They were so intimate that in 1878 it was Gull who was chosen to write the introduction to Hinton's biography and collected letters. In this introduction he said 'It is now near twenty years ago that our acquaintance began. Sympathies in common on the nearest subjects of human interest brought us much together'.

It is interesting that Gull chose as his best friend and most intimate confidant a man who was obsessed, and that James Hinton's strange obsession was *the prostitutes of Whitechapel*. This developed during the year 1839 to 1840 when he worked as a cashier in a wholesale woollen draper's in the heart of

Whitechapel. This experience, wrote his biographer Ellice Hopkins, 'came crashing down on his young heart with a most cruel force, and the degradation of women possessed him with divine despair'. All his life, wrote Hopkins, Hinton was 'divinely mad' about the prostitutes.

In 1855 he was a constant companion of Gull, and every morning they took their English constitutional together, 'wending their way, deep in discussion, through the comparatively deserted London streets'. At this time Gull was assistant physician at Guy's Hospital, which is just across London Bridge on the south side of the Thames and within easy walking distance of the East End. Is it conceivable that Hinton, with his all-consuming obsession about Whitechapel and its degraded inhabitants, did not take Gull there many times during those morning walks, to share with his friend those 'nearest subjects of human interest'? He would have taken Gull into the very alleys where the prostitutes slunk drunkenly through the shadows—the very alleys where Jack the Ripper was to destroy those same pathetic women in 1888. For some years before moving to Brook Street, Gull had a practice at 8 Finsbury Square, right on the borders of central London and the East End. He knew the stalking ground of the Ripper intimately, and in all probability he had been given a personal and exceedingly passionate grounding in the lives and characters of the whores of Whitechapel.

How deeply Gull was affected by Hinton's obsession it is impossible to say. Though his motive for becoming Jack the Ripper was Masonic, perhaps there was also in his unbalanced mind an element of what was described in *The Times* as 'an earnest religionist with a delusion that he has a mission from above to extirpate vice by assassination'.

We shall never know.

In March 1974 I visited Gull's grave in the churchyard at Thorpe-le-Soken, Essex, a grave which he is supposed to share with his wife. By coincidence his headstone bears the same text as the wall of the Working Lads' Institute at Whitechapel where the first two Ripper inquests were held: 'What doth the Lord require of thee, but to do justly, and to love mercy, and to walk humbly with thy God?' It was Gull's favourite biblical text. I was shown the grave by an affable verger, a sixty-six-year-old pillar of the Church called Mr Downes. His father before him had been verger there too, and he recalled his father telling him that as a small boy he had walked twenty miles from their home at Clacton with a throng of mourning villagers to be at Gull's funeral.

Downes's comments as we gazed at the grave brought to mind the story of Dr Howard, which said the eminent physician who was Jack the Ripper had been confined in an asylum while a sham death and burial were staged. Downes had no idea why I was interested in Gull, so I was astonished when he said, 'This is a large grave, about twelve feet by nine, too large for two people. Some say more than two are buried there. It's big enough for *three*, that grave.'

He fell silent a moment or two, then said pensively, 'Burial places for two just aren't normally that big'.

Then, half jokingly, he mused, 'Of course, it's *possible* somebody else is buried there, without anyone knowing who.'

I pressed him for more information, but he quickly changed the subject. This did not appear to be because he had any sinister knowledge, but because he held Gull in the most profound reverence. Gull is Thorpe-le-Soken's only claim to fame, and Downes did not want seriously to ponder even the possibility that something 'not quite right' may have happened. But even though he knew nothing sinister about the grave, nor of any connection between William Gull and the Ripper, his words were based on an honest man's assessment of a strange phenomenon—a grave for two which is big enough for three.

There is every indication that Gull was the doctor referred to by Howard and Lees and that he was committed to an asylum under the name Mason. Meanwhile a bogus funeral was gone through and a coffin filled with stones was lowered into his grave. But what happened when Gull actually died? Either he was buried somewhere under the name Mason or pressure was brought to bear and he was secretly laid in his rightful grave, taking up the third place in the grave for two.

In later years Gull's most intimate friend and companion was Sir James Paget, another Freemason. Paget was Serjeant Surgeon to Queen Victoria. It will be remembered that in examining the cover-up of the Prince Eddy–Annie Elizabeth Crook episode, it was hard to see how—after her incarceration —Annie was moved from workhouse to workhouse without any of the normal paperwork or removal procedure being gone through. The explanation lies in the convenient presence on the Boards of Guardians dealing with Annie Elizabeth of one

Rev. Henry Luke Paget. The Rev. Paget was one of the
elected members of the St Pancras Board of Guardians—to
whom Annie Elizabeth was chargeable for the first half of her
thirty-one years in workhouses. Only one of the guardians
could have arranged for Annie Elizabeth to be moved in such
a way that every rule was waived. Paget was Vicar, and later
Rural Dean, of St Pancras and went on to become Suffragan
Bishop of Ipswich (1906), Suffragan Bishop of Stepney (1909),
and Bishop of Chester from 1919 to 1932. More importantly,
he was the son of Sir James Paget, Gull's best friend. Judging by
the example set by his family, and by the more high-ranking
members of the Church of England at that time, it is virtually
certain he was a Freemason, though the Grand Lodge have
refused to allow me access to their records to check this or any
other point.

*Two important points arose in the months after this book was delivered to the pub-
lisher. As the typed manuscript was already in the hands of the printer it was impossible
to make any changes in the body of the text, so the new evidence has been inserted here,
the end of the relevant chapter, at proof stage.*

*In 1975 Richard Whittington-Egan discovered in a London bookshop a handwritten
letter from Dr Benjamin Howard, whose testimony has proved such strong support of
Sickert's story. The letter, reproduced in Whittington-Egan's A Casebook on Jack the
Ripper, was addressed to The People newspaper, which had published an article
based on the Chicago Sunday Times-Herald story. In the letter, Howard denied all
knowledge of the report attributed to him, and denied he was even in America at the
time the disclosures were said to have been made. Whittington-Egan comments that this
denial rules out the Howard story.*

*On the contrary. Dr Howard would hardly have admitted that he had become drunk
and broken the solemn oath binding him to secrecy about the Masonic lunacy commission proceedings. I find it perfectly credible that Howard would deny this betrayal of
Masonic secrets most vehemently. And though Whittington-Egan is to be heartily
congratulated on his coup in finding the letter, its existence is by no means surprising.*

*The second point, possibly coincidence but nevertheless worthy of note, could indicate
the identity of the police inspector whom Lees led to the Ripper. Lee's family roots were
at Bournemouth. When Inspector Abberline retired he moved to Bournemouth. This in
itself is hardly startling. Bournemouth was, and is, a favourite town for those planning
a comfortable retirement. What is interesting is that Abberline died in 1928, having
appointed one Nelson Edwin Lees as his executor. I have been unable to discover if
Nelson Edwin Lees was related to Lees the medium. If he was, and it does seem a strong
possibility bearing in mind the coincidence of location and the relative rareness of the
name, the case in favour of the Lees story is surely conclusive.*

CHAPTER TWELVE

John Netley

John Netley, the second member of the Ripper party according to Sickert, is a man without a face. He is the one character named by Sickert who is quite unknown. As such he provides one of the strongest pieces of evidence that the story is true. The whole of Sickert's narrative examined up to this point has been shown to be correct. If the old painter had been lying about those involved in the killings the weakest part of his story is likely to have been that part concerning John Netley, the mysterious figure of whom no 'Ripperologist' had previously heard.

To recall Sickert's description of Netley and his part in the affair:

He was the young man who first became involved in the case when he regularly picked up Eddy from a prearranged spot and ferried him to his secret meetings with Sickert and Annie Elizabeth in Cleveland Street. Netley was not on the official Palace staff, but he owned his own coach. How he came to know Eddy in the first place Sickert did not explain. At the rendezvous Eddy would transfer from the royal coach into Netley's vehicle in order to outwit any royal aides who might have happened to be keeping an eye on his carriage.

When Gull and his extreme Masonic colleagues were organizing the elimination of the blackmailing whores Netley was inveigled into taking part in the operation. According to Sickert the coercion was not necessary. Sickert thought he was not too far from the truth in saying that because Netley was a short man—a fact about which he was hypersensitive—he would go to any lengths to boost his ego and reach the state where he felt, not equal to other men, but their superior. He was prepared to take part in any plan, however obnoxious, to further his own ends. He was appallingly ambitious, and though an inveterate womanizer, it was said that he had taken part in homosexual activities with wealthy homosexuals to help him in what he somehow imagined would be his climb to the top. The top of what, Sickert could not imagine. He did not know if Netley was a Mason, but whether he was or was not, he was prepared to do all he could to help the secret brotherhood purely for his own sake. Sickert never ceased to marvel that Netley was quite insensitive to the fact that he was despised by those who used him for *their* own ends.

He was enlisted by the killers firstly because he was already involved in the case, and secondly because he knew Cleveland Street and the people there. He would be invaluable, they thought, in making the initial discreet inquiries at Cleveland Street and its neighbourhood after the disappearance of Kelly. Thirdly, he was a working-class man, and would be useful and inconspicuous making inquiries, with the aid of a picture of Kelly, in the East End.

During the murders Netley drove the party around the East End in his coach. As he drove the two Masonic murderers carried out their ghastly work in the relative darkness of the vehicle. Later Netley placed the bodies of the victims where they were found. This was true only of Nichols, Chapman and Eddowes; Kelly was murdered in her room and Stride was killed at the spot where her body was found.

Walter Sickert was unclear what happened to Netley when the murders were at an end. All he knew was that the abominable coachman somehow developed the fixation that selling his body to notable homosexuals was no longer the path to power. Perhaps because he had gained an insight into the workings of Masonry, he wanted now to ingratiate himself with influential Freemasons rather than their puppets, the aristocracy. It suited his ends, and he switched his allegiance from Eddy to Freemasonry with as little compunction as he had shown in performing his part in the murders. This loathsome, misguided creature, whose greatest attribute was his inferiority complex, continued a lone campaign against Alice Margaret, the daughter of Eddy and Annie Elizabeth. At the height of the Ripper murders the child was knocked down by Netley's coach in Fleet Street or the Strand, said Sickert. She was nearly killed, but after months in St Bartholomew's Hospital she recovered. The incident was repeated in February 1892. On this occasion Netley charged along Drury Lane in his carriage just as Alice Margaret was crossing the road with an elderly relative who was helping to bring her up. The child was not so badly hurt on this occasion because she was spun out of the way of the wheels when the corner of the carriage struck her. She was taken to hospital unconscious but released after a day, having been treated for concussion. The elderly woman who had been with her later described the driver of the coach to Sickert. He knew at once it was Netley. It was with grim satisfaction that he recounted to his son that after the coach struck Alice Margaret on this occasion it careered into the kerbstone and the wheel was damaged. Unable to get the coach moving again, and desperate that he should not be apprehended, Netley was seen to jump down from the cab, and in the ensuing confusion he passed through the crowd and fled to Westminster Bridge, several passers-by in hot pursuit. Despite his smallness, however, Netley was fleet of foot, and he threw off his pursuers long before he reached the Thames. Sickert heard later that for some inexplicable reason Netley threw himself into the river from Westminster Pier, where he drowned. That, said the old painter, was the end of Netley, and the final chapter of the Jack the Ripper mystery was closed.

Netley was difficult to investigate. To begin at the beginning, there was no proof that he had even existed.

After six weeks of research, Karen de Groot discovered Netley's birth certificate. He was born in May 1860 in Kensington, and christened John Charles Netley. The certificate showed he was the son of an omnibus conductor, which at least made it likely that he would have become something similar. It was a period when the old song about following in father's footsteps was more apposite than today.

Even though a man may do nothing all his life, one thing is virtually certain: he will leave a record of his birth and a record of his death. John Netley definitely existed. Now it was time to examine the most positive part of Sickert's narrative about Netley, his alleged suicide in the Thames in February 1892.

But according to the records at Somerset House, no John Netley did die in 1892; nor, it was later proved, did such a death occur in 1891 or 1893. And the Thames Police have no record of a suicide for the whole of February 1892.

Nothing appeared that looked anything like an explanation until Karen de Groot found this brief report in *The Observer* of 7th February 1892:

> Shortly before one o'clock yesterday, attempted suicide from Westminster Pier. A respectably dressed young man took off his boots and coat and hid them under a seat in a waiting room, jumped off the pier and swam for a few yards. Rescued by Mr Douglas, Pier Master, but struggled. Taken to Westminster Hospital. Gave name of *Nickley*, but refused his address.

This episode tallies so closely with Sickert's account that it seems beyond coincidence. The attempted suicide reported in *The Observer* occurred at the same place and in the exact month that Sickert said Netley jumped into the Thames. Admittedly the man rescued by the Pier Master gave his name as Nickley and not Netley. But apart from the obvious similarity between the two names, there is also the fact that the name Nickley was false. No one called Nickley was alive at that time—certainly no one that could be described as a young man. Assuming the 'respectably dressed young man' of the *Observer* report to have been anything between fourteen and thirty-five, I checked the eighty-four registers of births at Somerset House covering every month from 1878 back to 1857, but no one called Nickley was born in those years. The registers almost invariably jump from Nickless to Nicklin. Nor does the name Nickley appear in the *Dictionary of British Surnames*. The odd behaviour of the young man in giving this false name (so similar to Netley), and in refusing to give his address, is consistent with his having something to hide, as Netley most certainly had. The attempted suicide of *Nickley* corresponds closely to the reported suicide of Netley; the conclusion that they were one and the same is irresistible. That Sickert imagined Netley had drowned is understandable. This part of his story obviously relies on what someone else had told him. The records of Westminster Hospital, where 'Nickley' was taken, are now lost, so it is impossible to confirm the episode beyond the report in *The Observer*.

There was still some way to go. It had not yet been shown that Netley was a cab-driver or that he was anything to do with Cleveland Street or the Whitechapel Murders; the two attempts on Alice Margaret's life were equally unsubstantiated; and if Netley did not die in the Thames in 1892, when did he die?

Any record of the two attempts on the child's life seemed non-existent. Police and hospital records—such as had survived two wars—were useless. For a long time it seemed impossible to verify the story of the two incidents, until a copy of the *Illustrated Police News* of Saturday, 6th October 1888 came to the rescue. It will be remembered that Sickert said the first attempt on Alice Margaret's life took place in Fleet Street or the Strand at the height of the Ripper murders. The report said:

> Shortly after four o'clock on Monday afternoon [two days after the 'double event'] a little girl was run over by a hansom cab in Fleet-street, opposite Anderton's Hotel. The child was placed in the cab and conveyed to St Bartholomew's Hospital in an insensible condition, one of the wheels having passed over her body. From the serious nature of the injuries the little sufferer is not likely to recover.

Once again, though no names are mentioned, the story tallies too closely with Sickert's version of events to be coincidence. The time and place of the accident are exactly right. Sickert claimed Alice Margaret was nearly killed in the collision. This is confirmed by the report. Finally, he said she was taken to St Bartholomew's Hospital, just like the child in the newspaper story.

The gaps were beginning to disappear, but still there was no indication of what happened to Netley after he left hospital following his suicide attempt in 1892.

Here it is interesting to recall the content of the Masonic code, described in Chapter 10. The *Protocols* declare that a Freemason will, in certain circumstances, die by his own greatest achievement. It has been shown that Sir William Gull, in his element certifying the troublesome as insane on behalf of the Masons, was himself certified and incarcerated under the name Thomas *Mason*.

By a miracle of research, Karen de Groot discovered that when Netley did die it was in such an 'accident' that he too seems finally to have fallen victim of those he wished desperately to serve. For Netley, whose best achievements on behalf of the Masons were ferrying the Masonic killers around in his coach, and later using his coach in his mistaken attempts at eliminating Alice Margaret, *died under the wheels of his own vehicle.* The 'accident' did not happen until 1903, but it seems a similar happening occurred about 1897, from which he recovered. The

astonishing part of this story is the place of Netley's death. The
unlikely notion of a man falling under the wheels of his *own*
coach is difficult enough to accept. When we learn that he died
at *Clarence* Gate, Regent's Park, the memory of the wry Masonic
humour that surrounded Gull's removal cannot be erased from
the mind.

The story of Netley's death appeared in two local newspapers. The *Marylebone Mercury and West London Gazette* of 26th
September 1903 reported:

SHOCKING FATALITY IN PARK ROAD

An inquest was held by Coroner Danford Thomas on
Wednesday afternoon on the body of John Netley aged 43
years.

Evidence was given to the effect that the deceased was in
the employ of Messrs Thompson & McKay, carmen, to the
Great Central Railway Company. On Sunday afternoon he
was driving one of their pair horse vans along Park Road,
Regent's Park, when one of the wheels of the van collided
with a stone rest, and he was thrown from his seat into the
roadway. As the deceased lay on the ground, one of the
horses kicked him on the head and the wheel passed over
him. He had no strap round him.

Dr Norris of 25 Park Road said he was called and saw the
deceased lying dead in the roadway near Clarence Gate.
There were extensive injuries to the head. Death, which was
due to fracture of the skull, was instantaneous. The jury
returned a verdict of accidental death.

The *Marylebone Times* of the previous day reported Netley's
father as saying he had fallen from a van about six years before,
but had fully recovered from the effects of the accident.

That Sickert got the story of Netley's death wrong is stronger
support of the fact that he was telling the truth. If Sickert had
been a fantasist who had created a sensational story by which to
be remembered (hardly necessary for a man acknowledged as
the greatest English painter since Turner) then he would have
been eager to get details right, and certainly would have used
the Clarence Gate death to 'sell' the story.

The truth about Jack the Ripper has already been so obscured by wanton speculation that it is dangerous to depart
from certainties. But there are inevitable gaps in the evidence
now traceable. For instance, only informed speculation can
help to explain Netley's death. If indeed it was Masonic, why

would his erstwhile masters have disposed of him at all? The answer to this must lie in Netley's repeated attempts to gain the favour of the Masons by such acts as his attempts on the life of the infant Alice Margaret. His 'help', beyond his part in the Ripper episode, was unsolicited and would no doubt have outraged the Masonic elders in whose name he mistakenly imagined he was working. The fact that in 1903 he was no more than a carman seems to indicate that his fortunes had taken a tumble. Did he too make the fatal mistake of trying to blackmail the Masons with his knowledge of the Ripper murders?

CHAPTER THIRTEEN

Yours truly, Jack the Ripper

I'm not a butcher,
I'm not a Yid,
Nor yet a foreign skipper,
But I'm your own light-hearted friend,
Yours truly, Jack the Ripper.

'The above queer verse', as it was described by Sir Melville Macnaghten, was one of the more palatable communications received at Scotland Yard during the Ripper's reign of terror. It is important at this point to take an unbiased look at this welter of correspondence, hurled at the police and Press from all corners of the globe. It has been estimated that Scotland Yard received about a thousand letters a week at the height of the murders. Many were from people with suggestions about how to snare the Ripper. Hundreds more were from cranks who derived a perverted sense of fun from sending crude little notes signed 'Jack the Ripper'.

Almost every theory so far expounded in print has relied to a large extent on several of these letters purporting to be from the murderer. The messages arrived in all shapes, sizes and forms, and from all over the world. Some were in conventional envelopes, some in home-made envelopes, some on postcards, some scrawled on telegram forms. They were in every conceivable style of handwriting, some obviously educated, others by educated people imitating an illiterate style and yet others by genuinely ill-educated pranksters. The one factor common to most of the correspondence is the opening address, 'Dear Boss', and the signature, 'Jack the Ripper'.

These were in imitation of the first two missives received. From the fact that the second, a postcard, referred to the contents of the first, a grubby letter, it has been concluded they are of common authorship. The handwriting does differ markedly, but as the second message was received before the first had been published it is almost certain the two pieces of correspondence do come—if not from the same individual, at least from the same group of people.

I have closely examined the contents of the *Letters* file at Scotland Yard, and feel that only one of the hundreds of letters received is at all likely to have come from Jack the Ripper.

If this is true it cripples many previous theories about the identity of the Ripper, most effectively Harrison's elaborate theory indicting Prince Eddy's tutor, James Kenneth Stephen. Harrison's thesis is built almost entirely upon a comparison of the poetry of Stephen and the 'style' he detects in the so-called Ripper correspondence. He cites as the work of the Ripper poems, postcards and letters which are definitely of different authorship.

Donald Rumbelow was almost at the truth when he wrote:

Few of the letters signed 'Jack the Ripper' or purporting to come from him, are of any real value—in fact, a ruthless weeding-out process leaves only two.

In fact Rumbelow decided *three* messages were genuine, but the first two—being from the same source—he counted as one. These are the letter posted on 28th September and the follow-up postcard from the same group of hoaxers received after the double murder. Rumbelow's second vote of confidence goes to the 'From Hell' letter received on October 16th. The first letter is important because it was the first use of the name Jack the Ripper:

25. Sept. 1888.
Dear Boss

    I keep on hearing the police have caught me but they wont fix me just yet. I have laughed when they look so clever and talk about being on the right track. That joke about Leather Apron gave me real fits. I am down on whores and I shant quit ripping them till I do get buckled. Grand work the last job was. I gave the lady no time to squeal. How can they catch me

now. I love my work and want to start again. You will soon
hear of me with my funny little games. I saved some of the
proper <u>red stuff</u> in a ginger beer bottle over the last job to write
with but it went thick like glue and I cant use it. Red ink is fit
enough I hope <u>ha ha</u>. The next job I do I shall clip the ladys
ears off and send to the police officers just for jolly wouldnt
you. Keep this letter back till I do a bit more work, then give it
out straight. My knife's is nice and sharp and I want to get to
work right away if I get a chance. Good luck.
yours truly
Jack the Ripper

Dont mind me giving the trade name.

Then at right angles to the rest of the letter:

wasnt good enough to post this before I got all the red ink off
my hands curse it. No luck yet. They say I'm a doctor now
<u>ha ha</u>.

The postcard received after the double murder said:

I was not codding dear old Boss when I gave you the tip,
you ll hear about saucy Jacky s work tomorrow double event
this time number one squealed a bit couldnt finish straight
off. had not time to get ears for police thanks for keeping
last letter back till I got to work again,
Jack the Ripper

The last two sentences are direct allusions to the contents of the
first letter, which had not been published by the time this
second message was received. Rumbelow believes this is the
work of the murderer for the same reason that every major
author on the subject has believed the same thing. He wrote:

The second letter was posted on 30 September, the day of
the 'double event'. . . . Details of the 'double event' were not
known until they were published in the newspaper on the
following day, Monday 1 October, and for twenty-four hours
at least they would have been confined to Whitechapel and
some of central London. Only the murderer could have
known that he had not been able to finish the first victim off
and had not had time enough to 'clip her ears'.

Few authors on the subject of the Ripper have paid enough

attention to detail. Many have taken the word of previous writers without checking basic facts for themselves. Hence the continuing misunderstanding about the addresses of the victims—resolved in Chapter 9. It has resulted, too, in one of the greatest fallacies concerning the murders—namely that the 'double event' postcard was posted on Sunday, 30th September, when only the killer could have known the details of the murders.

Donald McCormick, Tom Cullen, Robin Odell, Daniel Farson and Donald Rumbelow have all made the misleading statement that the postcard was mailed on Sunday, 30th September. If any one of them had looked at the postmark they would have seen it read, 'OC 1', which meant it could well have been posted on Monday, 1st October, when full details of the double murder were general knowledge. This seems to be confirmed by the records department of the Post Office, who point out that in 1888 there were collections from post-boxes made each Sunday. They say that any letter posted on a Sunday would have been stamped with that date. So if the 'double event' message had been posted on the Sunday as we have been led to believe, it would almost certainly have borne the postmark 'SEP 30'.

The other letter Rumbelow selects is that which was sent to Mr George Lusk, chairman of the Whitechapel Vigilance Committee, which had been set up to patrol the streets after the murder of Annie Chapman. Part of a kidney was enclosed with the letter, which read:

> From hell
>
> Mr Lusk
>   Sir
>   I send you half the
> Kidne I took from one women
> prasarved it for you tother piece I
> fried and ate it was very nise. I
> may send you the bloody knif that
> took it out if you only wate a whil
> longer
>   signed   Catch me when
>   you can
>   Mishter Lusk

Note that the one letter claimed to be genuine is not in fact signed, 'Jack the Ripper'. This letter did more than any other to whip up panic in the East End, the reign of terror so sacred to the Masons. I do not believe it to be the work of an illiterate man, although the writer took pains to make it appear so. An illiterate is far more likely to write 'nife' than 'knif', or 'wile' rather than 'whil'. And someone who believes 'wait' is rendered as 'wate' is unlikely to know the sound *bludee* is rendered as 'bloody', which the writer spells correctly.

The Ripper's 'From hell' letter

It has been held that the section of kidney enclosed with the letter provides strong evidence that this communication is genuinely from the killer or killers. The first reaction of the Press, before any examination had been carried out, was that the kidney had been taken from a dog, or that the letter was a medical student's prank. What finally convinced many people that the letter must have come from the Ripper, was the reported outcome of the examination of the kidney by Dr Openshaw, pathological curator of the London Hospital Museum. Dr Openshaw was said to have stated that it was a 'ginny' kidney such as would be found in an alcoholic (like most of her class, Eddowes was an alcoholic), that it belonged to a woman of about forty-five (Eddowes was forty-three), that it had been removed in the previous three weeks (Eddowes had been killed two weeks and two days before the kidney was received by Lusk) and that it was in an advanced state of Bright's disease (the kidney remaining in Eddowes's body was in exactly the same state). What seemed conclusive proof that it was indeed part of Eddowes's kidney was the reported fact that two inches of renal artery remained in her body. The renal artery is about three inches long—and one inch of artery was attached to the kidney sent to Lusk.

Anyone convinced the identity of the murderer is revealed in a previous theory has only to eliminate from his mind the 'evidence' of all correspondence except the Lusk letter to see that the case against most suspects is pretty threadbare.

The authenticity of the Lusk letter seems to be confirmed by the findings of Canadian handwriting expert Miss C. M. Mac-Leod, who wrote in *The Criminologist* in 1968, 'If there was only one real Jack the Ripper, I should cast my vote for the writer of sample 1 (the Lusk letter)'.

But if this is true who wrote the message? More than one murderer made up the lethal identity of Jack the Ripper. The identity of the writer is to be found in the same analysis of the writing. Miss MacLeod wrote:

I would have looked for this killer among such men as cab-drivers, who had a legitimate excuse to be anywhere at any time. I should have sought a hail-fellow-well-met who liked to eat and drink; who might attract women of the class he preyed on by an overwhelming animal charm. I would say in fact he was a latent homosexual (suggested by lower-zone strokes returning on the wrong side of the letter) and passed as a 'man's man'; the roistering blade who made himself the life and soul of the pub and sneered at women as objects to be used and discarded.

In saying also that 'This writer was capable of conceiving any atrocity, and of carrying it out in an organized way', Miss MacLeod might be accused of being wise after the event. But her character sketch of the killer based upon his handwriting is remarkable, and banishes all doubts as to the author of the letter 'From Hell'. It is a perfect description of Netley.

CHAPTER FOURTEEN

Maniacs and Woman-haters

Despite all the anti-social diseases that plague modern society, a cross-section of humanity in any major city is unlikely to reveal great numbers of lunatics, woman-haters or sexual maniacs. In considering Jack the Ripper from a present-day standpoint then, it would seem reasonable to suggest that if a man could be shown to have had a strong hatred of women, *on that fact alone* he should rank as a major suspect. Much of the sympathy that Michael Harrison's theory has earned is based on the undisputed fact that James Kenneth Stephen hated women. This is one of Stephen's verses:

> If all the harm that women have done
> Were put in a bundle and rolled into one,
>> Earth would not hold it,
>> The sky could not enfold it,
> It could not be lighted nor warmed by the sun;
>> Such masses of evil
>> Would puzzle the devil
> And keep him in fuel while Time's wheels run.

Because misogyny is today such an unusual phenomenon, it seems plausible to argue that anyone displaying Stephen's disgust with the feminine sex is inescapably a strong candidate for the Ripper. This argument falls down rather badly, however, in the face of evidence contained in the Scotland Yard *Suspects* file. The file reveals that in 1888 lunatics, sexual maniacs and woman-haters were almost two a penny.

It contains some amazing stories, and provides a rich commentary on the sort of world in which Jack the Ripper operated, and an alarming insight into the sort of effect the Whitechapel Murders had on many minds. A five-page report written in the hand of a man who walked into Scotland Yard on Boxing Day, 1888, is an outstanding example:

I beg to draw your attention to the attitude of Dr Morgan Davies of — Street, Houndsditch, E. with respect to these murders. But, my suspicions attach to him principally in connection with the last one—committed in-doors.

Three weeks ago, I was a patient in the London Hospital, in a private ward (Davis) with a Dr Evans, suffering from typhoid who used to be visited almost nightly by Dr Davies, when the murders were our usual subject of conversation.

Dr Davis [sic] always insisted on the fact that the murderer was a man of sexual powers almost effete, which could only be brought into action by some strong stimulus—such as sodomy. He was very positive on this point, that the murderer performed on the women from behind—in fact, *per ano.* At that time he could have had no information, any more than myself, about the fact that the post mortem examination revealed that semen was found up the woman's rectum, mixed with her faeces [this is quite untrue].

Many things, which would seem trivial in writing, seemed to me to connect him with the affair—for instance—he is himself a woman-hater. Although a man of powerful frame, &, (according to the lines on his sallow face) of strong sexual passions. He is supposed, however, by his intimates, never to touch a woman.

One night, when five medicos were present, quietly discussing the subject, & combatting his argument that the murderer did not do these things to obtain specimens of uteri (wombs) but that—in his case—it was the lust of murder developed from sexual lust—a thing not unknown to medicos, he acted (in a way which fairly terrified those five doctors) the whole scene. He took a knife, 'buggered' an imaginary woman, cut her throat from behind; then, when she was apparently laid prostrate, ripped and slashed her in all directions in a perfect state of frenzy.

Previously to this performance I had said: "After a man had done a thing like this, reaction would take place, & he would collapse, & be taken at once by the police, or would attract the attention of the bystanders by his exhausted condition?" Dr D— said "NO! he would recover himself when the fit was over & be as calm as a lamb. I will show you!" Then he began his performance. At the end of it he stopped, buttoned up his coat, put on his hat, & walked down the room with the most perfect calmness. Certainly his face was as pale as death, but that was all.

It was only a few days ago, after I was positively informed by the Editor of the "Pall Mall Gazette" that the murdered woman last operated on had been sodomized—that I thought—"How did he know? His acting was the most vivid I ever saw. Henry Irving was a fool to it. Another point. He argued that the murderer did not want specimens of uteri, but grasped them, & slashed them off in his madness as being the only hard substances which met his grasp, when his hands were madly plunging into the abdomen of his victim.

I may say that Dr Davies was for some time House Physician at the London Hospital, Whitechapel, that he has lately taken this house in Castle St Houndsditch; that he has lived in the locality of the murders for some years; & that he professes his intention of going to Australia shortly should he not quickly make a success in his new house.

Roslyn D'O Stephenson

PS I have mentioned this matter to a pseudo-detective named George Marsh of 24 Pratt St., Camden Town N.W. with whom I have made an agreement, (enclosed herewith) to share any reward which he may derive from my information.

R.D'OS

PPS I can be found at any time through Mr Iles of the "Prince Albert", St Martin's Lane—in a few minutes—I live close to; but do not desire me to give my address.

R.D'OS

Gummed to the statement is a torn sheet of paper dated 24th December 1888 and bearing the words:

I hereby agree to pay to Dr R D'O Stephenson (also known as "Sudden Death") one half of any or all rewards or monies received by me on a/c of the conviction of Dr Davies for wilful murder.

Roslyn D'O Stephenson MD
29 Castle St WC
St Martin's Lane

One can only wonder at the state of mind of the author of this intriguing document. Apart from the dubious content of the accusation, it is full of so many imponderables it is hard to know where to begin in analysing it.

The inconsistencies begin with Dr Roslyn D'O Stephenson (can that be genuine?) obviously being unprepared to give the address of his suspect, because he describes him as 'Dr Morgan Davies of — Street, Houndsditch, E'. Yet later he thwarts his own intentions by explaining that Dr Davies has taken a house in *Castle* Street, thus filling in his own blank. He then mentions by way of a postscript that he has struck a bargain with a man for whom he clearly has little respect, describing him as he does as a 'pseudo-detective'. He next expresses his desire not to give his own address, but appends an agreement *on which his address is written*. The address itself is curious, for it also is in Castle Street, but a Castle Street in the W.C. district, not Houndsditch. The agreement attached to the statement is absurd, for it is a promise to pay Dr R. D'O Stephenson money—yet it is signed by Dr R. D'O Stephenson himself! The situation becomes even more intriguing when, several papers down in the file, one discovers another statement, this one by Stephenson's 'partner'. It was made on Christmas Eve. The statement is written by Inspector J. Roots at the Yard, who reports:

Mr George Marsh, ironmongery salesman (now, and for two months out of employment) 24, Pratt St, Camden Town, came here at 7 p.m. and made the following statement:—

"About a month ago at the Prince Albert P.H., Upper St Martin's Lane, I met a man named Stephenson and casually discussed the murders in Whitechapel with him. From that time to the present I have met him there two or three times a week and we have on each occasion discussed the murders in a confidential manner. He has tried to tell me how I could capture the man if I went his way to work. I simply told him I should go my own way about it and sooner or later I'd have him. I told him I was an amateur detective and that I had been for weeks looking for the culprit. He explained to me how the murders were committed. He said they were committed by a woman hater after the forthcoming manner:-

"The murderer would induce a woman to go up a back street or room and to excite his passion would 'bugger' her and cut her throat at the same time with his right hand, holding on by the left.

"He illustrated the action. From his manner I am of opinion he is the murderer in the first six cases, if not the last one.

"Today Stephenson told me that Dr Davies of Hounds-ditch (I don't know the address although I have been there and could point it out) was the murderer and he wished me to see him. He drew up an agreement to share the reward on the conviction of Dr Davies. I know that agreement is value-less but it secured his handwriting. I made him under the influence of drink thinking that I should get some further statement but in this I failed as he left me to see Dr Davies and also to go to Mr Stead of the Pall Mall Gazette with an article for which he expected £2. He wrote the article in the Pall Mall Gazette in relation to the writing on the wall about Jews. He had £4 for that. I have seen letters from Mr Stead in his possession about it; also a letter from Mr Stead refusing to allow him money to find out the Whitechapel Murderer.

"Stephenson has shown me a discharge as a patient from the London Hospital. The name Stephenson is obliterated and that of Davies is marked in red ink. I do not know the date.

"Stephenson is now at the common lodging house No. 29 Castle St., St Martin's Lane, W.C. and has been there three weeks. His description is:- Age 48, height 5 ft 10 in, full face, sallow complexion, moustache heavy—mouse coloured—waxed and turned up, hair brown turning grey, eyes sunken. When looking at a stranger generally has an eyeglass. Dress, grey suit and light brown felt hat—all well worn; military appearance: says he has been in 42 battles: well educated.

"The agreement he gave me I will leave with you and will render any assistance the Police may require.

"Stephenson is not a drunkard: he is what I call a regular soaker—can drink from 8 o'clock in the morning until closing time but keep a clear head.

Despite a marginal note by Roots that Stephenson's agreement is attached, there is no longer any sign of it in the file. There is one last report on this episode, a character sketch of Stephenson by Roots, written after Stephenson's visit to Scotland Yard on Boxing Day. Under the subject heading 'Whitechapel Murders, Marsh, Davies & Stephenson', Roots says:

With reference to the statement of Mr George Marsh, of 24th inst., regarding the probable association of Dr Davies and Stephenson with the murders in Whitechapel.

I beg to report that Dr Stephenson came here this evening and wrote the attached statement of his suspicions of Dr Morgan Davies, Castle St, Houndsditch; and also left with me his agreement with Marsh as to the reward. I attach it.

When Marsh came here on 24th I was under the impression that Stephenson was a man I had known 20 years.
I now find that impression was correct. He is a travelled man
of education and ability, a doctor of medicine upon diplomas
of Paris & New York: a major from the Italian Army—he
fought under Garibaldi: and a newspaper writer. He says
that he wrote the article about Jews in the Pall Mall Gazette,
that he occasionally writes for that paper, and that he offered
his services to Mr Stead to track the murderer. He showed
me a letter from Mr Stead, dated Nov 30 1888, about this
and said that the result was the proprietor declined to engage
upon it. He has led a Bohemian life, drinks very heavily,
and always carries drugs to sober him and stave off delirium
tremens.

He was an applicant for the Orphanage Secretaryship at
the last election.

The statements were passed to Inspector Swanson but no action
appears to have been taken to investigate Dr Morgan Davies
(who surely *had* to be classed as a suspect if the Ripper were still
on the loose, however unlikely Stephenson's story), and no
further interview with either Stephenson or Marsh appears to
have been undertaken. This is odd, especially in view of the
fact that from the contents of his own statement and the suspicions expressed by Marsh, Stephenson was more likely to have
been the murderer than Davies. Not only was his behaviour
before Marsh identical to that which he attributed to Dr
Davies, his own statement seems to be strewn with deliberate
clues pointing the finger at himself. That his suspect and himself both lived in streets of the same name; that he on one
occasion alluded to his suspect as 'Dr D—', which would also
fit himself; and that he referred to himself as 'Sudden Death'
all support the argument that he would have been investigated
if Jack the Ripper had still been at large.

The value of these strange allegations and counter-alle-
gations goes beyond psychological insight into the effect of the
Ripper and a behind-the-scenes look at the day-to-day problems of the men at the Yard. The essential fact is that the dozens
of papers in the *Suspects* file indicate the police *knew* the Whitechapel Murders had ended with Kelly's death on 9th November. This is true, because no allegations after that date were
followed up by the Yard. Arrests certainly did not cease
immediately. As far as the average bobby on the beat and his
superiors at the station were concerned, Jack the Ripper was

still at large and might strike again at any time. But the Yard obviously knew something, or they would not have been content to let the allegation reports build up without taking any action to investigate suspects. Farson has suggested that police activity on the case ceased because they knew Druitt was the killer. This is untrue, for the Yard papers show no real investigation into the case took place after the death of Kelly, seven weeks before Druitt's body was found. The allegations against Stephenson and Davies, for instance, were made on Christmas Eve and Boxing Day respectively, and Druitt was not retrieved from the Thames until 31st December. Unless the police already knew who the murderer or murderers were, they would certainly not have received Marsh's statement accusing Stephenson on 24th December and done nothing to investigate it. It appears no steps would have been taken at all, even to obtain a character sketch of Stephenson, if the suspect himself had not turned up of his own accord two days later.

Another woman-hater story emanated from the office of the Chief Constable of Rotherham on 5th October 1888. The *Suspects* file contains the correspondence received from Rotherham but there are no copies of Inspector Abberline's replies. The content of these can be guessed, however, and the Rotherham letters are what count:

Sir

I have the honour to inform you that I have just had a visit from a man named James Oliver, residing at 3 Westfield View, Rotherham, a discharged soldier of the 5th Lancers, who is firmly persuaded in his own mind that he knows the perpetrator of the Whitechapel Murders. He was perfectly sober and made his statement clearly and circumspectly and it is of such a nature that I consider it should be laid before you without delay.

He states that there was a man named "Dick Austen" who served with him in R. Troop in the 5th Lancers, who previous to joining the Army had been a sailor, he would now be about 40 years of age—5–8 in height, an extremely powerful and active man, but by no means heavy or stout. Hair and eyes light. Had, in service, a very long fair moustache, may have grown heavy whiskers and beard. His face was fresh, hard and healthy looking. He had *a small piece bitten off the end of his nose*. Although not mad, he was not right in his mind, "he was too sharp to be right". He used to be very temperate, but sometimes used to get out of bed in the night and walk about the barrack room. He never would say where he came from and often said he had no friends.

He used to sometimes brag of what he had done previously to enlisting in the way of violence but more often of what he could do, "as though qualified to do anything".

While in the Regiment he was never known to go with women and when his comrades used to talk about them in the barrack room he used to grind his teeth—he was in fact a perfect woman hater. He used to say if he had his will he would *kill every whore and cut her inside out*, that when he left the Regiment there would be nothing before him but the gallows.

He had gone through great hardships and rough times in various parts of the world, having been a sailor in sailing ships, he was a very sharp and witty man and a capital scholar. Oliver believes he could recapture his handwriting. He was most plausible. His hands were long and thin.

He had 12 months for breaking into the Orderly Room and tearing up his defaulter sheets.

He is believed to have drawn his deferred pay. (about 24£) and used to say he would make London his home.

He is a man who is most abstemious and will live on dry bread. "He used many a day to save his money and live on what was knocking about in the Barrack Room".

Probably he would always be respectably dressed but more often the description of a sailor than a soldier.

Oliver's idea is that he would probably be working at Docks or on board ship by day—possibly, if the murderer, that he may take short voyages on some vessel and commit the murders shortly before leaving—the dates of the murders tally with this theory.

"He always had revenge against women brooding in his mind."

I have cautioned the man Oliver to say nothing about this, and he tells me that he has not as yet told anyone his suspicions excepting his own wife.

I have also promised him that unless his suspicions prove true, or of material help that his statement to me will be considered in confidence.

I have the honour to be

Sir

Your obedient servant

L. R. Barick [?] Captain, C.C.

At this stage, after only four Ripper murders, this sort of clue was being followed up, as Abberline's report shows:

Referring to annexed correspondence from the Chief Constable, Rotherham, I beg to report that I have caused an insertion in the Informations asking if anything was known in Divisions respecting Austen giving his description and other particulars . . . but up to the present time with no result.

Perhaps it would be well to ask the Chief Constable of Rotherham, to cause James Oliver to be seen again and requested to furnish the date of Austen's discharge from the 5th Lancers, giving the name of the Station discharged from, and any other information.

A further letter from Rotherham dated October 19th said:

Sir

I have the honour to acknowledge the receipt of your letter of yesterday's date, relative to mine of 5th instant, and to inform you in reply that I have seen James Oliver this morning, he is unable to state the date or place of Austen's discharge—but as stated in my former letter he is positive that Austen intended to reside in London. Application to the 5th Lancers at Aldershot would produce the date and place of discharge, and should he be entitled to draw any future deferred pay or Army Reserve Pay, his whereabouts could by that means be ascertained—Oliver says several photographic groups of the Troop were taken, he has no copy, but could, if a copy was obtainable, pick out Austen—I should like a copy of some or any of the alleged letters from the murderer, as Oliver, as stated before, believes he could identify Austen's handwriting.

I have the honour to be etc.

The final letter in the episode came from Rotherham on October 24th:

Sir

In reply to your letter of yesterday's date enclosing Metropolitan Police Notice I have the honour to inform you that I have shown the facsimile handwriting to the man Oliver, who says that it is extremely like that of Austen, especially that of the letter (written with steel pen). That of the post card (written with quill) he does not think so like—although of course it is easy to see they are written by the same person—Austen's signature could of course be obtained from the Troop Pay Sheet of the 5th Lancers even if a large example of it could not be got from the same source.

I have the honour to be etc.

And there the matter ended. No further investigation was carried out into the whereabouts of Dick Austen. In Chapter 8 evidence was produced to show that the truth about the Ripper was suppressed. For the cover-up to have been successful it would have been vital to have the assistance of the man in charge of the investigation, Inspector Abberline. Abberline was clearly not involved in any conspiracy when he first took over the case, for his notes in the Yard file show beyond doubt his untiring efforts to track the Ripper. The files relating to the first two murders, Nichols and Chapman, are crammed with reports. The Stride file is smaller than its predecessors, but still displays a fair amount of evidence that an investigation by Abberline was taking place. Eddowes, of course, was murdered in the City Police district, so her case was not handled by the Yard. But in Kelly's file there is nothing in the way of relevant reports about the murder investigation. Abberline's only contribution to this file is a report of the Kelly inquest, which is worthless. The file shows that the Yard did virtually nothing to track the Ripper after the third week in October. A study of Abberline's paperwork indicates that it must have been about this time that he was brought into the cover-up. No other explanation justifies the fact that, in the middle of the Ripper's reign of terror, serious police activity simply stopped. Only Abberline's involvement in the conspiracy at the time of the Ripper would explain his reappearance less than a year later to run the Cleveland Street cover-up at police level. It will be remembered that in the Cleveland Street case Abberline deliberately allowed vital witnesses to escape from the male brothel and leave the country, while his men were watching the house.

The day before Kelly died, Warren resigned. Four days later Abberline abandoned the Ripper case. And even though three Ripper-like murders took place in Whitechapel after Kelly's death, Abberline did not return. He *knew* the Ripper's day was done.

CHAPTER FIFTEEN

The Secrets of the Files

When Roy Jenkins became Home Secretary in 1974 he insisted on having personal control over all his department's secret files. Among other changes, this meant that requests from authors and researchers to see closed files would henceforth be examined by him and not, as before, by senior civil servants. His general policy has been to release documents to legitimate investigators, rather than withhold them as was the case before. This attitude, though unpopular among some of the higher members of the Civil Service, is an important step forward. As a result of it, I have been able to examine all the Home Office files on the Whitechapel Murders, which are due to remain closed until 1993.

With both the Scotland Yard and Home Office files in my hands, I at last had at my disposal the material 'Ripperologists' have been speculating about for nearly ninety years. The first point of interest is that Daniel Farson's claim, in the revised edition of his *Jack the Ripper*, that the Home Office file confirms Montague Druitt as the prime suspect, is wrong. There is no mention of Druitt anywhere in this file.

The early chapters of this book show the immense value of the files in getting the Ripper investigation back to basics. By drawing purely on the reports of policemen engaged on the murder investigation it has been possible to eliminate the distortion which the Ripper story has undergone at the hands of newspapers, film-makers and unreliable authors like Leonard Matters. The files also contain vital information which has been left until now to examine. The widely accepted rumour that they hold the solution to the mystery in any explicit sense is unfounded. There is no dossier, yellow with age and officially stamped, which reveals the identity of Jack the Ripper. The information embedded in the hundreds of secret documents only now available is more subtle than that—but it shows that crucial points in Sickert's narrative are perfectly correct.

Old Sickert provided considerable detail in his tale of the murders, and it will be useful to recall the essence of his account.

Mary Nichols, he claimed, was picked up in Netley's coach, ritually slaughtered as it jogged along the streets of the East End, and then her body was deposited in Bucks Row, where it was found.

Annie Chapman was likewise butchered in the vehicle and carried through the passage of 29 Hanbury Street to the backyard by Netley and Sir Robert Anderson, whose alleged part in the affair is examined in the final chapter.

Elizabeth Stride was a different case. She was drunk, and with a good-natured wave of her arm she walked off along the road when the carriage stopped and Gull offered her a lift. In her alcoholic stupor she was impervious to Gull's gentlemanly appeal to her vanity. Netley consequently parked the carriage in a back street and, leaving Gull alone inside it, he and Anderson followed the shambling form of Long Liz, said Sickert. At the corner of Berner Street Netley accosted Stride and walked with her into the darker areas further along the street, while Anderson kept watch on the opposite side of the road. Time was of the essence, for Stride's refusal of a lift in the carriage and the killers' subsequent action to nail her down had taken up more time than had been allowed for. Somehow the unholy trinity already knew that the woman who was to be their final victim was in the cells at Bishopsgate Police Station, and in common with most drunks arrested by the City Police, was likely to be released any time after midnight. Sickert said Netley went with Stride into the darkness of the yard behind the International Workers' Educational Club at No. 40 Berner Street, threw her down and cut her throat with one slash of his knife. The two men then returned to the carriage and drove on to Bishopsgate Street, now simply Bishopsgate, which they planned to patrol until their final victim appeared from the police station. How the killers knew she was under arrest for drunkenness, the old painter never explained.

By the time the carriage reached Bishopsgate Eddowes (whom the killers believed to be Kelly) had already been discharged, and she was found making her way back to her doss-house in Spitalfields. There was no difficulty in luring her into the carriage, where the devilish work of killing her and Masonically mutilating her was carried out with a vengeance. In the hope that she would not be identified, part of her nose was cut off and her face was otherwise attacked. This, as far as the murderers were concerned, was the final killing—and as far as they knew this victim was the cause of the whole ghastly affair. When the work inside the vehicle was complete Netley drove to Mitre Street and he and Anderson heaved Eddowes out of the carriage and into the nearest corner of Mitre Square, by chance the darkest, where her intestines were thrown in a Masonic flourish over her shoulder.

It was not long before they realized they had eliminated the wrong woman, but they could not strike down Kelly immediately because of the upsurge of panic and vigilance on the part of police and residents that succeeded the double murder. When she was finally found Kelly was approached by Netley, whom she invited to her room. She too was drunk. The final details of Kelly's butchery Sickert never imparted to his son. He had known her as a friend and helper, and even after so long the memory was too painful for him, he explained.

There is evidence to support Sickert's claim that three of the women were not murdered at the spots where their bodies were found. Inspector Spratling's report of the Nichols murder in the Yard file records that he interviewed three people who were in Bucks' Row on the night she was murdered, 'none of whom heard any screams during the night, or anything to lead them to believe that the murder had been committed there'.

This was confirmed by Inspector Helston, who informed *The Times* on the morning of the murder that 'viewing the spot where the body was found, it seems difficult to believe that the woman received her death wounds there'. Beyond the discoloration ordinarily found on pavements, said Helston, there was no sign of stains. Dr Llewellyn, who was called to Bucks Row to examine the body of Nichols, noted that there was only a small amount of blood in the gutter—'not more than would fill two wine glasses, or half a pint at the outside'. Rumbelow suggested that the apparent lack of blood may have been attributable to Nichols's clothing soaking most of it up, but the minutely detailed reports of her murder in the secret files provide no evidence to support this theory. It is unlikely that the clothes did absorb much blood. If they had it would have been instantly obvious, and the police would never have speculated, as they did, that the murder had taken place elsewhere. It is true that Inspector Spratling testified at the inquest that he had not seen any wheel-marks in the road, but this does not disprove Sickert's account. There was a day and night traffic in 'knacker's' wagons from the slaughterhouse in Bucks' Row. Presumably if the road conditions were such that *they* left no marks, neither would Netley's coach.

Annie Chapman was not murdered in the backyard of 29 Hanbury Street, where she was found. This is confirmed in a report by Chief Inspector Swanson in the Home Office file. It referred to a man called John Richardson who at 4.45 on the morning of the murder had gone to the yard and had sat on the steps, close to which the body was later found. Richardson was certain that if the corpse had been there then, he would have seen it. Medical evidence showed that Chapman had been dead at least twenty-five minutes when Richardson went to the yard. Swanson's report reads:

> If the evidence of Dr Phillips is correct, as to time of death, it is difficult to understand how it was that Richardson did not see the body when he went into the yard at 4.45 a.m., but as his clothes were examined, the house searched and his statement taken in which there was not a shred of evidence, suspicion could not rest upon him, although police specially directed their attention to him . . . He [Phillips] was called and saw the body at 6.20 a.m. and he then gives it as his opinion that death occurred about two hours earlier, viz: 4.20 a.m.

Phillips' exact words were, 'I should say the deceased had been dead at least two hours, *and probably more*'. Annie Chapman was murdered at 4.20 a.m. at the latest, but at a quarter to five her body was still not in the yard at 29 Hanbury Street. Where was it? Only Sickert offers an answer. It has been incorrectly reported by several authors that no blood was found anywhere but immediately adjacent to Chapman's body. The reporter of the *East London Advertiser*, likely to have been one of the first journalists on the scene, reported that blood was found not only in the passage leading to the yard but also in Hanbury Street itself. This is quite consistent with the body having been carried from Netley's coach into the yard, as is another major point which no one has yet explained. The uterus and its

appendages were missing. Was this bloody trophy carried off by
a mad lone killer, or was it simply left unnoticed in the place
where she was murdered—Netley's coach?

Bearing in mind Sickert's description of the Stride murder, a
hitherto unpublished statement recorded in the Home Office
file is of crucial importance. A report by Chief Inspector
Swanson says:

> 12.45 a.m. 30th Israel Schwartz of 22 Helen Street,
> Backchurch Lane stated that at that hour on turning into
> Berner Street from Commercial Road and had got as far as
> the gateway where the murder was committed he saw a man
> stop and speak to a woman, who was standing in the gate-
> way. The man tried to pull the woman into the street, but
> turned her round and he threw her down on the footway and
> the woman screamed three times, but not very loudly. On
> crossing to the opposite side of the street, he saw a second
> man standing lighting his pipe. The man who threw the
> woman down called out apparently to the man on the oppo-
> site side of the road, "Lipski" and then Schwartz walked
> away, but finding that he was followed by the second man
> he ran as far as the railway arch, but the man did not follow
> so far. Schwartz cannot say whether the two men were
> together or known to each other. Upon being taken to the
> Mortuary, Schwartz identified the body as that of the woman
> he had seen and he thus describes the first man who threw
> the woman down:—age about 30, ht. 5ft. 5in. comp. fair,
> hair dark, small brown moustache, full face, broad shoul-
> dered; dress, dark jacket and trousers, black cap with peak,
> had nothing in his hands.
> Second man age 35, ht. 5ft. 11in. comp. fresh, hair light
> brown, moustache brown; dress, dark overcoat, old black
> hard felt hat, wide brim, had a clay pipe in his hand.

Schwartz's statement, which Swanson described as reliable,
provides an uncanny parallel with Sickert's version of the
murder. Admittedly Sickert did not mention that Netley had
called out 'Lipski', a way of insulting Jews that became the
vogue after a Jew of that name was hanged for murder in 1887.[1]
Nor did Sickert say that Anderson had followed anyone during
his wait on the opposite side of the road. In fact he made no

[1] Later reports in the Home Office file make it clear that when the woman's
assailant shouted 'Lipski' he was addressing Schwartz and not the man on
the other side of the road as Schwartz at first imagined.

mention of anyone passing along Berner Street as the attack on
Stride was taking place. Despite these omitted details, however, it cannot be denied that the scene Sickert described was
exactly that witnessed by Schwartz. And even taking into
account a marginal note on Schwartz's statement, written by
Home Secretary Matthews, that 'the police apparently do not
suspect the 2nd man whom Schwartz saw on the other side of
the street', can there be any doubt that that man was keeping
watch precisely as Sickert described? We have no proper
physical description of Netley except the word of Sickert that
he was short and the evidence of his birth certificate that shows
he was twenty-eight years old at the time of the murders. The
attacker seen by Schwartz was 'about 30, height five feet five
inches', which fits closely.

Despite speculation by Chief Inspector Swanson that the man
Schwartz saw accosting Stride may not have been her murderer,
logic shows he was. The man was seen to turn Stride round and
throw her down on the footway, on the self-same spot where
she was found murdered only fifteen minutes later. It is inconceivable that this man left her and by coincidence another
man appeared and carried out the same sort of attack on the
same woman at the same place. The timing of the assault witnessed by Schwartz confirms that the scene he saw was the
killer in action. At the inquest on Stride at the Vestry Hall in
Cable Street, Dr Blackwell said, 'I consulted my watch on my
arrival (at the scene of the murder) and it was just 1.10'.

Asked how long Stride had been dead, he replied, 'From
twenty minutes to half an hour when I arrived'.

Counting back the minutes from 1.10 when the doctor
arrived, we find that death is unlikely to have taken place later
than 12.50, which was five minutes after the attack witnessed
by Schwartz. According to Blackwell's evidence, the time of
death is more likely to have been in the ten minutes preceding
12.50, which sets the murder *almost exactly* at the time Schwartz
saw Stride attacked.

Schwartz's statement provides incontrovertible evidence that
Sickert's description of Stride's murder was accurate. There is
no possibility of Sickert having adapted his story to fit
Schwartz's observations because until now the Schwartz story
has never been published. Even though he was the only person
ever to witness a Ripper murder taking place, *Schwartz was not
called to give evidence at the inquest.* Here was yet another piece of
vital testimony that was suppressed.

Sickert's assertion that Gull induced unconsciousness in four of the victims by feeding them poisoned grapes is another bizarre aspect of the case that connects with previously unknown facts contained in the secret files.

Grapes have an established connection with Jack the Ripper, and have become bound up in the folklore of the case. Cullen quoted the case of an elderly Polish woman called Annie Tapper who told him she had sold a bunch of grapes to Jack the Ripper when she was a girl of nine. Cullen explained the presence of the grapes in the Ripper legend as being based on the 'erroneous' report that grapes had been found clutched in the dead hands of a murder victim. Robin Odell tends to support Cullen's notion that the report of the grapes was incorrect. He told me, 'Most "Ripperologists" follow the line of the inquest on Stride which reported that she had *cachous* in her hand when found dead, *not grapes*'.

It is true that at Stride's inquest it was stated that her hand contained cachous. How then did the story about grapes get into circulation? The answer is found in a report which appeared in *The Times* on Monday, 1st October which said 'In her right hand were tightly clasped some grapes, and in her left she held a number of sweetmeats'. Now it is curious that *The Times* should have been mistaken in such a detail because in all other respects its minute description of Stride's corpse was totally accurate. In a separate report, the *Evening News* confirmed the finding of grapes in Stride's right hand, and it even found a witness who claimed he had sold grapes to a man he had seen with Stride. Yet at the inquest Dr Phillips, the doctor who had tried to hide evidence implicating the Freemasons at the Chapman inquest, went out of his way to discredit the reports about grapes being found.

He said, 'I am convinced that the deceased had not swallowed either skin or seed of a grape within many hours of her death'.

But he admitted that stains on Stride's handkerchief were fruit stains.

The existence of the grapes is confirmed by a single statement of fact in the Home Office file. Chief Inspector Swanson wrote:

two private enquiry men acting conjointly with Vigilance Committee and the press, upon searching a drain in the yard *found a grape stem which was amongst the other matter swept from the yard* after its examination by the police. . . .

Only the dubious evidence of Freemason Dr Phillips cast the truth in doubt, a truth supported not only by *The Times* and the *Evening News* but by the police themselves. As the quote from the Home Office file shows, the evidence of the grapes was literally swept down the drain. We are doubtless close to finding who was responsible when we remember that Phillips was an active participator in the cover-up, and also the person most likely to have removed the Masonic symbol laid out at Annie Chapman's feet.

A Berner Street greengrocer called Matthew Packer was reported in the *Evening News* as having sold grapes to a man with Stride shortly before her murder. *Yet he was not called at the inquest.* Why?

The explanation for this perversion of justice has been that Packer's story was probably untrue, that either he or the *Evening News* had invented it. But this is not so. The Scotland Yard file contains documents that show beyond doubt that Packer was regarded by the police as a key witness and that his claim to have sold grapes to Stride's murderer was being taken very seriously by the authorities. The documents are contained in the slim folder on the Stride murder. The first is a report by Sergeant Stephen White and is countersigned by Abberline and Superintendent Arnold:

I beg to report that acting under the instructions of Insp. Abberline, I in company with P.C. Dolden, C.I. Dpt., made inquiries at every house in Berners Street, Commercial Road, on 30th ult, with a view to obtain information respecting the murder. Any information that I could obtain I noted in a book supplied to me for that purpose. About 9 a.m. I called at 44 Berner Street, and saw Matthew Packer, fruiterer in a small way of business. I asked him what time he closed his shop on the previous night. He replied, "Half past twelve in consequence of the rain. It was no good for me to keep open." I asked him if he saw anything of a man or woman going into Dutfield's Yard, or saw anyone standing about the street about the time he was closing his shop. He replied, "No, I saw no one standing about, neither did I see anyone go up the yard. I never saw anything suspicious or heard the slightest noise, and knew nothing about the murder until I heard of it this morning."

I also saw Mrs Packer, Sarah Harrison and Harry Douglas residing in the same house but none of them could give the slightest information respecting the matter.

On 4th inst, I was directed by Inspr. Moore to make further inquiry and if necessary see Packer and take him to the Mortuary. I then went to 44 Berner Street and saw Mrs Packer, who informed me that two detectives had called and taken her husband to the Mortuary. I then went towards the Mortuary where I met Packer with a man. I asked him where he had been. He said, "This detective asked me to go to see if I could identify the woman." I said, "Have you done so?" He said, "Yes, I believe she bought some grapes at my shop about 12 o'clock on Saturday." Shortly afterwards they were joined by another man. I asked the men what they were doing with Packer and they both said that they were detectives. I asked for their authority. One of them produced a card from a pocket book, but would not allow me to touch it. They then said that they were private detectives. They then induced Packer to go away with them. About 4 p.m. I saw Packer at his shop. While talking to him the two men drove up in a hansom cab, and after going into the shop they induced Packer to enter the cab, stating that they would take him to Scotland Yard to see Sir Charles Warren.

From inquiry I have made there is no doubt that these are the two men referred to in the attached newspaper cutting who examined the drain in Dutfield's Yard on 2nd inst. One of the men had a letter in his hand addressed to Le Grand & Co., Strand.

Apart from showing that the police thought of Packer as an important witness (why else would they call on him three times and conduct him to the mortuary?), this report also indicates something peculiar was going on. White was obviously surprised to find that Packer was already at the mortuary and that he was in the company of two 'detectives', when he called at the shop on 4th October. Clearly knowing nothing about the activity of the so-called detectives, White set off for the Mortuary. On the way he met Packer, along with two men who claimed they were private detectives. *They then induced Packer to go away with them.* From the words White used to describe their egress it is plain he was suspicious of the two men and their unorthodox methods. His suspicion was justified. What sort of detectives take away a witness even before the police running the investigation have interviewed him? On the second occasion when White met the men they claimed again they were private detectives, but refused to let White handle their identity card. Then they made what appeared to be the most outrageous claim of all, that they were taking Packer to see Sir Charles

Warren. Who were these men? What authority did they have
for carrying on an investigation of Packer independently of the
CID and uniformed men? How did they hope to get into the
presence of Warren? What possible interest could the Chief
Commissioner of the Metropolitan Police have had in the
evidence of a lowly greengrocer?

Such questions could all be answered by the possibility that
the so-called detectives were in fact journalists deceiving
Sergeant White in order to get a good story, and to be first with
the news. Such tactics were not unheard of. Just one thing
disproves this—the second important document in the Yard file.
This is an official statement by Packer, written in the unmistakable spider-like hand of *Sir Charles Warren*. This is
strange indeed. It means Packer *was* taken to the Yard to see
Warren by the two detectives. It must also mean they were not
detectives but some sort of special investigators working quite
independently of the CID and the uniformed branch. What is
more important, they must have been working under the
express instructions of Warren himself. For some reason Warren
wanted to outwit his own officers, to find Packer and learn
exactly what evidence he had before the policemen on the case
got a chance to interview him. There are no other statements
or reports in the file in Warren's own handwriting. He had
taken no other direct part in the investigation except to erase
the Masonic writing from the wall on the morning of 30th
September. It is important to note that his undercover men
were not engaged on the general details of the case. They had
just two functions. The first was to pre-empt Packer's evidence
about selling grapes to the Ripper. The second was to remove
all trace of grapes from the drain in Dutfield's Yard.

If Warren had employed these men in the cause of justice he
would have made sure that Packer's evidence was heard. But
like Schwartz, the only other really important witness, he was
not called at the inquest and his knowledge was suppressed.

Why should Warren have wanted to conceal the facts about
the grapes? It has been shown that only evidence that could
have helped identify the real killers was carefully and deliberately suppressed during the Ripper inquiries. But what possible
use could grapes have been in identifying Jack the Ripper?
Though it has never been recognized, grapes were a strong
indication of the truth. Unusual in so many respects, Sir William
Gull never went anywhere without raisins or grapes. In a letter
written eleven years before the murders, and never before

Matthews Packer

keeps a small shop in Berner St —

have a few grapes in window. Black & white

On Sat night — about 11 pm. a young man

from 25–30 — about 5.7. with long black coat —

buttoned up — soft felt hat —. kind of yankee hat —

rather broad shoulders — rather quick in speaking.

rough voice. I sold him ½ pound black grapes

3. A woman came up with him from Bath church

end (this [illegible] and of [illegible] —) She was dressed

in black frock & jacket —. fur round bottom of jacket —

a black crape bonnet, she was playing with a

flower like a geranium white outside and red

inside — I identify the woman at the P. George

mortuary on the one I saw that night —

They passed by in [illegible] they were going up the [illegible]

Road, but — instead of going up the crossed [illegible]

Packer's statement

published, Gull incriminated himself. The letter, now in the library of the Royal College of Physicians, says:

Dear Dr Duckworth

When I read your remarks on my evidence [before the Lords' Committee on Intemperance] I thought you had misapprehended them. I have not a copy of the evidence I gave but what I intended to say was that when fatigued I personally refreshed myself by eating raisins.

I have been in the habit of doing this for many years. I never travel or I may say go anywhere without raisins. They are always in my travelling bag and when in Scotland or the hills they form my luncheon with a biscuit and water. I eat no cane sugar but the sugar of the grape seems to supply the readiest refreshing material of which I have in my own person any experience. I take but little wine but I am not by any means a total abstainer. I believe in the use of wine as I have said in my evidence but I repeat that in my work when fatigued I prefer grapes and raisins and water.

Yours sincerely
William W. Gull
16 Dec 1877

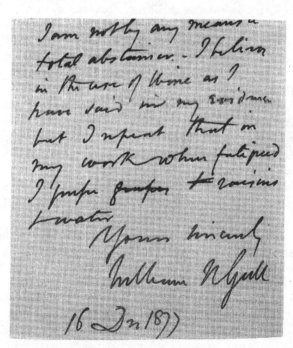

Part of Gull's letter

CHAPTER SIXTEEN

The Third Man

By now it was a far cry from that weird morning in 'Hobo' Sickert's front room when he first divulged the details of his father's rambling saga. A year and a half of energetic research had culminated in a report which showed that the most unlikely story ever told about the Whitechapel Murders was indeed the long-sought solution. Walter Sickert appeared to have been transformed from a dubious story-teller into the one man in eighty-seven years of 'Ripperology' who had spoken the truth, the whole truth, and nothing but the truth. It remained only to examine his final statement, the sobering but by now no longer astonishing identification of Sir Robert Anderson as the third man.

Anderson was a Freemason of high standing, and he was appointed Assistant Commissioner of the Metropolitan Police on the very day Mary Nichols was murdered. As explained in Chapter 10, his non-Masonic predecessor, an able and enthusiastic detective called James Monro, had been the butt of an all-out attack from Warren for months. Warren was determined to be rid of Monro. And on the day he succeeded in removing him from office, Mary Nichols was killed.

There is no *concrete* evidence to incriminate Anderson in the murders. The worst that can be said of him is that he was a liar, and that his behaviour at the time of the murders was highly suspicious. He is arguably the most unlikely of the three men named to have been connected with the Ripper crimes in any direct sense.

His strange conduct began almost immediately after he took

over as head of the CID. He stepped on to the scene hours after
the death of Nichols, did his new job unremarkably for a week,
and the day after the murder of Annie Chapman he left for a
holiday in Switzerland—hardly the most responsible action to
have taken. The Metropolitan Police area was a seething caul-
dron of vice and crime. Violence all over England was reaching
new and disquieting heights, and in London the situation was
critical. In addition to this existing turmoil a cold-blooded
killer who even at that stage was regarded as a maniac was on
the loose in the East End of London, having struck twice
already. Yet Sir Robert Anderson deserted all his new responsibilities *to go on holiday*! In his autobiography *The Lighter Side of
My Official Life* Anderson gave the reason for his untimely
departure as ill-health. If he was so ill that he could not cope
with his duties at a time when he was vitally needed, it is surprising he was appointed Assistant Commissioner at all. And
it is intriguing that with such a serious incapacity he was able
to make the long journey to Switzerland.

One other comment sheds light on Anderson's character but,
it must be admitted, by no means incriminates him. When
referring directly to the Ripper case he lied outrageously. In his
memoirs he stated quite categorically that he knew the identity
of the murderer:

> One did not need to be a Sherlock Holmes to discover that
> the criminal was a sexual maniac of a virulent type . . . and
> the conclusion we came to was that he and his people were
> certain low-class Polish Jews. . . . And the result proved our
> diagnosis was right on every point. For I may say at once
> that 'undiscovered murders' are rare in London, and the
> Jack the Ripper crimes are not within that category.

He went on to say that the 'double event' postcard was 'the
creation of an enterprising London journalist'. He continued:

> Having regard to the interest in this case I am almost
> tempted to disclose the identity of the murderer and of the
> pressman who wrote the letter referred to. But no public
> benefit would result from such a course, and the traditions
> of my old department would suffer. I would merely add that
> the only person who ever had a good view of the murderer
> unhesitatingly identified the suspect the instant he was
> confronted with him; but he refused to give evidence against
> him. In saying he was a Polish Jew I am merely stating a
> definitely ascertained fact.

In this, we are not only expected to believe the Ripper was known to be a certain immigrant, but that he was in police custody and had even been identified by a witness who had seen him at the scene of a crime. Even the most gullible of readers would find this hard to swallow, and even harder the ludicrous claim that the police's single witness refused to give evidence against the killer. It was no doubt with a philosophic shrug of the shoulders that the arresting inspector watched Jack the Ripper walk free out of the police station!

Three years before he wrote this, Anderson told another story when he reported in his book *Criminals and Crime* that the Ripper had been 'safely caged in an asylum'. None of the police of the day agreed with either of Anderson's views, as is shown by the wealth of writing on the case penned by policemen of all ranks; none of his claims is supported by a single word in the files of Scotland Yard or the Home Office; none of the so-called 'facts' he claimed were 'definitely ascertained' were ever more than his own airy speculation. Either Anderson was inventing his stories to throw investigators off the scent of the Masons, or he was fantasizing to inflate his own ego. The puerile boast, 'I know who Jack the Ripper was, but I'm not telling!' has been surprisingly prevalent among supposedly mature men. Either way, Sir Robert Anderson, Freemason, one of the most high-ranking policemen connected with the Ripper case, dealt in fiction.

Whatever the truth about Anderson and his connection with the murders, one fact was becoming clear: Sickert had told the truth but not the whole truth. Everything he had said about Prince Eddy, Annie Elizabeth Crook, Sir William Gull and the murders themselves was true. Too many independent facts, and corroboration unhinted at by Sickert, have come to light for this to be otherwise. But he knew too much for his story to end at Cleveland Street, as he repeatedly told his son. It is clear from the depth and accuracy of his knowledge that Walter Sickert knew more than he claimed. To find out exactly *how* much more he knew, it is helpful to examine some of the least tangible aspects of his story.

One of the minor mysteries of art is contained in the paintings of Walter Sickert. An undisputed master, and regarded by many as the best of only a small group of English painters this century worthy of the name, Sickert produced a tremendous number of works. His output was reportedly 'greater than

Constable's and Corot's taken collectively'. The exact number is unknown, as he had four major bases, Dieppe, Camden Town, Venice and Bath, and he was never particular about where he discarded his works. The riddle of his paintings surrounds odd inexplicable details and deliberate inconsistencies they contain, and also the seemingly irrelevant titles of some of his works. These have never been explained. Walter told his son that he had half unconsciously recalled the main events of the murders in some of his paintings, and that he had planted clues in his titles. One example of this, he said, was his picture called *Lazarus Breaks His Fast*, an impressionist portrait of a man eating black grapes with a spoon. The painter said the picture was a veiled accusation of Gull, who had induced unconsciousness in the victims by feeding them poisoned grapes. This was specialist knowledge indeed, and there is now no realistic way of finding out if the victims were poisoned before being mutilated. The notion is in part supported by Dr Llewellyn, who examined the corpse of Nichols. A report by Abberline in the Yard file says:

> The inspector acquainted Dr Llewellyn who afterwards made a more minute examination and found that the wounds in the abdomen were in themselves sufficient to cause instant death, and he expressed an opinion that they were inflicted *before the throat was cut.*

Sickert is consequently one of the few who have claimed that the cutting of the throat was not the cause of death, a claim confirmed by the official post-mortem report. Bearing in mind the artist's accuracy in all other points so far examined, and taking into account that the secret file (of which he could have known nothing) contained a medical opinion that at least one of the victims was dead before her throat was cut, it seems likely Sickert was right in his description of Gull's method of killing. There is still one slim chance that the truth might be discovered even at this late date. If the bodies of the victims were exhumed, tests of their bone marrow might possibly reveal traces of the poison. Sickert's specific reference to grapes also ties up with Gull's self-confessed partiality for the fruit; with the grapes found clutched in Stride's dead hand, the existence of which was carefully covered up; and with the story of the greengrocer Packer, which Sir Charles Warren wanted desperately to suppress.

If Sickert's knowledge of the method of the killers is accurate his involvement in the affair must have been much closer than he admitted. Walter Sickert, not Sir Robert Anderson, was the third member of the Ripper party. Psychologically, this explanation is far more consistent with Sickert's compulsion to tell the story before he died, and with his painting clues about the case into his pictures. His story about the motive for the killings, their Masonic significance, and the involvement of Gull and Netley is all true, as has been shown. But a man whose story in reality ended at Cleveland Street could not have had at his fingertips such a wealth of detail about the actual crimes. And he would not have been so obsessed with the case. If Sickert had been directly involved, he had participated in the perfect crime, which might explain his fixation with the case. For in real terms there is no such thing as the perfect crime; if no one is ever caught only the perpetrator knows of its perfection. The pressures on such a compulsive conversationalist as Sickert to reveal his own 'perfect' crime must have been immense. But he knew that if he told the *whole* truth the perfection would have been shattered by his own implication. Cleverly, he substituted his part in the operation with that of a man he knew was supposed to have been out of the country during much of the Ripper's reign, a man who had no alibi. Anderson's indictment by Sickert, and the peculiar events surrounding Anderson's appointment as Assistant Commissioner, indicate that Anderson was involved in the conspiracy. The fact that as a Freemason he was the man Warren wanted so much as second-in-command for the duration of the Ripper crimes suggests he actively abetted Warren in the cover-up, which was probably Warren's sole purpose in becoming Commissioner in the first place.

By a coincidence of the sort which abound in Ripper research, two hours after deciding Sickert was deeply involved in the actual murders, I read this passage in McCormick's *The Identity of Jack the Ripper*:

> Yet another suggestion made is that Walter Sickert, the painter, was Jack the Ripper. The reason for Sickert being suspected is that he was believed to have made sketches and paintings of the Ripper crimes. . . .

Someone had already pointed an accusing finger at Sickert. But who? In the fifteen years that had elapsed since McCormick wrote his book, his notes on Sickert had been lost. But the fact remained that Sickert had been accused for reasons completely unconnected with the unintentional clues contained in the story he told his son.

At the time of the murders Sickert was living in various rooms and lodging-houses all over the East End. This was the period when he was painting his famous music-hall pictures, all set in and around East London. He would go out nightly and pick up women of the streets to pose as his models for the paintings he did of squalid interiors and poverty-stricken inhabitants. At this time he was unable to afford professional models, who would anyway not have possessed the tired and often sagging figures so essential to the harsh truths he was striving to depict. In *The Life and Opinions of Walter Richard Sickert*, Dr Robert Emmons wrote:

> He used to go nightly to music halls and walk home from Hoxton, Shoreditch, Canning Town or Islington, across Primrose Hill, and so on to Hampstead. He wore a loud check coat, long to the ankles, and carried a little bag for his drawings. One night in Copenhagen Street a party of young girls fled from him in terror, yelling, "Jack the Ripper, Jack the Ripper!"

It is easy to see why such an incident occurred; Sickert bore a striking resemblance to the Jack the Ripper of the popular imagination. In retrospect, we can now see that the universal image of the Ripper was in fact based on the descriptions given by witnesses who saw Sickert at the scene of at least two of the murders. One of the most reliable descriptions of a man seen with a victim shortly before her death, that of P.C. Smith in Berner Street, said the suspect's age was twenty-eight. This was noted by the trained eye of a police constable, who was quite specific in his estimate. In 1888 Sickert was exactly twenty-eight.

In the late eighties, despite his growing reputation as a painter and his large circle or highly placed friends, Sickert spun out his life on a shoestring. Though his clothes were invariably well cut, he did not as yet have the resources to replace them as often as he might have liked. He was nearly six feet tall, and at this stage in his life, according to his friend, the Irish writer George Moore, wore a little fair moustache that was 'a frizzle of gold'. Compare Sickert's appearance at that time with the following description of a man seen with Catherine Eddowes

in Duke Street, leading to Mitre Square, shortly before her
murder. It is generally regarded as one of the most valuable
descriptions of the Ripper. *The Times* stated:

> He is of shabby appearance, about 30 years of age and
> 5ft 9in in height, of fair complexion, having a small fair
> moustache, and wearing a red neckerchief and a cap with a
> peak.

In all essential details the description fits Sickert. Is it coincidence that another reliable witness, George Hutchinson, who
saw a man conduct Marie Kelly to her room, described him too
as having a red handkerchief? Remembering that red is an
unusual colour for a handkerchief, and that it was even more
so in the conservative days of Victoria, one final observation
on this point is crucial. Sickert possessed a red handkerchief
that, in the words of his friend Marjorie Lilly, appeared to have
'some mysterious connection'. Miss Lilly recalled in her book
on Sickert that his red handkerchief

> was an important factor in the process of creating his picture,
> a lifeline to guide the train of his thought, as necessary as the
> napkin which Mozart used to fold into points which met
> each other when he too was composing.

The mystery which surrounded Sickert's red handkerchief Miss
Lilly never knew. It was closely associated in his mind with two
seemingly contradicting ideas—in some vague way with the
Church, and more definitely with murder. And according to
Miss Lilly, murder to Sickert meant Jack the Ripper. When he
was painting his *Camden Town Murder* series it was never out of
his sight. Miss Lilly remembered him while he was painting

> While he was reliving the scene he would assume the part of a
> ruffian, knotting the handkerchief loosely around his neck,
> pulling a cap over his eyes and lighting his lantern. Immobile,
> sunk deep in his chair, lost in the long shadows of that vast
> room, he would meditate for hours on his problem. When the
> handkerchief had served its immediate purpose it was tied to
> any doorknob or peg that came handy to stimulate his
> imagination further, to keep the pot boiling. It played a
> necessary part in the performance of the drawings, spurring
> him on at crucial moments, becoming so interwoven with

the actual working out of his idea that he kept it constantly before his eyes.

It was so vital to him because this was the handkerchief he had worn on the nights he was Jack the Ripper. Unless this is true, that Sickert was the man with the red handkerchief seen by two independent witnesses on the nights of two Ripper murders, what explanation is there for his obsessive connection of the article *with murder?* Corroboration fell from his own lips, for he told his son that *The Camden Town Murder* series was based on the murder of Marie Kelly.

Parts of Sickert's character cannot be reconciled to the idea of a man who knew the truth of the Ripper murders but was not personally involved. One aspect is inconsistent even with the man whose interest in the case was passionate, unless that passion were based on complicity. For after a stroke late in his life, Walter Sickert came to think he was Jack the Ripper. Before she had any notion of my thoughts on her old friend, Marjorie Lilly told me, 'After the stroke Sickert would have "Ripper periods" in which he would dress up like the murderer and walk about like that for weeks on end. He would turn down the lights in his studio and literally *be* Jack the Ripper in word and mood.'All his life he would go out in the middle of the night and, like Dickens, simply walk around the streets of London until morning. He found that the thinking which is so vital for a painter he could best do wandering completely alone through the dark streets of Kentish Town or the East End.'

They say, and not without some justification, that a criminal always returns to the scene of his crime. Were Sickert's nocturnal excursions a sort of psychological return to the atmosphere of which he had been so much a part? And after his stroke, when he no longer had the presence of mind or the superhuman control to hide the real truth, did the character of fifty years before become dominant in a mind well known for its tortuous complexity? Miss Lilly refers again and again in her book to Sickert's compulsion, whenever he was walking in London, to dart down dark alleys and explore all manner of unknown passages. This practice gave him just the sort of detailed knowledge of London's geography that has been repeatedly attributed to Jack the Ripper.

Studied in the light of his claim that they contain hidden references to the Ripper crimes, Sickert's paintings are rich evidence of the state of his mind. He used often to give his paintings names which appeared to bear no relation to their content, like several quite different pictures called *Jack and Jill*. Joseph Sickert says his father used this title because he was remembering the piece of doggeral penned by a frequenter of Cleveland Street, which has been mentioned already:

> Jack and Jill went out to kill
> For things they couldn't alter
> Jack fell down and lost his crown
> And left a baby daughter.

That his mind was constantly turning on the Ripper saga and its roots in Cleveland Street is shown most clearly in one particular picture. This is the richest evidence of all that Sickert littered his art with clues about the case. It is a disturbing painting about which he made no comment to his son. It depicts a gaunt Victorian room with a high ceiling. On the wall in the centre of a fireside alcove is some sort of ornament whose definition is indistinct, but which can be nothing other than a death's head. This age-old harbinger of impending doom is gazing down upon a woman dressed poorly in a blouse and long skirt. She is averting her face from its baleful gaze, her hand has been brought to her cheek in despair and a look of anguish is passing across her features. In suggesting that this woman is Marie Kelly with Death staring her in the face, I could justly be accused of allowing my imagination to run riot, except for one thing—the mysterious title of the picture. Like so many of Sickert's titles, it has never been explained. He gave it two names, *X's Affiliation Order* and *Amphytrion*. Remembering that an affiliation order fixes the paternity of an illegitimate child, can we escape the conclusion that Sickert was recalling the events of Cleveland Street? And who is X? Bearing in mind Sickert's story about the highest in the land disguising himself as a lesser being, and in that form seducing an ordinary girl and making her pregnant, consider the alternative title of this picture, *Amphytrion*. The legend of Amphytrion tells how Jupiter, King of the Gods, *the highest* in Olympus, *disguised himself as a lesser being to seduce an ordinary woman, who became pregnant by him.*

Old Walter spoke about another picture, which he had given two names. This was a full-face portrait of a square-chinned woman wearing a large hat. It is called *Blackmail* or *Mrs Barrett*. No one has been able to explain why it was given either of these titles. Sickert told his son it was a picture of Marie Kelly, and indeed Kelly did have a square chin, and the portrait bears a strong resemblance to drawings of Kelly which appeared in the newspapers after she was murdered. He called it alternatively *Mrs Barrett* because when she got to Dorset Street Kelly took up with a man called Barrett and was known as his wife. In this Sickert was mistaken, because Kelly's common-law husband was called Joseph *Barnett*, not Barrett. The painter's intention was nevertheless as he described it. He called it *Blackmail* because Kelly was the centre of the blackmail involving the royal bastard.

He painted a picture of a line-up of music-hall chorus girls, each with a blood-red dress and some sort of neck scarf. These, he said, represented the Ripper victims. The swirling coloured borders of their dresses represented their mutilations, and the scarves were the wounds in their throats.

The Camden Town Murder series is called alternatively *What Shall We Do For The Rent?* Once again, said Sickert, these paintings were inspired by Kelly. They show a naked woman sprawled out on a bed. As well as the prostrate nude, a man appears in these pictures. In some of them he is sitting on the end of the bed wringing his hands, in others he stands over the body of the woman. Sickert said he used the alternative title *What Shall We Do For The Rent?* because Kelly was long overdue with her rent. Her body was in fact discovered by a man sent to collect some back rent from her. The other title, *The Camden Town Murder*, is more readily understandable. This was a real-life murder which took place in 1907 and in which a woman had her throat cut as she lay in her own bed. While reflecting that the murderer was never caught, it may be interesting to remember Sickert's dictum that a painter cannot paint something of which he has no experience—and the fact that some years after the death of Sickert's second wife, his French cook Marie Pepin unaccountably vanished, and as far as his friends knew was never seen again. The connection between *The Camden Town Murder* series and Marie Kelly does not end there. According to Robert Emmons, Sickert used to tell people that the model for the series had been called Marie.

It is interesting that Robert Wood, the man who was tried and acquitted of the Camden Town Murder, was a friend of

Sickert's, and even acted as his model for the series. It was
Wood's friends, doubtless led by Sickert, who hired a solicitor
to defend him. By coincidence, that solicitor was Arthur
Newton, the same man who had conspired with the Government in hushing up Eddy's connections with Cleveland Street
in 1889.

Another picture called *Blackmail,* this one in pastel, depicts
a young woman sitting demurely in a high-backed chair. Her
eyes are glazed, the end of her nose appears to be missing and
the lack of definition in the lower part of the face renders the
mouth almost non-existent. To a far greater extent, this is
what Jack the Ripper did to Marie Kelly.

Perhaps a more obvious indication of Sickert's psyche,
though, is contained in *The Painter In His Studio,* a self-portrait.
In the foreground is a headless sculpture of a woman, the limbs
incomplete. Unlike a real sculpture, however, this piece has not
crumbled through the ravages of time. The limbs appear to
have been torn or *ripped* from the torso, as if the woman has
been the victim of some vile butchery.

His preoccupation with death is apparent in several works.
A good example is *Le Journal,* which appears to be a straight-
forward portrait of a woman lying down and reading a newspaper, which she holds in the air above her head. 'That woman
is dead', Sickert confided to his son, and pointed out the detail
most people miss—that the bottom of the newspaper is partly
obscured by the woman's hair. This means she is not reading it
at all. It lies on the floor behind her. And, without doubt, she is
dead.

In *Ennui,* a picture within the picture depicts Queen Victoria.
What appears to be a bird fluttering near her head is in fact a
gull, Sickert told his son.

Even in his later pictures Sickert could not forget Eddy and
the events he had set in motion. In 1935 he painted *King
George V and Queen Mary,* a portrait of the royal couple in their
car. The front half of the Queen is obscured by the window-
frame of the vehicle. This, said Sickert, was in memory of the
fact that half of Mary belonged to Eddy (they had been engaged to be married when Eddy died).

The painter displayed his abiding interest in prostitutes in
various pictures, painted at all stages in his career. *Cocotte de
Soho* and *The Belgian Cocotte* are the two best.

Finally, his *La Hollandaise,* painted in 1905, and another
version of *Mrs Barrett* lead us back to Miller's Court and the

nightmare of 9th November 1888. This *Mrs Barrett* was also based on Kelly, Sickert claimed. It is more disturbing than the versions so far mentioned. The subject is this time shown in profile. Her eyes are sunk in deep black shadow like a skull, and her face is deathly pale. *La Hollandaise* is an abomination. It depicts a large-limbed nude reclining awkwardly on a bed in a melancholy room. Her face is quite unrecognizable, and the difficulty presented in trying to discern her features is similar to that experienced in studying the Scotland Yard photograph of Kelly's mutilated face. The nose of *La Hollandaise* seems to have been cut off, like Kelly's, her eyes are blurred and the whole effect is that she has the head of an animal rather than a human. The same nauseating feeling is gained from the picture of Kelly.

Psychologist Dr Anthony Storr, formerly a Harley Street consultant, agrees that Sickert's behaviour in painting clues into his pictures could be consistent with his having taken part in the Ripper murders. 'It is certain', he said, 'that people with guilty secrets do suffer from a compulsion to drop clues, as Sickert claimed to have done in his paintings'.

The two major writers on Sickert, Robert Emmons and Marjorie Lilly, who were both closely associated with him, have each remarked on a strange, morose side to his character which most of the time lay hidden beneath sparkling wit and charm, but which would appear, in the words of Emmons, in flashes of coldness. Referring to one such manifestation of the darker side of his nature, Miss Lilly recalled 'how completely Dr Jekyll had assumed the mantle of Mr Hyde'. Emmons made the comment that 'The serpent lay dormant in the basket of figs'. He went on:

> Sometimes, when a mood of depression or misanthropy caught him, he would remain invisible for weeks at a time, and then suddenly reappear as gay and debonair as ever.

Moving to the documentary evidence against Sickert, two of the best descriptions of the Ripper (P.C. Smith's and Hutchinson's) say he was carrying a parcel. Smith described it as 'a parcel wrapped in newspaper, about eighteen inches long and six to eight inches broad'. Its dimensions preclude it from being a knife, as some writers have suggested. Smith's observations do tie in with Sickert's statement that the murderers tracked down Kelly with the help of a portrait. He omitted to explain, however, where the killers could possibly have come by such a portrait. There is not likely to have been a photograph of Kelly, so it must have been a painting or sketch, probably the latter. Sickert is drawn more definitely into the web when we realize only he would have been in a position to provide a picture of Kelly, probably one sketched from memory. We already know that Sickert had rooms all over the East End at this period, and nightly employed prostitutes as models. The fact that he had not one but several retreats in the heart of Jack the Ripper's territory, and that he was a familiar figure among the East End tarts, would have put Sickert in the best possible position to track down Kelly and her accomplices on behalf of the conspirators.

The parcel was seen for the second time by Hutchinson on the night of 9th November. He described it as 'about eight inches long with a strap round it, covered in dark American cloth'. Because this description naturally inspired the vision of a knife, it has been assumed the parcel Hutchinson saw was *narrow*. But Hutchinson gave no hint as to the parcel's breadth, so it might just as easily have been six inches wide. This is far more likely, because a thin parcel would not have required a carrying strap. Once again, with Hutchinson's description there is the connection with the artist, for American cloth was used for wrapping pictures. It is true that though P.C. Smith's description does fit Sickert, Hutchinson's does not. It has been unanimously decided the two witnesses had seen different men. But the colourful description Hutchinson provided, regarded by the police as genuine, better fitted a stage villain than anyone in real life. Greasepaint ran in Sickert's veins as surely as blood and oil paint. He loved the theatre, he was a trained actor, *and he loved adopting eccentric disguises*.

Sickert's story of the murder of Stride by Netley (with Anderson keeping watch on the opposite side of the road) tallies with previously unpublished facts revealed in the Home Office file, except for one point. The description of the man who was standing watch does not fit Anderson. Israel Schwartz, who saw Stride murdered, described the watcher thus:

Age 35 [Sickert was twenty-eight], height 5ft. 11in. [Sickert was just under six feet], complexion fresh [Sickert had a fair complexion], hair light brown [Sickert's hair was light brown], moustache brown [Sickert had a fair moustache]; dress, dark overcoat, old black hard felt hat, wide brim, had a claypipe in his hand [According to Marjorie Lilly, Sickert smoked only cigars when she knew him. It is impossible to discover his smoking habits when young].

The descriptions do not tally precisely. The age, for instance, is seven years out. In Schwartz's hurry and nervousness he is not likely to have got a clear picture of the man he saw, but one thing he could be positive about, however uncertain the light, and that is the man's height. He said quite definitely that the man he saw was about five feet eleven inches tall, a stature less common in Victorian times than today. Sickert was a little under six feet.

The substitution of Sickert for Anderson as the third man resolves several inconsistencies in the Sickert story. It makes sense of Lord Salisbury having entered his Dieppe studio and paid him £500 for a picture for which he might otherwise have received £3. The incident could well have happened. Salisbury regularly used to holiday in Dieppe in the eighties, and Osbert Sitwell referred to the incident in his introduction to *A Free House!* But when Sickert told the story to Sitwell he did not involve himself in it. He said the subject of Salisbury's generosity was the artist Vollon. Only when he came to disclosing the real background to the Ripper case to his son did he also explain the truth of the Salisbury episode. Until then he had used the amended version in much the same way he had used the veterinary student story. It satisfied his compulsion to talk about the subject, but shed no light on the real facts, which he regarded, even until a few years before his death, as highly dangerous. It is inconceivable that Salisbury would have bribed Sickert into silence. Far more plausible is the idea that the money was *payment* for his part in the plan, and his assistance in making it work. To be fair, it is likely that Sickert was coerced into helping the Freemasons, and that it was abhorrent to him to have been a party to the destruction of Kelly, whom he had personally brought from the East End to help Annie Elizabeth. But in the words of his son, 'The old man would do anything to get on'. It is certain he would have stopped at little to save himself from the sort of fate that befell Annie Elizabeth. He was, after all, a prime mover in the Cleveland Street episode, and knew far too much to be left alone. There may even have been in one of his acts a peculiar sort of bid for redemption: an attempt to save Kelly. An operation of the sort Gull was executing would never have resulted in such a basic mistake as a confusion of identities, as Sickert claimed happened the night Eddowes died. If the conspirators believed Eddowes was Kelly they had not made an error; they had been deliberately misled. Sickert must have been the man responsible, and a tardy attempt at saving Kelly seems the only explanation.[1]

Three episodes in particular bear the singular mark of Sickert, and display the same sort of mentality that would plant clues to a murder in works of art. These episodes are the careful placing of rings and coins at Chapman's feet, the writing

The writing on the wall in Goulston Street, and an example of Sickert's handwriting

of the chalk message on the wall and the planting of the grapes in Stride's hand. These acts must have been performed by one of the Rippers; the first, it seems, was removed by Dr Phillips and the last two were both covered up by Warren because they pointed the finger at Masons in general and, in the case of the grapes, at Gull in particular.

For one of the killers to have written the message on the wall he would have had to go *east* from Mitre Square, because

[1] Allied to this is the question of Kelly's rent. The average weekly rent for a man and his family was about 2s. 10d., yet Kelly's room cost 4s. 6d. a week—a sum she certainly could not have afforded. Who was paying to keep her in hiding?

Goulston Street is in the heart of Whitechapel. This is inconsistent with Sickert's report in that Gull would surely have headed straight back into the West End. But Sickert had various rooms in the East End at this time. After the Mitre Square murder he is likely to have parted from his accomplices and scurried to one of his hideouts. Did he live in Wentworth Dwellings, Goulston Street, where the writing was found? It is impossible to find out. Lodgers' names never appeared in the rate books. But in writing on the wall, 'The Juwes are the men that will not be blamed for nothing', the Ripper was doing exactly what Sickert did later in his paintings. And the careful copy of the writing on the wall in the Home Office file, reproduced (p.260) for the first time anywhere, bears a certain resemblance to Sickert's handwriting.

Sickert is almost certain to have been the man who arranged the rings and coins at Chapman's feet and who bought grapes from Packer, which he planted in Stride's hand to point a camouflaged finger at Gull. Not surprisingly, on all three occasions his clues were misinterpreted or removed. So he began painting the same sort of esoteric hints into his pictures.

Obviously Joseph Sickert found it impossible to accept that his father was not the knight in shining armour who alone carried the banner of truth to a future generation. He could hardly be expected instantly to believe that the story he has nurtured in secret most of his life missed out on one major point, that Sickert was not a helpless bystander but actually one of the Rippers. He may or may not have killed, but he was an accomplice to the most savage crimes of his generation.

It was in complete innocence, not to say naivety, that one day shortly after I began pondering the old man's entanglement in the actual murders, Joseph Sickert showed me some of his father's belongings. They included a dark brown doctor's bag, which meant a great deal to old Sickert and in which he used to carry his paints. This must have been the 'battered old Gladstone bag to which he was greatly attached', recalled by Marjorie Lilly. A bag just like this one has become woven into the fabric of Ripper lore. Many people who carried such bags at the time walked in danger of being lynched because the populace were convinced from several descriptions of suspected men that the bag was a trademark of the Ripper. Where Sickert came by the bag I have no idea. It was definitely a doctor's bag, divided into numerous compartments for the storage of medicines and surgical instruments. The second item I noticed in the pile of belongings was a small metal case about six inches long and one and a half inches wide. It had a small stain on it that looked like blood. I asked about it and Joseph handed it to me. It contained three surgical knives, razor-sharp.

'I don't know where the old man got those, or even what he used them for', he said ingenuously. 'I think he was given them as a young man.'

The items may have no significance. I merely mention them as extra detail in the abundantly colourful portrait of a near-perfect murderer, which I will leave as it stands, except to repeat one further comment made to me by Walter's own son:

'He was a strange man. He would start weeping for no reason sometimes, terribly moved by something long ago.'

Afterword by Joseph Sickert

When my mother died she was deaf, nearly blind, and paralysed. The deafness she inherited from her father, the Duke of Clarence, whose blood I think of as a taint to our family. Some descendants of royalty have found their ancestry a source of pride. I find mine disgusting. Had I been a plumber descended from a long line of plumbers, I'd have been a far happier man; none of the events so carefully documented by Stephen Knight would have happened. If my mother's deafness was a direct result of Clarence's intrusion into our family, her blindness and paralysis were indirectly attributable to the same cause: they were the after-effects of her encounters with John Netley. Apart from the physical after-effects of the injuries she received on the two occasions Netley tried to kill her, she also suffered terrible stress and nervousness for the whole of the rest of her life. In her teens this tension receded a little but after she was about twenty, with each year that passed she became quieter, more introspective, more nervous of strangers, and more preoccupied with the idea that her life was in danger. I saw my mother slowly destroyed, not only physically but mentally too. Believe me, there is no pleasure or pride in being an illegitimate descendent of the Duke of Clarence.

At last the burden of knowledge I have carried so long has been lifted from me. In a strange sort of way my mother and grandmother have been revenged. Those who caused their suffering are now named. They cannot hide their guilty faces from the world any longer. Though I took a long time to accept it fully, it is true that a truth such as this should be made known to everyone.

When the author told me his conclusions about my father's involvement in the case I was disturbed. There is no point in denying that I was also angry. I felt he had let me down and betrayed my trust. But later I had to admit that my father must have known more than he told me. It was a fact that I had half realized all along. And possibly one of the reasons I allowed my story to be investigated in the first place was that I hoped new facts might be uncovered that would somehow dispel my worst private fears about my father. In the event the investigation has had the opposite effect and my fears have been confirmed.

I should like to say that my concern all along has been for my mother and my grandmother. The old man was always able to look after himself and I've always thought of him, in a way, as an interloper like Clarence. I did not see all that much of him as a child but we did like each other and I did trust him. If Stephen Knight is correct in his conclusions, and I am forced to admit, reluctantly, that his reasoning is sound, I do not bear my father any malice. As it says in the final chapter of this book, 'it is likely that Sickert was coerced into helping the Freemasons, and that it was abhorrent to him to have been a party to the destruction of Kelly'. Apart from fear for his own life, which I agree *could* have induced him to participate in the elimination of the five East End women, I think it is more than likely that he received more persuasive threats even than that. How the monsters who masterminded this whole disgusting affair would have worded their insane threats I don't know, but if my father's assistance was so vital to them I can well believe the burden of their message was, 'Help us, Sickert, or we'll not only kill you. We'll kill the child as well.'

None of this justifies, but it might begin to explain why an essentially good man would do what it seems my father did.

POSTSCRIPT

The events surrounding the death of Prince Eddy in 1892 prompted a large number of letters after the first edition of this book appeared. It was widely rumoured at the time of his death that Eddy had been the victim of a judicial murder—carried out so that someone more suitable could come to the throne. There were also reports that his fingernails blackened during his last hours, which could indicate poisoning.

A former employee of Osborne House, Queen Victoria's Isle

of Wight hideaway, contacted me and said that a rumour had persisted among the staff at Osborne for many years that Eddy had not died in 1892 but that, hopelessly insane, he had been incarcerated at Osborne and died in 1930. A plain marble tablet in the grounds is supposed to be his only memorial. But here we are entering into the fascinating, but factually insecure, area of hearsay. None of this can be considered as evidence, but legend—as I suggest in chapter four—has its value when set in context and is worth recording. It is often anchored in some obscure reality.

For this reason it is worth while telling the story passed on to me by Mrs Anita Adams of Wanstead, Essex. I do not present it as evidence but as an interesting anecdote much older than the Sickert story and quite independent which might—I put it no stronger than that—which might have some basis in truth.

Mrs Adams explains that her great grandfather Charles Wingrove ran a company in the East End in the eighties and nineties of the last century. The company hired out carriages, wagonettes, gigs and coaches of every description. One of their regular customers, a contemporary advertisement boasts, was the Prince of Wales.

It has been tradition in the Wingrove family for many years that one of the Ripper murders was committed inside a coach hired out by the company. The coach, it is said, was later burned because of this.

Other evidence, which requires deeper investigation than such unverifiable legend, has also come to light. I am in the process of examining this and expect some conclusions in time for the next edition.

AFTERWORD
by Nigel Cawthorne

Since the publication of *Jack the Ripper: The Final Solution*, Joseph Sickert's story – that the Duke of Clarence had an illegitimate child and made an illegal marriage has become widely accepted. However, some Ripperologists have remained sceptical and have sought to pick holes in Stephen Knight's theory that the Queen's doctor Sir William Gull, coachman John Netley and the painter Walter Sickert together committed the Ripper murders. But further confirmation that the murders were not the work of one perverted madman but a conspiracy by men at the heart of the establishment has been forthcoming.

Before Stephen Knight had finished writing *Jack the Ripper: The Final Solution* he had fallen out with Joseph Sickert. This is partially because he rejected Sickert's story that Assistant Commissioner of the Metropolitan Police Sir Robert Anderson was the third man in the killings. Instead Knight insisted that Joseph Sickert's own father, Walter Sickert, was the third man. Joseph Sickert was not unnaturally offended by this suggestion and withdrew his co-operation and held back part of the story. From what Joseph Sickert told him, Knight concluded that Sir William Gull was the evil genius behind the Ripper murders. Sickert later claimed he kept back the name of the ringleader because he did not want to bring shame on the culprit's family. But as Knight's story came into general currency Sickert found that his omission had rebounded on him. The shame was now being heaped on his family. He was particularly upset when the 1985 TV film Murder by Decree portrayed the Duke of Clarence as the heartless seducer of the naïive Annie Crook, who he intended to dump. Sickert was offended by this, believing that his grandparents had shared a great love. They had suffered enough in their lifetime, he thought. It did not seem fair to him that they should be slandered after their deaths and he resolved to reveal the vital details he had withheld.

In doing so he confirmed everything that he had told Stephen Knight. Sir Robert Anderson, not Walter Sickert, had been the third man he insisted. But there were more men in the gang – maybe as many as twelve. These included Lord Euston and Lord Arthur Somerset, two of the principals in the Cleveland Street Scandal.

The reason Stephen Knight concluded that Walter Sickert, not Sir Robert Anderson, was the third man was because Sickert knew too much simply to have been a bystander. When he had told his son what he knew of the Ripper murders, he divulged details that only someone who had been there when the murders happened would have known. But Joseph Sickert had withheld the source of his father's information. Walter Sickert had been told the inside story of the Ripper murders by Inspector Frederick George Abberline, the policeman in charge of the investigation. Abberline, in turn, had been told the story by one of the men involved – Prince Eddy's tutor J.K. Stephen, one of the favoured suspects of the lone-madman theory of the murders. Stephen, Sickert said, was one of the Ripper gang and part of the conspiracy. Abberline had written down what Stephen had told him in three diaries which he had given to Walter Sickert, who passed them on to his son. Both father and son regularly referred to the diaries to keep the detail of the Ripper murders fresh in their minds.

One of the reasons that Knight discounted Anderson as a member of the Ripper gang was that he had been out of the country at the time of the double murder of Elizabeth Stride and Catherine Eddowes. But Sickert maintained that Anderson's role, as a detective, was to collect and collate information on the whereabouts of Mary Kelly and the other blackmailers. The fact that Catherine Eddowes was not one of the blackmailers and was killed by mistake, because she had been unfortunate enough to use the pseudonym Mary Kelly, seems to confirm that whoever was in charge of tracking the women down had slipped up or was not available at the time.

Sickert continued to maintain that Sir William Gull and John Netley were the men who actually performed the murders and mutilations. However, he later revealed that Gull had not begun his murderous campaign on his own initiative. He was acting on the orders of more prominent men. His orders came from his masonic superiors in the Royal Alpha Lodge No 16. The chief conspirator, Sickert maintained, was none other than Lord Randolph Churchill, father of wartime leader Winston Churchill. Although the freemason's deny Lord Randolph Churchill was ever a member, Sickert maintained that he was Magister Magistrorum – the master of masters. There are other indications that he was a mason, but had joined under the alias Spencer. Like his son, he often used the double-barrelled surname Spencer Churchill.

Lord Randolph Churchill had a twisted reason to hate women. By 1888 he was already suffering from bouts of madness, caused by the tertiary syphilis that would kill him. He blamed his condition and the loss of his meteoric political career on the woman who had given him the disease. It seems that Sir William Gull, an expert on syphilis, was treating him. By 1886, because of his condition, Lord Randolph Churchill ceased having sex with his wife, the beautiful American Jenny Jerome. She began to take lovers. This left Lord Randolph Churchill alone and bitter. His condition left him reliant on drugs. Like his son, he was a big drinker. He was also audacious and brooked no opposition. He even defied the Prince of Wales, threatening to publish incriminating letters which would lose him the throne if the Prince did not back down in an affair involving Churchill's brother Lord Blandford. The Prince of Wales did as Churchill demanded but refused to speak to him again for eight years. Lord Randolph Churchill believed that he had been robbed of the chance to be prime minister and did anything he could to exercise power behind the scenes. He saw himself as a second Machiavelli and was known to be unscrupulous. He was certainly a man who could have cooked up the Ripper conspiracy and would have had the expertise to pull it off.

Winston Churchill was a tireless defender of his father, whitewashing him in his biography Lord Randolph Churchill. As Home Secretary in 1910, Winston Churchill was in a perfect position to remove any evidence linking his father to the Ripper murders from the police files. When they were opened in 1988, the Ripper files were found to be far from complete. Soon after, Winston Churchill quit the freemasons. There were other connections between Churchill and the conspiracy. Walter Sickert gave Winston Churchill painting lessons and Churchill had been induced into the masons by Lord Euston.

Joseph Sickert believed that J.K. Stephen, Prince Eddy's tutor at Cambridge, had a homosexual affair with him. Stephen was also related to Annie Crook and may have introduced Eddy to her. Sickert believed that Lord Randolph Churchill got carried away with the power the Ripper conspiracy gave him. After killing Mary Kelly and the other blackmailers, he intended to finish the job by killing Annie Crook, her daughter Alice and Prince Eddy himself. It was then that Stephen broke with the other conspirators and, breaking his masonic oath, talked to Inspector Abberline. Like so many others involved in the conspiracy, Stephen died in a lunatic asylum. He starved himself to death after being told of Eddy's death in 1892. Four days later, Abberline retired from the police force.

As *Jack the Ripper: The Final Solution* points out, the conspiracy among the highest echelons of the police force and the establishment was such that even though Abberline knew the truth there was nothing he could do about it. The Ripper case had to remain officially unsolved or it would have opened the can of worms the conspirators had sought to conceal.

Joseph Sickert told the rest of what he knew to Melvyn Fairclough, who recounted it in his books *The Ripper and the Royals*. The book confirms the thesis of Stephen Knight's book and adds a myriad of detail. However, Fairclough's book over-eggs the pudding, tying the Ripper conspiracy to an assassination attempt on Queen Victoria and the abdication crisis of 1936. Distraught at being forcibly parted from his wife, Prince Eddy intended to exact his revenge by killing his own grandmother. And, apparently, Prince Eddy did not die in 1892. Being thought unsuitable to ascend to the throne, he was proclaimed dead then hidden away in Glamis Castle – ancestral home of the Bowes-Lyons – until he died in 1933. In recompense, the master of Glamis, the Earl of Strathmore, was to see his daughter, a commoner, sit on the throne of England. Elizabeth Bowes-Lyon – Queen Mother at the time of writing – was romantically attached to the Prince of Wales who became Edward VIII before marrying his brother the Duke of York who became George VI. Apparently Edward – or David as he was known before ascending to the throne – had discovered the secret of Glamis and had decided to abdicate in protest at the treatment of Eddy, who was rightfully king, before he even met Mrs Simpson. Hence Ms Bowes-Lyon's change of partner.

For my money, this is one conspiracy theory too far. But that does not undermined Stephen Knight's thesis. Not withstanding the additional information that Joseph Sickert has revealed since *Jack the Ripper: The Final Solution* was written, Stephen Knight remains the Ripperologist who really did come up with the final solution.

Bibliography

BOOKS

Acland, Theodore Dyke
William Withey Gull, A Biographical Sketch (Adlard and Son, 1896).
Anderson, Sir Robert
Criminals and Crime (J. Nisbet, 1907).
The Lighter Side of My Official Life (Hodder and Stoughton, 1910).
Archer, Fred
Ghost Detectives: Crime and the psychic world (W. H. Allen, 1970).
Barker, Richard H. (Editor)
The Fatal Caress and Other Accounts of English Murders from 1551 to 1881 (Duell, Sloan and Pearce, 1947).
Barnard, Allan (Editor)
The Harlot Killer: The Story of Jack the Ripper in Fact and Fiction (Dodd Mead, 1953).
Baron, Wendy
Sickert (Phaidon, 1973).
Battiscombe, Georgina
Queen Alexandra (Constable, 1969).
Besant, Sir Walter
East London (Chatto and Windus, 1901).
Blake, Robert
The Conservative Party from Peel to Churchill (Eyre and Spottiswoode, 1970).
Brewer, John Francis
The Curse Upon Mitre Square A.D. 1530–1888 (Simpkin Marshall, 1888).
Bridges, Yseult
How Charles Bravo Died (Jarrolds, 1956).
Browne, Douglas G.
The Rise Of Scotland Yard: A History of the Metropolitan Police (Harrap, 1956).

Browse, Lillian
Sickert (Hart-Davis, 1960).
Buckle, George Earle (Editor)
The Letters of Queen Victoria: Third Series, Vol. 1 (Murray, 1930).
Carter, Dr Alan Barham
All About Strokes (Nelson, 1968).
Crowley, Aleister
The World's Tragedy (Paris, 1910).
Cullen, Tom
Autumn of Terror (Bodley Head, 1965).
Emmons, Dr Robert
The Life and Opinions of Walter Richard Sickert (Faber and Faber, 1941).
Farson, Daniel
Jack the Ripper (Michael Joseph, 1972).
Gaunt, William
The Pre-Raphaelite Tragedy (Cape, 1965).
Griffiths, Major Arthur
Mysteries of Police and Crime (Cassell, 1898).
Halsted, Dennis
Doctor in the Nineties (Johnson, 1959).
Hannah, Walton
Darkness Visible, A Revelation And Interpretation of Freemasonry (Augustine Press, now Britons Publishing Co, 1952).
Harrison, Michael
Clarence (W. H. Allen, 1972).
Hirschfeld, Magnus
Sexual Anomalies and Perversions (Encyclopaedic Press, 1938).
Hyde, H. Montgomery
Their Good Names (Hamish Hamilton, 1970).
Jones, Elwyn, and Lloyd, John
The Ripper File (Weidenfeld and Nicolson, 1975).
Lilly, Marjorie
Sickert, The Painter and His Circle (Elek, 1971).
Longford, Elizabeth
Victoria R.I. (Weidenfeld and Nicolson, 1964).
MacKenzie, Norman (Editor)
Secret Societies (Aldus, 1967).
Macnaghten, Sir Melville
Days of My Years (Edward Arnold, 1915).
McCormick, Donald
The Identity of Jack the Ripper (Jarrolds, 1959; Pan, 1962; Arrow and J. Long, 1970).
Magnus, Sir Philip
King Edward the Seventh (John Murray, 1964).
Matters, Leonard
The Mystery of Jack the Ripper (Hutchinson, 1929; and W. H. Allen, 1949).

Morgan, William
Freemasonry Exposed (Glasgow, 1836).
Newton, Joseph Fort
The Builders: A Story and Study of Masonry (Hogg, 1917; Allen and Unwin, 1918).
Odell, Robin
Jack the Ripper In Fact and Fiction (Harrap, 1965; Mayflower, 1966).
Rumbelow, Donald
The Complete Jack the Ripper (W. H. Allen, 1975).
Sitwell, Sir Osbert
Noble Essences or Courteous Revelations (Macmillan, 1950).
A Free House! or The Artist as Craftsman, being the Writings of Walter Richard Sickert (Macmillan, 1947).
Sparrow, Gerald
Vintage Edwardian Murder (Arthur Barker, 1971).
Stewart, William
Jack the Ripper: A New Theory (Quality Press, 1939).
Stow, John
Survey of London (1598).
Van Thal, Herbert (Editor)
The Prime Ministers, Volume Two (Allen and Unwin, 1975).
Whittington-Egan, Richard
A Casebook on Jack the Ripper (Wildy, 1976).
Wilks, S., and Bettany, G. T.
Biographical History of Guy's Hospital (Ward Lock, 1892).
Wilson, Colin
A Casebook of Murder (Leslie Frewin, 1969).

DIRECTORIES

Dictionary of British Surnames
Dictionary of National Biography
Masonic Records 1717–1894
The Medical Directory
The Medical Register
Post Office Directory of London

JOURNALS

The Criminologist
Daily Express
Daily News
Daily Telegraph
East London Advertiser
Evening News

Freemasons' Magazine and Masonic Mirror
Freemasons' Monthly Remembrancer
Freemasons' Quarterly Review
Illustrated Police News
The Lancet
Marylebone Mercury and West London Gazette
Marylebone Times
The Nineteenth Century
North London Press
The Observer
Pall Mall Gazette
The People
Reynolds' News
The Star
The Sun
Sunday Times-Herald, Chicago
The Times
Truth

PAMPHLETS

The Coming K – – –
What Does She Do With It?

DOCUMENTS

Public Record Office file DPP/1/95 relating to Cleveland Street scandal of 1889.
Scotland Yard files MEPOL 3/140, MEPOL 3/141 and MEPOL 3/142 relating to the Whitechapel Murders.
Home Office files A49301, 144/220 A49301A, B, C, D, E, F, G, H, J and K relating to the Whitechapel Murders.
Protocols of the Learned Elders of Zion (Eyre and Spottiswoode, 1920).

Index

Index

Index